Sarah Bernhardt's
First American
Theatrical Tour,
1880–1881

Sarah Bernhardt's First American Theatrical Tour, 1880–1881

by PATRICIA MARKS

McFarland & Company, Inc., Publishers
Jefferson, North Carolina, and London

Frontispiece: Sarah Bernhardt. Cabinet card by Napoleon Sarony, 1880. Harry Ransom Humanities Research Center, the University of Texas at Austin.

LIBRARY OF CONGRESS CATALOGUING-IN-PUBLICATION DATA

Marks, Patricia, 1943–
    Sarah Bernhardt's first American theatrical tour, 1880–1881 / by Patricia Marks.
      p. cm.
    Includes bibliographical references and index.

    ISBN 0-7864-1495-2 (softcover : 50# alkaline paper)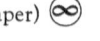

    1. Bernhardt, Sarah, 1844–1923—Performances—United States. I. Title.
PN2638.B5M37 2003
792'.028'092—dc21
                                                                              2003001321

British Library cataloguing data are available

©2003 Patricia Marks. All rights reserved

No part of this book may be reproduced or transmitted in any form or by any means, electronic or mechanical, including photocopying or recording, or by any information storage and retrieval system, without permission in writing from the publisher.

On the cover: Sarah Bernhardt in costume for *Froufrou* (photograph by Napoleon Sarony, circa 1880, Harry Ransom Humanities Research Center, the University of Texas at Austin)

Manufactured in the United States of America

McFarland & Company, Inc., Publishers
  Box 611, Jefferson, North Carolina 28640
    www.mcfarlandpub.com

To D.W.M.

Contents

Acknowledgments ix
Introduction 1

CHAPTER 1. Lady Liberty Sets Sail 9
CHAPTER 2. Sarah and the Four Hundred 33
CHAPTER 3. "Bust-on" Beans and Other Delicacies 60
CHAPTER 4. "Ehue, Jaques! How frail we are!": Bernhardt and
   the Sympathetic Barbarians 80
CHAPTER 5. "We are hardly good colonists": Bernhardt's
   Southern Odyssey 109
CHAPTER 6. "We be men of little wit": Audiences in the
   Midwest 130
CHAPTER 7. Home, Sweet Home 156

Appendix I. Plays Performed in the United States, 1880–1881 .. 175
Appendix II. Bernhardt's Traveling Art Show 176
Appendix III. Performance Chronology 178
Notes 187
Bibliography 201
Index 207

Acknowledgments

I appreciate the assistance of the countless individuals who supported me in my research and writing. Faculty research grants from Valdosta State University helped to fund travel and photocopying costs, and a Mellon grant from the Harry Ransom Humanities Research Center at the University of Texas in Austin allowed me access to a treasure trove of Bernhardt photographs. I am grateful for the interested help of the librarians there, as well as those at the Harvard College Library, and I with to express my thanks to those institutions for permission to reprint photographs in their holdings.

Without the knowledgeable assistance of librarians and archivists in libraries and historical societies in the towns Berhardt visited, this book would not have been possible. Of especial help was Denise Montgomery, who, at the Valdosta State University Odum Library, tirelessly helped locate out-of-print and rare resources. Many thanks go as well to the librarians in the rare book room of the New York Public Library's Billy Rose Theatre Collection and those in the serials and reference collections of the Library of Congress.

To acknowledge all those who took time from busy schedules to verify Bernhardt's appearances or to check references and dates would be impossible, but among those individuals or institutions who helped were the following: The Maryland Historical Society; Julie Thomas, Chicago Historical Society; Dennis Northcott, Missouri Historical Society; Clyde Weeks, St. Joseph Historical Society (Missouri); the Mobile Public Library (Alabama); Mary Oliver, Montgomery County Historical Society (Ohio); Patricia Tomczak, Brenner Library of Quincy University (Illinois); James

Hanson, State Histori cal Society of Wisconsin; The Historical Society of Western Pennsylvania; Nancy Gaudette, Worcester Public Library (Massachusetts); Forest Turner, New Jersey Historical Society; Jeff Korman, Enoch Pratt Free Library (Maryland); and many others, including Grady Lacey, who made sense of the fractured French in the satires.

For friends who during this manuscript's preparation listened, exhorted, and encouraged, and for those who let me borrow books or who shared anecdotes about Bernhardt, I am grateful; and especially for the support of Tom Dasher, friend and colleague, who, as head of the Department of English and Dean of the College of Arts and Sciences at Valdosta State University, sought to foster opportunities for research.

Most of all, I celebrate the boundless support of the person who feeds me and fixes my computer, who travels to libraries with me, who views my ever-increasing piles of photocopies with equanimity and good humor, and who cheerfully reads every word I write—my husband, Dennis.

Introduction

On October 15, 1880, with great flurry and fanfare, at least two Sarah Bernhardts set sail for New York from Le Havre for a theatrical tour of the United States. One sought to introduce a selection of French drama to a decidedly unintellectual country; the other wanted to make money.

The first was as beautiful and admired as she was temperamental and dedicated. As a child, she had been educated first at an exclusive boarding school, where she learned how to please the social world, and then at a genteel convent school, where she was taught to discover her spiritual nature within the Roman Catholic tradition. She was then trained at the prestigious Conservatoire de Musique et Déclamation, an experience that satisfied her passionate love for ritual and pageantry while preparing her for membership in the Comédie Française. Socially, she belonged to a heady circle of intellectuals and public figures that included Victor Hugo, Gustave Doré, Alexandre Dumas—*père et fils*, Oscar Wilde, and the Prince of Wales. And then, because of her growing fame, the impresario Edward Jarrett sought her out to negotiate terms for a tour of the New World.

The other Sarah Bernhardt was the neglected daughter of Judith Van Hard, or Youle Bernard, as she was known, a Jewish courtesan from Amsterdam.[1] Left with a country nurse who negligently allowed her to tumble into an open fireplace, Bernhardt was virtually abandoned by her mother. A troublesome and inconvenient child, she had a tempestuous stay at a convent school, alternating between bouts of rage at the way the nuns combed her unruly mop of hair and bouts of religious fervor (she was inconsolable at the death of the Archbishop of Paris, Monseigneur Sibour, who was to officiate at her baptism). Her acceptance at the celebrated Conservatoire de Musique et Déclamation came about only because of the intercession of the Duc de Morny, one of Youle's lovers; her contract with the Comédie Française was terminated when she slapped a leading lady for pushing her little sister into a piece of scenery. Her subsequent experience in her mother's profession introduced her to one of the great loves of her life—the Prince de Ligne—and left her with a son, Maurice. Ten years later, she was reinstated at the Comédie Française, but persisted in making her own engagements and signing contracts without permission. Refusing to follow the rules that bound a *sociétaire*, she was dismissed and nearly bankrupted by the fine—until Edward Jarrett showed up.[2]

Bernhardt's multiple personas, her life roles, are what intrigued the American public from her first American tour in 1880–81 to her last in 1916, when her name, her eccentricities, and her genius had made her world-famous. The very success of this upstart actress, her *joie de vivre* and her refusal to follow rules and shape herself to cultural expectations, whether American or French, hint at the conflicts she both encountered and engendered. Followed by crowds and cheered by patricians and plebeians alike, she stormed the barriers of language, culture, and geography. She had an independent streak that Uncle Sam would have admired. As a young actress invited to a command performance for Napoleon III, she brazenly recited the exiled Victor Hugo's poetry; and in 1870, during the Franco-Prussian War, she turned the Odeón Théâtre into a hospital. Bernhardt represented the same brand of patriotic activism, egalitarianism, and self-sufficiency that had moved her American hosts to create a thriving nation from a colony.

By the time Bernhardt paid her first visit to the United States, her reception was complicated by the multiple and conflicting expectations Americans had of themselves and of foreigners, as well as by their assumptions about class, labor, and gender. While her enthusiastic supporters happily welcomed Bernhardt the *artiste* on the ground of theatrical expression, she was identified in the popular mind by her "otherness" from the "American way," an ethos predicated on a set of norms and assumptions that measured the outsider against local values. As an actress, she behaved in a fashion that amused and scandalized her viewers; as a foreigner, she had tastes and manners that, like her language, were interesting, unfamiliar, and not immediately understandable; as a woman, she was an unwed mother and a shrewd businesswoman. In no way was she a spiritual, self-effacing "angel in the house," nor, as a parvenu, did she have the social stature to gain immediate acceptance.

Yet "The Bernhardt," the one whose acting gained her audience's sympathy for adulteresses and murderesses, had much in common with her American hosts, who were cashing in on the Gilded Age. Their strong belief in individual freedom and fighting frontier spirit, which had metamorphosed into profit-making and consumerism, was reflected in Bernhardt's dedication to freedom, individualism, and money-making. As the contemporary periodical record shows, the New World entrepreneurs who made a *rendezvous* with an Old World actress had their own values called into question. Her very presence was disruptive; she was what the critic M. M. Bakhtin would call a carnivalizing force, both in terms of language and action.[3]

As Bernhardt mania erupted across the country, Americans became engaged in the complexities of language and communication. While their straightforwardness was proverbial, Uncle Sam's children were adept at linguistic play, as countless squibs, puns, and one-liners in newspapers and comic periodicals attest; but repeated cultural and linguistic misunderstandings also show that many critics proceeded on the assumption of cultural univocality. Those who attended her plays for enjoyment, however, had a different experience. Review after review suggests that Bernhardt's audiences put aside their translated librettos to hang spellbound on the actress's performance. Bernhardt, performing in her native tongue, "spoke" the language of emotions, and left her audiences both weeping and exhilarated. They understood, that is, on a level quite different from the logical level of accurate translation. Such nonverbal discourse, a form of "heteroglossia," was likely to have occurred unconsciously.[4] The audience probably learned some French words; but, more significant for a population that proverbially valued directness, they learned to speak on multiple levels.

Bernhardt, the *arriviste* who sought to rival the legendary Rachel, challenged assumptions and turned expectations upside down; as a result she was extravagantly praised and just as extravagantly condemned. Because seats were available in a wide range of prices in towns small and large, she attracted viewers from a spectrum of economic, educational, social, and professional levels, involving them in the ceremony and intensity of her performances so effectively that pulpit orators anathematized her publicly. Generously welcomed and vindictively burlesqued by the press, she became a cultural icon even for those who were unable to attend her theatrical performances. Americans found themselves in the uncomfortable position of criticizing her for what they liked to do best—make money. In the baldest sense they were called upon to welcome an upstart immigrant who spoke broken English and who attracted jobs away from her American counterparts, the very charges made against the stream of immigrants pouring into New York.

In Bernhardt's case, these charges were fostered by pervasive anti-Semitism. Her nose, hair, and facial characteristics were matched against a perceived Jewish profile, and many of the caricatures published early in her tour show exaggerations that stress her otherness, not as a French citizen, but as an ethnic and economic threat. Reports of her rapacity preceded her. Described in terms ordinarily reserved for money-lenders, she was accused of demanding an exorbitant percentage of the gate receipts and maintaining an unconscionably lavish lifestyle. She was thought to be more interested in profit than art; her paintings and sculpture were spoken of as wares hawked from a handcart, and her antecedents made her socially unacceptable. The reporters' genuine amazement at her naturalness and charm in face-to-face interviews bespoke a created stereotype that did not fit the actuality.

From anti-Semitism to commodification was a short step as critics extended their perception of her avarice to a willingness to sell herself. The ambiguities of gender definition complicated the issue: as a woman, Bernhardt was neither housewife nor society matron but rather public figure, and her lifestyle suggested that she would be willing to prostitute herself for the stage. As someone whose presence could be bought but whose freedom could not be curtailed, she posed a challenge to the popular press. Cartoonists pounced on the graphic possibilities of her rumored eccentricities, depicting her as an astonishingly attenuated skeleton sleeping in a coffin; advertisers incorporated her face, form, and name into posters and souvenirs; satirists gave her American nicknames; and columnists described her luxurious costumes in exquisite detail. Whatever was thin, slight, and allied to death was forgettable and irrelevant during the Golden Age, but Bernhardt's "nothingness" was clothed with great magnificence and given value according to the profit it commanded. Bernhardt was furious about many of the caricatures, but perhaps she also understood and participated in the journalistic impulse to create an image. As her *Memoirs* and even her publicly reported tantrums and melodramatic public appearances make clear, she lived her life and then rewrote it to accord with dramatic principles.[5]

The pervasive and sometimes invasive campaign carried on by her impresario, Edward Jarrett, contributed to making her name and face into stock in trade. If her explorer forebears like Cartier and Champlain came to the New World for a combination of adventure and trading possibilities, Bernhardt too came for both artistic and monetary reasons. As an invader, an explorer, she conquered the Americans, from the streets of New York to the bayous of Louisiana. Yet, recolonized in this way for their wealth, the Americans engaged in a typically capitalistic dynamic and demanded fair value for money. The sum totals that are associated with the newspaper reports—how many people were waiting in line, how many tickets were sold, how expensive the seats were, what her profits were, what her costumes cost, what value was set on her jewelry—suggest that her "Frenchness" was put on the market and exchanged for American dollars.

Although newspaper reviewers were at first judgmental, they were won over by her performances, so that the plethora of skeleton sketches and humorous verses gave way to headlines about "the great tragedienne Sarah Bernhardt." Such homage was hard-won for this woman of independent spirit, who refused to let herself be defined by American journalists. In initiating her audience into a new kind of dramatic understanding—theatrical intensity that overcame language boundaries—she introduced them to a species of gender talk that was in other venues unacceptable. The stage provided "free space" on which great movements of passion and untrammeled female sexuality were presented, quite outside the bounds of normal, socially acceptable behavior. Bernhardt, in acting the roles of transgressive women, leaped over the standards that her American hosts held to be permissible. At the same time she was perceived to be breaking rules, however, she was following a theatrical ritual that was highly rule-bound, entailing, as it did, stylized gestures, make-up, costumes, script, and stage plans for setting, props, and lighting. This paradox is buried both in the title and the advice in her little book *The Art of the Theatre*, which Marcel Berger assembled posthumously from her notes and dictations. While she writes that above all one must have both talent and an ineffable quality called charm, her insistence on discipline, determination, and hard work is clear. "The secret of our art consists in preventing the audience from recognizing it to be illusion," she writes, and the way to creating that illusion is "labour" (78). Her comment about "gesture" is a typical blend of her insistence on work and on an inherent vocation: "Gesture, like delivery, can be mastered by dint of study and becomes perfect in course of time. But in no case can study take the place of nature, the innate gifts which constitute the very essence of talent or of genius" (80).

In her mixing of modes and roles, Bernhardt blended a variety of typologies by which nineteenth-century American women have been identified. Even more, she is an early version of what her twentieth-century cultural sisters like Julia Kristeva, Luce Irigaray, and Hélène Cixous demand: one who attempts to "write the body" theatrically and who, in her American tour, challenges a phallocentric system of language and behavior, by adopting and modifying it. Her voice, delivery, physical characteristics, gestures, and, above all, her will, all part of the complex nature of the actor as she describes it in *The Art of the Theatre*, served to overcome the language barrier; and everything else, from her business sense to her love affairs, showed her co-opting a masculine set of rules. Although she refused to be marginalized, in a fundamental way Bernhardt does not fulfill the feminist model. Her allegiance is to a canon of theatrical greats and to Romantic inspiration combined with a Protestant work ethic. Her reiteration of the necessity of personal vitality and the "joy of creation" (*Art of the Theatre* 96) is, therefore, not a joyous submission to *féminité*, but rather the motivating power for an old-fashioned call to the service of art, and art created by male writers at that. As she says, "Art is ageless, and the artist must not know age. Not by indolence or by self-indulgence, but by the absolute possession and mastery of his personality will the artist be able to raise himself to the supreme glory of men whose lives are all creation, all labour, and all enthusiasm" (97).

On the other hand, she was in no way allied to the cult of "True Womanhood," the "[p]iety, purity, submissiveness, and domesticity"[6] that were the repressive and idealistic standards to which nineteenth-century American women were held. Bernhardt's career as a successful actress performing thousands of miles from her home, to say nothing of her proud acknowledgement of her illegitimate son, made these ideals alien to her. The model proposed by Frances Cogan in *All-American Girl* is more useful, suggesting a middle ground—the "Real Woman," who connected physical health and fitness with moral well-being, who was a proponent of higher education and careful preparation for marriage, and who was vocationally trained and employed, albeit putting her duties to home and family first. Bernhardt's vocational training allied her tangentially with such a model, as did her acknowledgment of separate gender spheres, but her peripatetic touring separated her from the "Real Woman's" belief in the value of her own activities in creating and preserving domestic and social order, especially through influence on the home front.

The devotion to separate gender spheres is what best distinguishes the earlier "Real Woman" from the later "New Woman." For the figure that emerged after the 1880s, a career was preferable to domestic influence, and independence, equal fellowship, and reform were the keys to fulfillment (Cogan 258–9). Bernhardt cuts across many lines: both a "Real" and a "New" woman, she embodies the contradictions through which she created her reputation. She wore trousers when she painted and sculpted, but she was not a "Bloomer Girl"; she insisted on Alençon, Bruges, and Languedoc laces on gowns embellished with hand-sewn pearls, but she was nearly always in want of ready cash. While she was at the apex of her acting career, women in the New York Four Hundred refused to meet her socially, yet she hobnobbed with royalty on the Continent. She clearly enjoyed being taken care of (she relied heavily on Jarrett, her maids, and Mme. Guérard, her friend), yet she was stubbornly independent. And, although she could resort to feminine wiles—she fainted when she wanted relief for an unwelcome situation, like being besieged by reporters—she shrewdly insisted on her contractual rights, at the same time honorably living up to workmanlike expectations. What speaks to her equivocal position is that when she returned to the United States in 1916 after more than three decades, she refused to endorse the suffragettes, despite their warm welcome and despite her own lifelong position as a working woman.

Studying Bernhardt's first American tour is, then, to uncover a series of contradictions that seem to reveal somewhat more about American cultural values than about Bernhardt herself. Ultimately, despite the best efforts of her hosts to Americanize her and her own best efforts to theatricalize her life, she cannot be labeled or pigeonholed. Perhaps it is precisely this quality of what might be called French *chutzpah* that energized her and prompted her to adopt as her motto *Quand Même*, a phrase that suggests "I will succeed, no matter what." As to how she herself was affected by her American experiences, her own words provide the key:

> In those few months my mind had matured and the brusqueness of my will was softened.
>
> My life, which I thought at first was to be so short, seemed now likely to be very, very long, and that gave me a great mischievous delight whenever I thought of the infernal displeasure of my enemies.
>
> I resolved to live. I resolved to be the great *artiste* that I longed to be.
>
> And from the time of this return I gave myself entirely up to my life [*Memories* 456].

1

Lady Liberty Sets Sail

> Oh, poor things! poor things! with their Promised Land! Dakota or Colorado... . In the day-time they have the sun which makes their brains boil, scorches the ground, dries up the springs, and brings forth endless numbers of mosquitoes to sting their bodies and try their patience. The Promised Land! ... At night they have the terrible cold to make their eyes smart, to stiffen their joints and ruin their lungs. The Promised Land! [Bernhardt, Memories 375].

Sarah Bernhardt's passionate complaint about the plight of the 760 emigrants crammed into the hold of *L'Amérique*, the ship that brought her to New York, came one day before she celebrated her birthday with a party, gifts, and a bouquet of fresh flowers. The contrast was so great between herself and her penniless compatriots that, as she writes, "I hurried away to my cabin to have a good cry, for I was seized with a great love for humanity and intense grief." But her party inspired another flood of tears for a different reason: "This little fête had evoked the tender and restful side of my life, and the tears that all this called forth fell without grief, bitterness, or regret" (*Memories* 376–7). These outbursts of emotion were typical of Bernhardt, who imaginatively recreated her first transatlantic crossing as a series of melodramatic set pieces. A scoundrelly attack thwarted—a baby delivered—a president's widow saved from certain death—the emigrant defended: these stories, woven into the fabric of her memoirs, were embellished with dialogue and retrospective emotion as she dictated them on her deathbed to her granddaughter Lysiane. Possessed by a storytelling daemon, Bernhardt mixed legend and biography into a colorful account. Her own mythmaking was compounded by a host of satirical portraits and half-

Bernhardt and her granddaughter Lysiane at the Congress Hotel, Chicago. Photograph by Eugene Hutchinson, 13 July 1918. Harry Ransom Humanities Research Center, the University of Texas at Austin.

truths partly fostered by the publicity created by Henry E. Abbey and Henry C. Jarrett,[1] the impresario and business agent who managed her first overseas tour. Both knew the public's thirst for the sensational and assured Bernhardt an enthusiastic welcome by dispatching details of her temperamental disposition, elegant costumes, and eccentric habits to the American press, so that well before she sailed from Le Havre on October 15, 1880, she had become a celebrity on foreign soil.

In her memoirs she denounced the myth about "La Bernhardt" that the press created as "often outrageous and always ridiculous" (*Memories* 385; Skinner 152). Although her much-discussed partiality for coffins, menagerie of wild pets, adventures in a hot-air balloon, and inordinate thinness were among the stories that attracted the curious, they conveyed little of her power as an actress, what the drama critic Francisque Sarcey called her ineffable "*je ne sais quoi*" (Gold and Fizdale 146). This power was fully recognized by Jarrett, whose prestige as a successful agent had been built over the years through a combination of professionalism and sound business sense. His task was to repackage the mixture of talent and bravado that typified Bernhardt's continental reputation for American consumption. He did more than that, fostering her international stardom and solving her financial difficulties without standing in the way of her desire for theatrical independence. An English horn player of high repute, Jarrett was a longtime member of the musical profession who achieved success serving as the business agent for such operatic stars as Christine Nilsson, Marie Van Zandt, and Pauline Lucca.[2] With Abbey as her manager, Jarrett as her agent, and the press as her advertiser, Bernhardt was prepared to take a place not only as leading lady of the day but also as theatrical spectacle.

The satire in the press shows Bernhardt as a talented actress, but one whose personal foibles were exploited for the sake of humor. Underlying the comments about her appearance and lifestyle were hosts of unexamined and perhaps unconscious prejudices and preconceptions. Bernhardt was a theatrical immigrant at a time when large cities in the United States were struggling with problems of assimilation; veiled references to her Jewish background appeared in her physical descriptions and in complaints about her interest in profit. An excellent businesswoman and indefatigable worker, she nonetheless conducted her personal life according to her own lights. Although she behaved like a *grande dame*, she was socially suspect; she conveyed an impression of upper-class charm and physical fragility, but she was not a typical angel in the home. These contradictions, which overturned assumptions about gender and ethnicity, made her difficult to define. In effect, the journalistic responses to Bernhardt embodied a cultural commentary even as they revealed the equivocal nature of the late nineteenth-century frame of mind.

Some of these issues surfaced before she arrived in America. As the events leading up to her 1880–1881 tour suggest, Bernhardt was in much need of a good agent. Unhappily contracted to the Comédie Française, she was eager to pursue a more professionally independent role. Initially, however, although her combination of generosity and spendthrift ways kept her in debt, Jarrett's offer to "make her fortune" did not appeal to her—what she did like was his idea that she present private parlor performances during the troupe's 1879 London season. The director, Emile Perrin, who learned of her decision in the newspapers, was furious; his anger amplified the company's jealousy over her stupendous success at the London Gaiety Theatre and fueled their indignation over her notorious friendship with the Prince of Wales, who provided her an excuse to miss rehearsals while she hobnobbed with the London social set. Off-stage, Perrin exercised even less control over his free-spirited woman of the hour, who horrified the staid residents of London's Chester Square when she acquired additions to her private menagerie, delivered in defiance of the "No Noise Permitted After 10 P.M." sign. Bernhardt took mischievous enjoyment in showing polite society that an energetic and imaginative woman needed neither pedigree nor pence to make her way. Predictably, it was she, not the exasperated Perrin, who moved toward breaking her Comédie Française contract. One purported reason was the irritable reaction of French reviewers to her personal success in England, which they interpreted as a slight to the entire troupe. Angered and distressed by the bombardment of bitter articles and fabrications, Bernhardt nonetheless met the hostility with characteristic verve. Even the threats she received[3] failed to keep her from appearing on stage: braving an expected anti–Semitic demonstration at the annual memorial celebration in honor of Molière, she faced the audience alone—and received an ovation.

Such individual recognition was what she sought: "It was one of the most beautiful moments of my career," she said (qtd. in Gold and Fizdale 156). Her histrionic public acts were part of her temperament, but they were also symptomatic of her desire to succeed on her own. As a member of the Comédie Française, Bernhardt shared top billing, but as an independent performer, she would be a celebrity. To hasten that day, she again double-engaged herself, signing a contract with the London Gaiety theatre and skipping Comédie Française rehearsals under the pretense of illness. Disciplined by Perrin, she publicly announced her displeasure by resigning. The consequent lawsuit, fine, and loss of pension seemed to invigorate her. She engaged Jarrett, who arranged the terms of Abbey's sponsorship, and, after a series of critically acclaimed performances at the Gaiety, she toured Brussels, Copenhagen, and twenty-five cities in France, at the same time assembling costumes and company for her American engagement.

In the United States, the newspapers feasted on the details of her planned visit, indulging in misinformation and editorial asides that spoke of varying degrees of xenophobia. Well before she sailed from Liverpool on October 15, 1880, Bernhardt was reported to be a "shrewder Shylock." Her artistry needed careful scrutiny, the *New York Times* warned, "for curiosity and fashion will pay her that abundant homage which the heart may or may not refuse" (4 July 1880: 7). The issues of anti–Semitism and Francophone distrust became increasingly important in shaping the public response to Bernhardt, as evidenced by the wealth of caricatures and reports that appeared after she arrived. Her challenge, then, was not only to succeed artistically but also to preserve the audience's focus on her professional accomplishments, rather than on ethnic and chauvinistic assumptions. Bernhardt's tour came at a time when the press increasingly catered to public tastes by popularizing celebrity lifestyles. This flood of commentary had two effects: it threatened privacy, but it also helped alter attitudes toward women on stage. A growing number of actresses in the 1880s, including Olga Nethersole, Geneviève Ward, Madge Kendall, Lillie Langtry, and Ellen Terry,[4] presented the spectacle of independent success that redefined perceptions about professional women (Kent 110–11). Bernhardt, one of the pioneers in altering these perceptions, blurred the lines of respectability more than some of her sisters, however, and so became a special target for the press, even before she arrived.

Some of the reports that appeared while she was en route to America were complete fabrications. Since nineteenth-century passengers were *incommunicado* during long sea voyages, fictionalized diaries and stories, farragoes of matter-of-fact details about seasickness, and histrionic recreations of shipboard adventures abounded. Actual details emerged once she arrived. Aside from Jarrett, her traveling companions included her old friend and now rival Marie Colombier, filling in for Bernhardt's sister Jeanne, hospitalized for morphine addiction; and Edouard Angelo, Bernhardt's leading man and sometime lover.[5] According to her memoirs, she began the journey prostrated by grief for the first three days. Skinner more prosaically points out that she was seasick (149), and Gold and Fizdale suggest that it was only the spectacle of Marie Colombier flirting with the captain that restored her (165). In any case, she apparently did prevent Mrs. Lincoln from being dashed down the stairs when a large wave rocked the ship; and, in light of the president's assassination by the actor John Wilkes Booth, she was aware of the poetic justice of her action (*Memories* 370). Some of her accounts of other adventures are down-to-earth—she admits that assisting the ship's doctor at a birth and washing the newborn made her sick—but more commonly she theatricalized her experiences. In writing about her visit below decks, for instance, she transmuted it into a shipboard stage setting, with extras carefully costumed and lighting discreetly muted:

> Everything was there mingled together in that human medley—men, women, children, rags and preserves, oranges and basins, heads of hair and bald pates, half-open lips of young girls and tightly closed mouths of shrewish women, white caps and red handkerchiefs, hands stretched out in hope and fists clenched against adversity[6] [*Memories* 371].

"I leaned over the table to embrace him, but dipped my bangs in his *potage a la Crécy*...." From "A Life on the Ocean Wave: Extracts from the Diary on Shipboard of Mlle. Sarah Bernhardt." *Chic,* 27 October 1880. President and Fellows of Harvard College.

Artistic sensitivity might have blinded Bernhardt to the contrast between her championship of the steerage passengers and her own situation in a flower-filled stateroom generously strewn with personal belongings—sable coverlet, embroidered linens, gold dresser set (Skinner 149)—but her complaint to the purser and captain about the condition of the steerage passengers was sincere in its own way. She was distressed about the shortage of rescue boats, since shipwreck would mean the death of those in the hold; but her idea of "justice" entailed separation, one ship for passengers like her, another for the emigrants (*Memories* 371). She presented a melodramatic plea on behalf of the "Poor things ... poor things ... with their Promised Land." After cataloging the hardships of making a new home in scorching heat and "terrible" cold, she continued with a diatribe against the "slave drivers who trade in white slaves." Before exiting tearfully to her cabin, she excoriated the purser who collected the fares—"[p]oor money economized, copper by copper, tear by tear"—for the kind of greed that she herself will be accused of by her American hosts (*Memories* 375–6). The cadence of her narrative suggests that she reshaped the scene theatrically, combining equal measures of sincerity and passion that made her stage performances so successful.

As these adventures occurred on board, the short-lived comic periodical *Chic* exercised poetic license on land to publish an elaborate satirical welcome in "A Life on the Ocean Wave: Extracts from the Diary on Shipboard of Mlle. Sarah Bernhardt." Skinner fulminates against such treatment of Bernhardt—"Hardly an issue of *Puck*, the humorous periodical, or of a shoddy little weekly called *Chic* appeared without one of these offensive jibes" (158), she complains. No matter how unsophisticated the humor, these periodicals were important in both mirroring and creating public response. *Chic*, along with others like *Puck*, *Life*, and *Judge*,[7] provides comic counterpoint to Bernhardt's own observations and to the themes common in more serious reports. In the *Chic* "diary," for instance, Bernhardt, having been advised to take "specifics" against sea-sickness, finds "brandy, chloral, a hearty dinner, the pork salted" to be of little use. Recuperating from *mal de mer*,[8] she joins a "professor of the mathematic" at dinner: "I leaned over the table to embrace him, but dipped my bangs in his *potage a la Crécy*.... He was disgoost, though why I know not, for there was more *potage* to be got, while my bangs were ruined. However, I have 672 other pairs." Her thinness was a pervading theme—the *New York Times* dubbed her, sight unseen, "the attenuated Sara" (18 Oct. 1880: 4). "Ze horrors, ze horrors," she exclaims: "As I was walking on the deck a brutal and short-sighted mariner seized me in the manner the most aggressive and prepared to mop the decks with me." She is inhaled through the speaking-tube by the steward, who "thought he was swallowing a straw: but recognizing the fact that straws do not wear diamond-hilted *bottines*, he promptly abstained...."; she is nearly spliced into the main-brace; and she strolls the deck with the captain, taking refuge behind "the starboard jibboom of his waxed mustache" whenever a "brawny mariner" appears (*Chic* 27 Oct. 1880: 5). Normally, humor domesticates the unknown to make it familiar: here, Bernhardt's juxtaposition to the hearty seamen underscores her exotic nature, which Skinner describes as an "effect of an incandescent, shimmering aura she gave forth as though she were creating her own eerie limelight" (162).

These fictional adventures, however humorous, reflect a prevailing attitude about women that Bernhardt faced throughout her tour. To the onlooker, she seemed to exemplify the assumption that women were by nature sensitive and unstable: her theatrical success depended upon her emotive powers, and off stage she rarely appeared without her coterie of friends or, in America, without Jarrett or some other escort. In addition, her lifestyle manifested other traits, like illogic and spontaneity, that were seen to be feminine—in many ways, she behaved like a child playing with adult toys. Driven by a mercurial temperament to impulsive acts and public tantrums, she nonetheless exhibited charming manners and beautiful clothing, both of which emphasized her femininity. Many of these characteristics were, however, part of her histrionic stance. Bernhardt, both on and off stage, was the incarnation of Freud's "performing woman," who cannot help her deceptions and who must be "translated" into the logical pattern of the male imagination, a pattern that deprives her of independence and volition. Yet, as Nina Auerbach points out, Freud himself was completely taken in by Bernhardt's convincing acting: "Nothing she said could have surprised me; I believed at once everything she said" (qtd. in Auerbach 26).

Although this "performing woman" in some ways displayed the trappings of the feminine stereotype, she by no means embodied the traits that defined Coventry Patmore's womanly woman:

> ... although in act and word
>   As lowly as a wife can be,
> Her manners, when they call me lord,
>   Remind me 'tis by courtesy;
> Not with her least consent of will,
>   Which would my proud affection hurt,
> But by the noble style that still
>   Imputes an unattain'd desert;
> Because her gay and lofty brows,
>   When all is won which hope can ask,
> Reflect a light of hopeless snows
>   That bright in virgin ether bask ...
>   [from Canto XII, "Husband and Wife"].

In some guises Bernhardt may have looked like an angel, but she more closely resembled the demon that Auerbach writes about. Well removed from the domestic sphere, she had neither home nor husband for whom she served as guiding moral and maternal spirit: rather, she lived in a series of hotels and railroad parlor cars, shared her bed with lovers, and had an illegitimate son whom she passionately and publicly adored. Moreover, many of the figures she portrayed on stage—Phèdre, for instance, or Tosca or Froufrou—were "fallen" women, and so by personal and theatrical reputation, Bernhardt was associated with the demimonde. Perhaps most difficult for the public to accept was her professionalism, which was compounded of the same qualities that had made American businessmen so successful: a tireless worker, she was equally concerned about her profits and her calling. In short, she presented mixed signals to her public. She was both fragile female and hardheaded businesswoman, maternal and loving, but outside of the bounds of acceptable behavior.

Unlike the comic diary in *Chic*, which created a laughable caricature whose dress, accent, body, and mannerisms emphasized her otherness, the press dealt with these contradictions by focusing on her external image. Many newspaper reports, both early and late in the tour, emphasized Bernhardt's clothing as a key to understanding her life and acting. Such commodification, a reflection of 1880s consumerism, suggested commercial prostitution: Bernhardt was "selling" her appearance, not her talent. Indeed, she seemed well aware that public image preceded critical acclaim and so played the public relations game with gusto, all the while striving for theatrical verisimilitude. In accord with the practice at the time, she provided her own stage wardrobe, but because of her interest in period dress, her costumes were detailed and authentic. Bernhardt's particularity about costuming is a function of her early training in the Conservatoire, where the combination of costume (especially when it involved drapery) and gesture was transformed into a vocabulary of its own (Taranow 123–8). Moreover, she was allied with the influential archeological and historical movement in spectacular theatre near the end of the century, when audiences were regaled with historically accurate costumes and huge panoramic effects that were in themselves a show.[9] For Bernhardt, such elaborate settings had a double disadvantage: difficult to take on the road, they also distracted from the actors, a dislocation that she was not likely to countenance. What she did instead for her American tour was to focus on costume authenticity by amassing an expensive collection of imported French silks, Italian velvets, and Russian furs; the embroidered details were of real crystal and mother of pearl (Gold and Fizdale 161; Skinner 147). A host of emotional factors, including her own love of luxurious materials, also came into play in assembling the wardrobe. For Bernhardt to engage her audience in the willing suspension of disbelief, to provide the kind of performance that Freud and others found so convincing, she required the real thing. In effect, her stage costumes were an American dowry that spoke to her social status: as a professional actress, she provided for herself clothing of better quality than wealthy stage-struck amateurs wore in their everyday lives.

In displaying the foreign parvenu as a commodity to the consuming public, the newspaper accounts also domesticated her by making her acceptable in terms of money and appearance. Attracting the fashionable reader, an important part of the *Times*'s editorial strategy, proved from Abbey's and Jarrett's perspective to be a means of free advertising. In the months before and after her arrival, the *Times* published long, detailed, and appreciative dressmakers' descriptions of her new 75,000 franc wardrobe, which, depending on the report, included as many as twenty-seven costumes for

eight plays, twenty-five dresses for everyday wear, and 350 pairs of gloves (17 Aug. 1880: 5; 5 Sept. 1880: 10; 27 Oct. 1880: 8; Richardson 90). This sartorial spectacle influenced the fashions for Fall 1880 and promised a feast for the eyes of those who could not understand either the plots or the language of Bernhardt's repertory. In late August and early September, the *Times* reported particulars about the costumes ordered from the "celebrated Felix of the Rue Boissy d'Angla[i]s in Paris." "A perfect mass of Alençon lace" in Louis XV style for *Adrienne Lecouvreur*, with Bruges and Languedoc lace used for other stage *déshabillés*; diamond pins to fasten both walking and indoor dresses; a bodice covered with "finely-cut jet beads": all these were eclipsed by the "perfect marvel" of a ball dress for *La Dame aux Camélias*, bedecked with "camellias *en relief* on white satin" and "waist and front of the skirt ... covered with fine pearls and bunches of camellias." "This style," the reporter states authoritatively, "is to be one of the great nov-

Opposite and above: Bernhardt's costumes fostered her versatility in playing the ingénue or the woman of the world. Photographs by Napoleon Sarony, 1880. Harry Ransom Humanities Research Center, the University of Texas at Austin.

elties of the Winter, and will be extensively used for ball dresses...." Another of Bernhardt's designs would seem to hold less promise for imitation. The toilet for *Le Sphinx*, for instance, featured "a skirt taken up on the sides by two enormous ravens," which, with masterly understatement, is said to "produce a most singular effect" (27 Oct. 1880: 8; 5 Sept. 1880: 10).

These descriptions, which created valuable publicity, testified to Bernhardt's financial and professional position, thereby effectively separating her from her mother's lifestyle. Importantly, the freedom to design her appearance without regard for money served a psychological purpose, a way of redeeming her youthful vulnerability. In her memoirs Bernhardt records a painful sensitivity to the vulgarity and inappropriateness of her dress when she auditioned at crucial stages of her early career. To prepare for the entrance examination at the Conservatoire de Musique et Déclamation, for instance, she was dressed by her mother in a new low-cut black silk gown of such inferior quality that it had to be mended immediately; too short, it hung above her drawers and her brown boots.[10] A white guimpe was tied around her neck, accentuating its thinness, and an out-of-season straw hat completed the outfit. She was accompanied by her friend Mme. Guérard and her governess Mme. de Brabender, who was arrayed in "a salmon-colored dress," "an Indian shawl," "a very large cameo brooch," and a densely ruched bonnet (*Memories* 66). Her confidence, already at low ebb, was further depressed by her appearance, and she passed the examination only through the good offices of her mother's friend, the Duc de Morny (Gold and Fizdale 43). Likewise, when she went to sign her much-coveted contract with the Comédie Française, her outfit was inappropriate: wearing a white hat trimmed in blue, a dress of "hideous cabbage green with black velvet put on in Grecian pattern," and a turquoise ring, Bernhardt remembered looking "like a monkey" (*Memories* 94).

Once she made her debut and settled into a life that in part mirrored her mother's (in private, a series of liaisons; in public, a series of engagements at the Gymnase Theatre, where she appeared in popular plays), she learned considerably more about couture and about behaving in front of an audience. The gawky teenager with long legs and unruly hair had become a fashionable woman. Like her mother, she had an *affaire de coeur;* her lover was the Prince de Ligne, by whom she had a son, Maurice. Bernhardt, however, wanted to act, not merely keep a salon, and this ambition, pursued with determination and an unquenchable sense of adventure, is what

Opposite: **Bernhardt in costume for *La Dame aux Camélias*. Photograph by Napoleon Sarony, 1880. Harry Ransom Humanities Research Center, the University of Texas at Austin.**

eventually made her "La Bernhardt," rather than her mother's daughter. Near the end of her life, when she warned about artistic indolence, she formulated what she had perhaps understood instinctively when she moved from being a member of the demimonde to a celebrated actress:

> In the theatre, the nervous tension never ceases, physical effort is added to and fused with intellectual effort.... [I]f will power be not invoked, if in their creation of this or that character, [the actors] were not sustained at once by their high artistic conscience and a determination that is proof against everything, they would very often be tempted to stick to the parts already mastered [Art 96–7].

What the public was initially aware of during her first American tour was not, however, her determination to succeed; rather, they saw a well-advertised product for which they were asked to pay dearly. As if to underscore that aspect of her tour, Bernhardt was immediately involved in an argument over tariffs; arriving in New York in the thick of a legal dispute about dutiable items, she had her belongings impounded. The customs law originally designed to exclude immigrants' household belongings and trade tools had customarily protected actors' effects as well, but had been abused, as the *Times* reports: "Actresses have been known to import fine dresses for ladies in private life on commission under this construction of the law" (27 Oct. 1880: 8). Consequently, Bernhardt was caught by a precedent set the previous year, when the impresario Col. Mapleson brought his opera troupe to New York and was made to pay duty on all costumes and stage sets. The conservative approach followed by New York Customs House Collector General G. A. Merritt may have been an effort to remove himself from the raging political battle in which General Arthur, accused of making political appointments to the customs houses, produced letters from President Hayes demanding that he make those very appointments. When Mapleson appealed, Secretary Sherman upheld Merritt, issuing a ruling that "theatrical properties owned and controlled by theatrical managers and used by individual actors under their management shall be dutiable" (*New York Times* 27 Oct. 1879: 8).

Because of the Mapleson precedent, Bernhardt's costumes were impounded in Booth's Theatre. Her colorful memories of the "chiffon court martial" suggest another reason for the strict enforcement of duty: a political argument about importing foreign (especially French) fashions. She was offended by the officer with his cigar and "melon" of a hat and by the "forty dirty hands" of the Customs inspectors; and she was equally offended by the two dressmakers, "odious shrews," who made the evaluation. She complained about the "Black Band" of inspectors who foraged

Bernhardt at 16 years of age. Carte de visite, unknown photographer, 1860. Harry Ransom Humanities Research Center, the University of Texas at Austin.

through her belongings and drew a vivid picture of the "Terrapin" and the "Seated Cow," who, fingering the luxurious materials, raised a hullabaloo over the "ruin of all the American dressmakers" caused by the "foreign invaders" (*Memories* 387). Other reports suggest that she was actually given special treatment: faced with luggage containing over three hundred pairs of gloves, seventy-five pairs of shoes, and at least forty dresses, the officers allowed her to take three unexamined trunks to the hotel. In the meantime Collector Merritt disallowed duty on dresses worn once and ruled that her sculpture, which she had brought to exhibit and sell, could be treated as "household goods" (*Philadelphia Bulletin* 28 Oct. 1880: 3; 30 Oct. 1880: 6). By the time Bernhardt entered a plea similar to Mapleson's, however, the response from Washington had changed, and Assistant Secretary H. F. French refunded Bernhardt $1,560, ruling her costumes to be "professional implements or tools of trade." As such, they fell under the provision for "wearing apparel in actual use and other personal effects (not merchandise), professional books, implements, instruments, and tools of trade, occupation, or employment of persons arriving in the United States" (*New York Times* 12 Dec. 1880: 5). Bernhardt, as a theatrical "immigrant," had won her first battle over money in the United States. She then proceeded to spend it: on her first hectic day in America, she went shopping, including a Fifth Avenue piano warehouse among her visits (*New York Sun* 29 Oct. 1881: 1).

Well before the customs officials dealt with Bernhardt, however, they had taken possession of her company's theatrical belongings. Those who arrived on the *Wieland*, the ship that docked at Hoboken at 1:30 P.M. on Oct. 4, were given little press coverage. The *New York World* reporter had a clear field. After presenting a lively picture of Abbey's winded agent arriving late at the bottom of an extremely steep gangway, he introduced the company according to their roles[11] and noted that they would be housed in privately run French boarding houses. What followed was a narrative of the various disasters that occurred before the trip, including a carriage accident that incapacitated the second leading lady, who spent the voyage recuperating from a broken knee-cap and playing "heavy" games of baccarat. Like Bernhardt's luggage, the troupe's fifty-nine trunks of varying sizes, twenty-two pieces of hand luggage, fourteen satchels, and an undetermined number of bundles, hat-boxes, and umbrellas were confiscated by "monsters" posing as customs officers (qtd. in *Philadelphia Bulletin* 27 Oct. 1880:1).

When Bernhardt arrived two weeks later, Abbey had invited 103 guests to form a welcoming party on the steamship *Blackbird* to meet *L'Amérique* after it left quarantine.[12] The 5 A.M. trip was cold and damp, especially since the hampers of food and drink remained closed to hungry reporters. When the two ships met, a French flag was run up the *Blackbird*'s bow and the band struck up the "Marseillaise," but "the high wind ... carried the inspiration of a dirge" and those on *L'Amérique* regarded the "dull and dismal stolidity" of the "ulstered reception party" with wonder. On board the ravenous welcoming party breakfasted on domino-sized pieces of ham as they waited for Bernhardt. When she suddenly appeared, swathed in furs, the reporter is unavoidably reminded of Dumas's comment about Bernhardt and her dog—"[I]t was the picture of a dog looking at a bone." Her feelings on the occasion are well documented; less so is the treatment of Mrs. Lincoln, who, a shabby figure with white hair and torn cloak, waited alone on board and then left, "unrecognized and unknown" (Verneuil 128), only to be brushed aside by a policeman so that the actress could be ushered with fanfare into her carriage (*New York Sun* 28 Oct. 1881: 3).

In her memoirs Bernhardt recorded the extreme discomfort of shaking hands endlessly and accepting effusive greetings in a foreign tongue, and she presented herself as a victim of satirical persecution and of "the basest calumnies" circulated not only by the reporters but by her enemies, among whom she numbered Marie Colombier (*Memories* 385). The *New York Times* and *Daily Graphic* provided a more moderate perspective. Despite Bernhardt's claim that she fainted from exhaustion during the early-morning shipboard breakfast (*Memories* 379–381), that ungracious episode received no coverage in these newspapers. Instead, the *Times* conceded that "no pen-picture of the 'divine Sara' has done her justice. The apparition was not gaunt, nor did it have red hair ..."; rather, she is described as a "lady ... ethereal yet womanly." Her personal features were anatomized— "a perfect head ... wealth of silken hair ... [w]onderful black eyes ... a faultless nose"; and she was said to possess "charming grace" and to be "animated" and "warm and earnest" as she "gossiped like a school-girl about her voyage and herself" (27 Oct. 1880: 8).

The *Daily Graphic* presented a more detailed and somewhat different report. It agreed that her face is "finer in its lines" than expected and "remarkably clear"; her blush is "natural," and her nose has "no such prominence" as had been depicted; her "tawny blonde hair" has a "reddish hue ... so unique as to lead to a possible suspicion of tonsorial interference with nature's work"; and her eyes are "true blue."[13] Bernhardt hid her discomfort well: the *Times* praised her "charming grace" and "animated conversation" and said that only "a few persons were favored with introductions" (27 Oct. 1880: 8), but what she remembered was the "terrible" and "tiring" line of people with names of "muffled vowels and hissing consonants," her hands swelling around her rings, her teeth chattering, and her histrionic faint. In the *Times* account, however, she sipped champagne, accepted a "floral trophy," listened to the band, and then drove away to the Albemarle Hotel. In the *Daily Graphic*, every detail of her costume "in excellent taste" was described and every gesture recorded, from the expressive movements of her hands and tapping of her "kid-covered feet" to her farewell to Mrs. Lincoln.

During her New York visit, the *Graphic* published sedate reviews, accounts,[14] and illustrations similar in tone to its first complimentary sketch heralding "La Divine Sarah." Published in July, the illustration showed the actress as a rising star, her long, slender body forming a comet's tail on which sit her maids carrying hairbrush and comb, "*poudre*," scent bottles, and brushes and easel, all followed by a crowd bearing placards announcing her plays (14 July 1880: 67). Upon her arrival, the *Graphic* showed her being welcomed by Father Knickerbocker (28 Oct. 1880: 900–901). This "pictorial tale" was produced, as the newspaper reports, by five enterprising reporters who scattered over the ship sketching and taking notes, while a sixth "told her in choice French how the American public hungered for the dawn of the day whereon she would give them the privilege of gazing on her charming presence and of being ennobled by her divine art"—an address that sounds tongue-in-cheek, except that the adulatory tone was mirrored in the sketches of Bernhardt in various elegant poses, captioned as a group "The Greatest Tragic Actress of the Age." Sarah in her stateroom, with heavily upholstered bed and ruffled drapes; Sarah gazing politely at "the grain elevators and other objects of interest around the harbor"; Sarah drinking tea with some two dozen strangers in the salon; Sarah, home at last, surveying her spacious rooms at the Albemarle: these seem well within the tradition of journalistic illustration rather than caricature. From the personal portraits to the small details, like the chandelier in the salon and the patterned teacups, the *Graphic*'s sketches conveyed an attempt to capture the moment with politeness and good taste.

The very different welcome accorded her by the *New York Clipper*, the well-known sporting and theatrical magazine, was typical of brash, breezy "American" humor.[15] Although it published a flattering drawing of the actress as Doña Sol on its front page, the *Clipper* dealt with Bernhardt in a casual way, domesticating her as "one of the boys." On a riff about the recent wave of spectacular and lavish presidential campaign demonstrations,[16] the reportorial staff mused about hijacking a torchlight political parade and diverting it to the dock, where they would "hail her with three American cheers and one Bengal tiger. This would have given her a very favorable idea of our republican form of government...." Fireworks, Barnum's chariots, and "elephants, camels, and educated mules" from the Forepaugh-Sells's circus were to be enlisted for transportation (30 Oct. 1880: 254). When Bernhardt actually did arrive, the *Clipper* recreated the debarkation as a music hall revue in which the "boys" embraced Bernhardt and handed her a bunch of sunflowers, singing:

> Oh, Sarah B., aint you coming out to-night,
>   Coming out to-night, coming out to-night?
> Oh Sarah B., aint you coming out to-night,
>   To dance by the light of the moon?
> She wears a brand-new sealskin sacque,
>   Sealskin sacque, sealskin sacque,
> And yellow hair all down her back,
>   Which cost a hundred francs.

Bernhardt responds in kind: "With the agility of an acrobat she sprang up the rattling and with one hand grasping the American flag and the other waving her little hat, she cried out: 'Oh, yes, indeed, I've come out to-night ... / To dance by the light of the moon'" (6 Nov. 1880: 252).

Rather than dancing, Bernhardt was peacefully napping at the Albemarle while Jarrett fulminated and her maid held off the admirers who wanted to meet her. Although the *New York Times* was circumspect, Skinner writes that when a number of reporters came to her hotel room, a replication of her Paris parlor with bearskin rugs, busts, flowers, and drapes, Bernhardt threw herself face down on the rug with a shriek and then locked herself in her bedroom and barred the door with a bureau (157). Her actual meeting with the New York reporters, whom she grew to detest not only for their questions about her religion but for their unflattering cartoons, was inauspicious: she answered their questions indifferently and, with mischievous weariness, claimed that she ate nothing but mussels at breakfast, lunch, and dinner. It was that kind of answer that prompted some of the doggerel verses, like the one published in *Chic*:

> I travelled with Sarah from Havre,
>   A quite lovely time too I had,
> She's the n-yum, n-yumer, n-yumest enslaver,
>   That ever bloomed into a fad.
> She was sick for at least half the passage,
>   And sulky the most of the way,
> Would eat nothing but onions and sassage,
>   Washed with gin and Imperial To-kay.
>
> Every man on the boat she set crazy
>   By a nod, or a beck, or a smile;
> As for me, I was luckily lazy,
>   And partly done up with the bile.
> The captain! oh, how he adored her!
>   He scarce left the seat by her side,
> I saw how completely he bored her,
>   When her yawns in her poodle she'd hide.

> The cook for that dog made up dishes,
>   That smacked of Phillipe's or Trois Frères,
> But they soon went their way to the fishes,
>   For the poodle was quite *mal-de-mer*.
> Her maids! how these soubrettes did suffer,
>   As they waited on Sara in gangs?
> The one that was oldest and tougher,
>   'Tween gasps, did her mistress' bangs...
>   [27 Oct. 1880: 7].

When Bernhardt's replies grew too absurd, Jarrett took over answering while she closed her eyes and withdrew to the comforts of her couch. In actuality, the reporters could hardly do better than quote her directly: complaining about giddiness because of the ship's motion, she says, "I have on still my 'sheep legs'—I believe it is called" (qtd. in *Philadelphia Bulletin* 28 Oct. 1880: 3).

Others, more unscrupulous, fabricated entire pseudo-biographies. One such scurrilous work—*"Too Thin;" Skeleton Sara. Her "Realistic" Life and Adventures in America*—purported to carry Bernhardt's imprimatur:

> I think *"Too Thin"* perfectly charmant, and I would like to (viskey) punch its author's head. Ze Melican man very funny. Please do not forget to send me one copy of ze very first edition. I will send you ze ten cents as soon as I make another, what you call, "raid" on my New York Manager.

The author, Isaac G. Reed, presents her American tour as a vehicle for self-advertisement and indulgence. Forgetting her four children, she leaps from the steamer, showing a quantity of petticoat and leg, plows through the food on the dinner table, and creates a sensation by "rehearsing 'Frou-Frou' with her pet skeleton—the skeleton of a man who had killed himself for love." She threatens to send for De Witt Talmage, a popular clergyman who preached against her, to inspire her at rehearsals; unpacks 2700 dresses, which, it is said, "if sewed together, would constitute a bridge of dry goods spanning (or rather *skirting*) the Atlantic, and uniting Paris and New York"; and auctions herself to the highest bidder. The entire screed ends with a scenario and a punch line: a "gentleman ... with banged eyes, swelled and cut cheek, lost teeth, crumpled collar, torn coat, and ... boots, had just passed through the 'fiery ordeal' of getting tickets ... for the purpose of seeing '*The best advertised woman in the world!*'"

Aside from this travesty, the kind of humor that offended Bernhardt was testimony to the reporters' over-eagerness to make headlines and their pique at being locked out of her hotel suite. The "horrible drawing of a skeleton with a curly wig" that she snatched from a reporter and tore up (*Memories* 384) may have been an early sketch for "Behind the Scenes: The Truth About Sara," published in *Chic* on 3 November; it shows a balding and skeletal woman whose attractive maids are trying to make presentable with wig and paint, while reporters are scrambling over a chest of drawers barricading the door (16). Other caricatures, like Frederick Opper's welcoming drawing in *Puck*—"The Bernhardt Boom in New York"—fit into a more traditional mode of comic exaggeration. In a city playing host to a famously slender actress, everything is elongated, including her coffin-shaped luggage, the wine bottle and loaf of French bread, her bed, and "The Telegraph Pole as an Advertising Medium" (27 Oct. 1880: 13). By the time Bernhardt left America in May 1881, this joke had been repeated countless times.

In the less innocuous sketches, however, a charming woman is disfigured into a skeletal shape, so that she is no longer an icon of fertility and regeneration, but rather an icon of death. To exaggerate a feature or an eccentricity is, of course, the way of satire; but the prevailing caricatural approach to Bernhardt carries implications of gender misrepresentation and cultural ill-health. As the immature response of an immature nation, such exaggeration devalues what seems threatening and seeks to impose its own frame of reference politically (i.e., whatever is foreign is allied to non-being). Too, it affirms by indirection that Bernhardt is indeed a very dangerous woman, sexually, economically, and politically. Stripping her to a skeleton to reveal what lies beneath the charm and costumes and finding only thinness, or nothingness, is a retelling of the story about the Emperor's new clothes; it is also an existential suggestion that the real Bernhardt is ungraspable aside from the masquerade. This attempt to control a disruptive force through disrobing is an effort to come to terms graphically with the contradiction between her fragility and her drive for success that the satirists dealt with verbally.

For her popular audience, Bernhardt's apparent delicacy validated her femininity, but it also defined her class status, placing a verifiable social distance between her and the factory woman whose robust physical nature allowed her to work long hours. Yet the conflict between Bernhardt's stature and her work ethic disrupted that comfortable class assumption, as did her dubious social antecedents. Moreover, because her slenderness was constitutional, she was unable to conform completely to the fashion of the time, which demanded a full bust and hips as well as a tiny waist (in the 1880s, the average waist measurement was twenty-two inches). This hourglass figure was achieved by lacing, which was not only a fashion statement but also a

Sarah Bernhardt's First American Theatrical Tour, 1880–1881

BEHIND THE SCENES.--The truth about Sara.

moral one about the confluence of "correct manners, bearing, and deportment" (Steele 161); nonetheless, as Helena Michie points out, achieving this shape required that "women live in two bodies at the same time"—the sensuous woman's and the schoolgirl's (23). Bernhardt's willowy figure seemed to cross the borderline that separated the appropriate moral "discipline of the corset" that taught submissiveness and "self-abnegation" and the far more dangerous area of sexual knowledge, since reducing the waist by four or more inches was thought to excite "the organs of Amativeness" (Steele 161–165; 182). That overall slenderness, then, suggested a paradox: her body, apparently the site of nothingness, was fraught with the forbidden knowledge of carnality.

As constructed and exposed to the public eye, Bernhardt's figure was inscribed with cultural values. In effect, readers critiquing her caricatures were like the 1860s sensation novel readers described by Pamela Gilbert: they become "the body of culture, observing itself clinically for signs of disease, voyeuristically for signs of pleasure, censoriously for signs of rebellion, above all anxiously for signs of vulnerability" (13). What these readers "saw" in the Bernhardt caricatures, then, was a society that was preoccupied with shaping women to its expectations about class and sexuality. It was, too, a society that enjoyed looking at, if not experiencing, the forbidden, since much of its enjoyment came from the moral satisfaction of resisting pleasure and thereby defining its identity by means of what it resisted. In a capitalistic nation that prided itself on freedom, such a stance seems contradictory, but is so only superficially; in effect, viewers could "have" Bernhardt without paying the price.

These contradictions are summed up humorously in "Bernhardt's Banquet," a parodic verse in *Puck* that suggests a reason for the outspoken reactions to the actress, both positive and negative: Bernhardt's "improprieties," her feistiness, her determination to make her own way are, in effect, American characteristics. In this verse the poet Walt Whitman, another breaker of traditions, rises with a prophetic toast, that the Americans will absorb Bernhardt as one of their own:

> Sadie!
> Woman of vigorous aspirations and remarkable thinness!
> I hail you. I, Walt Whitman, son of thunder, child of the ages,
>   I hail you.

The "horrible drawing of a skeleton with a curly wig" that Bernhardt snatched from a reporter and tore up may have been an early sketch for "Behind the Scenes: The Truth About Sara." Chic, 3 November 1880. President and Fellows of Harvard College.

> I am the boss poet, and I recognize in you an element of bossness that approximates you to me.
> Blast your impudence!—I like it.
> Your advertising dodges—your bogus sculptures—your painting—your impropriety—your coffin exhibited to all beholders and shown in the newspapers up.
> I like these things. I am these things. I, Walt, the son of a gun, I am all and every one of these things.
> I am the coffin and the painting, and the sculptures, and the improprieties—I am all these; I enter into them and become them...
>
> [27 Oct. 1880: 122].

Despite the imperialistic bravado of this verse, not all welcomed the actress in that way. The Woman's League of Orange, New Jersey, for instance, understood the social and sexual threats posed by the actress and took up cudgels to protect their families and class status. These women, described as "the wives and daughters of conspicuous gentlemen of North and South Orange," held a meeting to determine "how to defend our country against this European *courtisane* who is coming over to corrupt our sons" (Skinner 155). The discussion—"Does the private character of the actor concern the public"—ended with an informal poll. At least one member had been involved in women's suffrage; even so, only two or three of the twenty-nine present were willing to confess publicly that they felt comfortable going to Bernhardt's performances (*New York Times* 18 Nov. 1880: 1). Bernhardt not only embodied contradictions, she illuminated them in others: although the women at the meeting objected to her qualities—"bossness," for instance, and "aspirations," to say nothing of "impropriety"—those qualities could easily be identified as ones that had made successful businessmen of the husbands in Orange, New Jersey. This business ethic, a complex bundle of aspirations involving money, class, and respectability, largely concerned many of those who refused to welcome her into New York society, but it also motivated those who sought to make their fortunes by her means.

2

Sarah and the Four Hundred

> To be thin, to go up in balloons, to paint, to sculpt, to repose in coffins and to affect the society of skeletons ought to be enough to make any woman famous; but it appears that Mlle. Sadie Bernhardt has another specialty—she acts [*Puck* 17 Nov. 1880: 175].

Bernhardt's acting ability was often confused with other issues, particularly those involving economic matters. The actress and her business manager, however, were not the only ones interested in profit: the ticket scalpers were as well. Their role, already established as part of the American ethos of free enterprise, raised some of the same resentment about unfair ticket prices and overvalued goods that Bernhardt's role as profiteer did. The popular commentary, both serious and satirical, focused on the gender, class, and ethnicity issues that became evident when she stepped out of a prescribed female frame of maternalism and self-sacrifice and placed a monetary value on her talent. This commentary often found its expression in caricatures and satires involving the body. Since she sold her talent, she could not be a "lady," as her fragility suggested; rather, she was subtly accused of being engaged in a form of economic prostitution, so that her thinness became a double metaphor for libidinousness and avariciousness. Moreover, what seemed to be her primary interest in making a profit fell heir to prevailing anti–Semitic attitudes that blamed the Jewish population for local economic woes.

Before it interviewed her in person, the *New York Times* was suspicious about Bernhardt's professionalism. Announcing her contract with Henry

Abbey at Booth's Theatre, the newspaper warned that she was not to be depended upon to keep her agreement; she was money-hungry—her demands were "simply preposterous" and "betray in the actress a greed which harmonizes ill with her claims as an artist" (4 July 1880: 7). In the popular mind, this picture of Bernhardt as a money-grubber was borne out by her terms: as the *New York Times* reported, in addition to $500 for each performance as well as the proceeds from benefits, she was to receive $1000, plus one-half of the gross receipts over $3000 and a weekly expense account for herself and three servants.[1] By December she had reportedly amassed almost $100,000 (4 July 1880: 73; 5 Dec. 1880: 7). Abbey's successful entrepreneurship was envied, even though initially he was taken to task for his risky investment in a temperamental French leading lady. The opening night theatre boxes that he auctioned on November 4 aroused little interest: aside from one speculative investor who bought most of the seats, only four other bidders took part, the highest offering $300. On opening night, however, unsold tickets were at a premium, and patrons jammed the streets and lobby:

> Ah, ah! how husbands are sighing,
> Promising jewels, and satins, and laces.
> Wives know better; such trifles denying,
> They cry out, for "Booth's, and the *very* best places."
>   Sarah has come!
>   [*Chic* 27 Oct. 1880: 3].

If Bernhardt was willing to sell, then the public, it seems, was willing to pay: Abbey was rumored to have taken over $7000 in receipts for the first night, with regular admission prices ranging from $1 to $60.[2]

Even relatively naïve groups, like the mothers in Orange, New Jersey, were quick to make the connection between Bernhardt's economic shrewdness and her bodily stature: if she is always hungry, never satisfied, then her new "lover"—the United States—will have to pay dearly for the privilege of entertaining her. A verse in *Chic* played with the idea that American money would "fatten" Bernhardt:

> Even now the rush for tickets
>   Is so great each day
> That policemen range like pickets
>   Warning crowds away.
> Ah, the people will discreetly
>   Greet you with their tin;
> Just because you are so sweetly
>   Thin.

>   Yes, you'll capture in your drag-net
>   Piles of Yankee gold,
>   Most entrancing little magnet
>   Of the dreamy mold.
>   And we trust that you may star to
>   'Frisco e'en and win
>   Fortunes—then who'll say you are too
>   Thin?
>   [13 Oct. 1880: 2].

Chic's visual expression of the same idea—"Sarah Bernhardt.—New York's Latest High Pressure Craze"—equated Bernhardt's sexuality with her commercial value. In this double-paged lithograph, reminiscent of the sinuous lines of Aubrey Beardsley's work, Bernhardt poses theatrically, her gold gown reflecting the coins she walks through. The drawing portrays her as another Danae, impregnated by Zeus in a shower of gold; the implication is that the Americans have prostituted themselves by buying expensive tickets (27 Oct. 1880: 8–9).[3] Because audiences were alive to the business ethic and understood the value of advertisement, Bernhardt, already accused of self-salesmanship, became a lightning rod for existing complaints about theatrical commercialization. *Puck* adapts the last scene in *La Dame aux Camélias* into "A Sketch Which is Both a Prophetic Vision and a Practical Suggestion": all of the stage properties are labeled according to their manufacturers, from the "Carpet on installments by Kougan" on which Marguerite dies, to the trumpet by "Blowfree Music Company" (8 Dec. 1880: 223). Other satirists seemed aware that the public was accusing Bernhardt of its own mercenariness. In *Chic*'s continuation of her "Life on the Ocean Wave" "diary," she is mobbed by American entrepreneurs, but the satire is double-edged:

> To-day when I go out about one thousand enterprising youths inundate me with the fragmentary literature of the pavement, recommending me to drink these bitters, to wear those pantaloons, to read that paper, to 'ave my 'at block while I wait for 50 cents, as eef I would wait for 50 cents.

"Fortunately," she writes, "I concealed myself behind a lamp-post, and the infuriated mob passed by. I have seen the terrors of the Commune, but it was as nothing by comparison" (3 Nov. 1880: 4–5).

Once her art show at the Union League[4] was announced, she faced a press skeptical that she could divide her talents between acting and art, and convinced that her gallery show was another example of profitable self-advertisement. Some charged her with aesthetic chicanery: *Chic* announced,

4 CHIC.

Bernhardt confronts a shoe salesman. *Chic*, 3 November 1880. President and Fellows of Harvard College.

for instance, that she had "chiselled [a bronze bust] in two days." These suspicions were shared by polite society as well. Although her artistic talent attracted international admirers, in New York she was ostracized by the smart set. Bernhardt's unconventional lifestyle, her affiliation with business and theatre, rumors about her mother, and her Jewish background weighed heavily against her, despite her acceptance in court circles in both England and France. These fears are reflections of the anti–Semitic spirit of the time, when Jews were becoming increasingly unwelcome at private schools, resorts, and upper-class social clubs like the Union League, whose conservative members saw themselves as political and cultural guardians. This club, initially established to support Northern interests during the Civil War, was one of the social organizations that used exclusivity as a way to earmark social differences that were economically indistinguishable. As

Opposite: "Sarah Bernhardt.—New York's Latest High Pressure Craze." *Chic*, 27 October 1880. Harry Ransom Humanities Research Center, the University of Texas at Austin.

John Higham suggests, this developing sensitivity to class-consciousness derived from the insecurities faced by a population whose financial status outstripped its social acclimation ("Social Discrimination," rpt. in Gurock, 216, 238).

Complaints about Bernhardt's entrepreneurial activities seem to be related to growing anti-Semitic sentiment in the last quarter of the century, fueled by a general perception that Jewish businessmen were in control of American finance. The public activities of American Jews that began in the 1870s established a power nexus that had political and cultural overtones: Solomon Loeb and Joseph Seligman in banking and Emanuel and Mayer Lehman in railroads are only a few of those who became millionaires through hard work and determination. The success of the large international banking houses of Baron Rothschild and Lazard Frères furthered anti-Semitic paranoia, as did the political progress in England of Benjamin Disraeli (Handlin 329). During these years, the less threatening stereotype of the Jew as moneychanger was expanded to suggest infiltration and control on a global scale. As the socialist Laurence Gronlund noted,

> Our era may be called the *Jewish age*. The Jews have indeed had a remarkable influence on our civilization. Long ago they infused in our race the idea of one God, and now they have made our whole race worship a new true God: the Golden Calf.... "Jewism," to our mind, best expresses that special curse of our age, *Speculation* [qtd. in Handlin 332].

Gronlund's comment presents two stereotypes—economic and religious—that affected Bernhardt's public reception; a third, related to vulgarity and racial appearance, was most evident in caricature and in satire, where it was symptomatic of a developing tradition in American humor. In part, the strong jingoistic feelings that united the upper classes and the "plebian anti-Semites" were responsible in part for the stereotypes (Higham, "Anti-Semitism," rpt. in Gurock, 573). The sense that America was under European control, whether because of its investments or its large numbers of immigrants, fostered a pugnacious brand of nationalism that helped shape the distaste for "foreigners" that Bernhardt faced. If, as Higham says, the populists, the patricians, and the poor were the sources of much anti-Semitism in the Gilded Age, then indeed the hostility from the press on both ends of the scale is explainable, from the published concerns about whether to recognize the working actress in "polite society" to the raw American humor that lampooned her profit-making.

The sometimes-unfriendly reception of Bernhardt's artwork demonstrates some of these anti-Semitic elements. In bringing her paintings and sculpture to America for a series of gallery shows, she was seen as conducting a shyster business venture. Most reviewers did not take her efforts seriously, although her sculpture showed facility for the plastic arts; the members of polite society invited to her receptions reiterated the journalistic reaction by focusing more on the spectacle of Bernhardt than on her artworks. In light of the paucity of Jewish literary and artistic endeavors in the Gilded Age, this response is not surprising (Higham, "Social Discrimination," rpt. in Gurock, 236–37): those who saw her as a female Shylock would have few American Jewish artists to compare her to. Bernhardt's own attitude as an actress was a mixture of the entrepreneurial and the professional. She agreed to charge nominal admission prices to the gallery and willingly stood shaking hands with innumerable viewers, but she was serious about her artwork. Although she began her artistic vocation as an outlet for her energy between roles and performances at the Comédie Français (Skinner 95), she did have expert training, studying the basics with the sculptor Mathieu-Meusnier, whose works were popular but not enduring. Her friend and lover, the artist Gustave Doré, may have influenced her to sentimentalize her subjects, but more importantly, he motivated her to introduce psychological intensity.[5] A mixture of the peasant and the man about town, Doré exhibited a zest for life and social bonhomie much to Bernhardt's liking; he also provided her with artistic contacts. Because of their joint friendship with Charles Garnier, the architect of the Monte Carlo Casino, Bernhardt was successful in having her sculpture *Le Chant* serve as a pendant to Doré's *La Danse* on the façade (Gold and Fizdale 131–33), a major aesthetic achievement that moved her well beyond the avaricious amateurism she was accused of.

The negative reception of Bernhardt's artwork was also tinged with gender prejudice. As she entered wholeheartedly into a Bohemian lifestyle in the mid–1870s, she adopted an outfit of shirt and pants as her studio attire, a jaunty mixture of comfort and panache at a time when such clothing held strong significance. Cross-dressing in the theatre had a long and colorful history, although on the legitimate stage it was normally confined to men playing female roles. However, the picture postcards on which Bernhardt appeared in her new costume allied her in the public mind with the underworld of transvestism that violated assumptions about moral standards, particularly because this experiment in clothing was accompanied by a warm relationship with the talented painter Louise Abbéma.[6] Bernhardt's lifestyle caused a stir in the press: her detractors decried her friendship with Abbéma, whose short hair, mannish suits, and showy devotion spoke of her sexual preferences, and they took Bernhardt's white silk pants outfit to be proof of orgies held at her studio, where she played at

Bohemianism and served her guests undrinkable tea. Along with Abbéma, Bernhardt welcomed the painter Georges Clairin into her circle. The details of Clairin's life are obscure, but his Bernhardt portraits are well known; he brought the insight of a lover and then of a close friend to his paintings, many of which show her in private moments.[7] Even without the ordinary complement of satirists and scandalmongers, her experience as an artist in France was eventful. Émile Zola himself mounted a defense of her lifestyle, and she conducted a well-publicized tantrum over Baron Rothschild's disparagement of the bust he had commissioned (Gold and Fizdale 129–35; Skinner 97). Nonetheless, she had the support of well-known writers and artists, who found her to be an attractive artistic subject in her own right, and her sculpture, much praised, was ensconced in a public venue in Monte Carlo. No wonder, then, that she felt professionally confident about bringing her creations before the American public.

Ignoring her artistic and theatrical talent, some of the satirists reveled in moral disapprobation. She is shown to be guilty of impropriety and, perhaps more significant, not conversant with social protocol: in the parodic *Chic* "diary" she purportedly writes that she "cannot understand—the effrightful paucity of ... female relations" of those who visit her at the Union League and records naïvely the purported excuses the "misters Americans" give her—one "gentleman" said that "he did not think his wife was a proper person for [her] to associate with" (24 Nov. 1880: 6). Her response to real libels in England had been to write a letter in defense of her son: "I have a child; I love him.... If when he was born I had strangled him and thrown him into the gutter I should be at peace with society. But que voulez vous? I am so original that I prefer to be at peace with my conscience and with God" (qtd. in *Boston Globe* 4 Dec. 1880: 3). In America one of her few early champions was Jehan Soudan, who published a letter in the *New York Sun* deploring the insults she faced; they included a proposition from a small-time operator trying to find a partner in an "obscene libel" and a letter requesting a tête-à-tête accompanied by a gift of diamonds. Not all of her acquaintances were as gallant as Soudan. She was snubbed by James Stebbins, a wealthy art collector who had insisted on making her acquaintance in Paris. Even the well-meaning editor of the *New York Herald*, James Gordon Bennet, further compromised her by hosting an all-male supper-party at Delmonico's that the press unfairly sensationalized as an "orgy." Afterward, says Skinner, New York society women, even those who had importuned their husbands for tickets to her performances, held aloof from the Union League viewing (164–66; Gold and Fizdale 171–72).

The truth of that report must be balanced against the *Graphic*'s illustration, "Sarah Bernhardt Receiving her Friends at the Union League Theatre,"

Á Sarah Bernhardt, engraving after the original in the Gallery of the Théâtre Comédie. Portrait by Jules Bastien-Lepage (engraver, E. Champollion), 1879. Harry Ransom Humanities Research Center, the University of Texas at Austin.

which shows clusters of elegant women surrounding the actress. The editorial comment was cautiously generous: "[W]hile the great actress is not exactly a great artist she comes sufficiently near it to increase the legitimate admiration felt for the breadth and variety of genius exhibited by this remarkable woman." About the Orange, New Jersey, Woman's League boycott of the event, the reviewer was blunt, pointing out that Bernhardt "does not offer them [her morals], but her talents and her person, for public inspection"; he concluded with the tart suggestion that the League members needed to "ask themselves how many of them Mlle. Bernhardt would care or consent to meet socially" (16 Nov. 1881: 116, 119, 140). The *New York Sun* partly agreed, reporting with irony that the crush was such that the evening "was a complete social success," but deploring "the conflict ... between the love of virtue on one hand, and the love of notoriety on the other" (14 Nov. 1880: 4). The *New York Times* suggested that the truth lay somewhere between a social boycott and a wholehearted welcome, although the crowd was an eager one: "the crush become somewhat uncomfortable.... Mlle. Bernhardt ... was hemmed into a narrow circle of ladies and gentlemen, and Mr. Jarrett was obliged to hold her fast in order to prevent her from being swept into the line...." The *Times*' list of attendees (800 were invited; 500 accepted) names many women willing to brave the social contretemps, as well as well-known figures, including artist Winslow Homer, novelist John R. Dos Passos, and President Ulysses S. Grant (14 Nov. 1880: 1). Skinner's complaint that of the "New York 400," only half appeared and that "Sarah looked vainly about for a single woman other than the female members of her own company" (165) seems exaggerated.

The *Graphic's* brasher and more hostile counterparts *Puck* and *Chic* also castigated unmannerly guests but blamed Bernhardt for bilking her artistically naïve hosts. *Puck's* view of the Woman's League debate about "whether it is 'safe' to see Sarah" was skeptical: it pointed out the "small army of women of Jersey appearance skirmishing around Booth's Theatre for matinée tickets" and noted that the "best society" must have attended because the invitees "stared divine Sadie out of countenance ... shoved, and pushed, and fought ... made loud and vulgar remarks ... [and] pretended to speak French" (24 Nov. 1880: 187, 190). For *Puck*, Bernhardt's *noblesse oblige* is a quality lacking in New York society. Later, the magazine again lashed out against those who impolitely elbowed their way to see Bernhardt as "superior chromo swells and enterprising young Knickerbockers of the vulgarian order"; they were advised to take their "refined gymnastics" to the Garfield inauguration and seek jobs as postmasters and consuls (1 Dec. 1881: 205). Despite that defense, *Puck* warned its readers against making a bad investment in the actress. Frederick Opper's drawing of Bernhardt's long, grasping

Puck, 24 November 1880. President and Fellows of Harvard College.

fingers scooping up gold coins piled under childish artworks signed "Sarah Pinxt" and "Sarah Sculp" is accompanied by an editorial about her greed: "Sadie Bernhardt advertises herself by making a large collection of American money. This is her specialty ..." (24 Nov. 1880: 186, 202).[8]

Chic agreed with Opper's implicit message: Bernhardt is a charlatan as an artist, seeking to advertise her name and to make money. As she confessed to her *Chic* "diary," when she made an appointment to see a reporter, "I dress myself in the most artistic fashion, and have several litres of marble dust and chips strewn about the room, and posted myself in front of the bust as if I were giving it the finishing touches" (10 Nov. 1880: 6). The satirist hints that she bought her paintings from a Campaign Uniform shop and her sculptures from an Italian street-artist. More comically, he accuses her of using pastry dough to model "Shakespeare, Michael Angelo and Raphael crowning Sarah Bernhardt with laurels" and of planning to execute "a grand historico-allegorical picture" entitled "Sarah Bernhardt, Supported by Neptune, Rescuing the Shipwrecked Mariner from the Dragon of Indigence" (27 Oct. 1880: 5). The *Chic* reviewer who actually saw her works at the Union League Theatre liked them no better. His column, "Sara's Art Spasms," included a series of five sketches with commentary about the originals. "The Return to the House" lacks a house; "Breton Beauty" looks like a tulip turned upside down; and "The Model" is a combination of "a corkscrew, a cauliflower, a tobacco-pipe and a castor-oil-plant" (24 Nov. 1880: 5). Reportorial mischievousness aside, the lampoons and critical discomfort with Bernhardt's artwork are grounded in her lifestyle. On the continent, the studio arrangement was a recognizable one; in America, with a shorter artistic tradition, Bernhardt was asking a public who had not yet accepted her as actress to reinvent her as painter and sculptor, considered to be predominantly male roles.

The responses generated by her acting were more numerous and more complex, especially in New York, where the wealth of satire about her stature, finances, and eccentricities had the effect of domesticating her into a household word. The *Clipper*, which suggested that her thinness was "One Cause of Sarah's Success," recommended that someone compile a scrapbook of all the comments:

> It's largely due to the elongation
> Of Sarah's stays
> That the country pays
> The versatile lady such adoration!
> While, if her stays were made any shorter,
> She'd surely appear more staid than she oughter—
> The which, if you doubt, ask your wife or daughter!
> [12 March 1881: 406].

Such a scrapbook might have included an account of Bernhardt's supposed affair with an American attaché in 1878. According to the *Philadelphia Bulletin*, the unfaithful attaché fell in love with an underling actress, and Bernhardt, deciding to confront the two, concealed herself in his room:

> There was a shot gun standing in the corner ... into one of the barrels of which the star easily crawled after removing a few superfluous articles of apparel, which she slipped into the other barrel. ... [F]inally, getting tired of waiting, Sara tucked the wad of the charge under her head and went fast asleep [29 Nov. 1880: 3].

Much of the satire is shaped by the late nineteenth-century movement from rural humor to a new urban humor with political, religious, and cultural overtones. Most blatantly expressed in vaudeville and caricature, it thrived on stereotypes and was overtly critical of American idealism that did not accord with the reality of a large immigrant population struggling for survival (Appel and Appel 3). Urban humor of this type thrived on the profusion of dialects and accents that could be heard daily on the streets. Some humorists laughed at their own linguistic ineptness; others exercised Yankee verbal ingenuity and focused on the difficulties of translation and on the readers' cultural diversity. The *New York Clipper*, for instance, claimed to have enlisted Spanish, Choctaw, Sanskrit, Gallic, Dutch, and Chinese reviewers for *Adrienne Lecouvreur* and *Froufrou*. The Dutch reviewer commented, "Ven dot John Darms ... puds hees gun afore dem French voomans, you don'd saw her no more—she vas so din dot you don'd can see her dill dot firearms vas remofed; such vas her unropustfulness"; and the Chinese reviewer says, "Salle come uppee allee lightee; him arms makee nicee chopsticks; him queue alle samee Chinaman; an' she talkee, talkee likee Mary's little lam she goodee act like Ah Ling and Oh Mi! She smokee like hellee!" (20 Nov. 1880: 278). Although the *Clipper's* even-handed lampoon of foreign verbal idiosyncrasies was apparently directed at Bernhardt's slenderness, it partakes of a more serious chauvinism. Applied to the Jewish population, whose increasing economic power caused a measure of fear, anti–Semitic urban humor promoted two stereotypes. The first, which focused on language, behavior, and appearance, eventually supplanted an earlier Shylock image. The Jew, uncertain about social protocol in his newly acquired wealth, came to be seen as "the quintessential parvenu—glittering with conspicuous and vulgar jewelry, lacking table manners, attracting attention by clamorous behavior, and always forcing his way into society that is above him" (Higham, "Social Discrimination," rpt. in Gurock, 236). The second, which seemed to reflect constitutional degeneracy, was a racial stereotype. Jews were seen to be narrow of shoulder and chest; lacking in muscular strength;

and prone to disabilities, premature senility, neuroticism, and sexual complexes (Singerman 346–50). Bernhardt, arriving as an artistic immigrant with her accent, wealth of costumes, and penchant for spectacle, seemed to fulfill both of the stereotypes: not only did she seek success, but her proverbial thinness hinted at something constitutionally unhealthy.

What neutralized the prejudice against Bernhardt's Jewish background was her overwhelming talent. When *Puck* turned to serious reviewing, it reminded its readers that "Sadie's Show" was more than a parading of eccentricities: "she acts," she has "polish and keen intelligence," "[s]he reads with a splendid melodious clearness," and she gives "the most effective, even and brilliant portrayal of the character of *Gilberte* this country has seen" (17 Nov. 1880: 185). The next week *Puck* admitted that in *Hernani*, her "touching impersonation of the chastened and broken-hearted woman [was] much too sweet and pathetic for any cap-and-bells business on our part." The *New York Sun* agreed: her performance is "superb," "impressive," "rich and picturesque" (19 Nov. 1880: 3). Less friendly commentators took aim at the supporting cast. Their forte was comedy, *Puck* decided, and rewrote *Hernani* to incorporate the argument of the day over political corruption and imposition of customs duties. In the parody, Don Carlos says: "Look here, Don Juan de Etcetera, what you want is a nice quiet place in one of my custom-houses—something out of the way of investigating committees, where you can fix things to suit yourself. Leave this young woman to me— that's all right" (24 Nov. 1880: 191). *Chic's* reviewer indulged in a two-page illustrated article, beginning with a catalog of the New York papers' responses to *Adrienne Lecouvreur* that ranged from outright hostility to unmitigated praise. Only the "surpassing badness" of her company "redeemed" Bernhardt's acting, he concluded; although she has a "musical voice ... she never forgets that she is Sara Bernhardt" or that she is playing to the crowd's expectations. The accompanying sketches, unattractive renditions of frizzy hair and hooked nose, indicate the reviewer's negative mindset, from "A Study of Back Hair" and "Sara's Rapture" to "Sara Dies All Over the Place" (17 Nov. 1880: 4–5).

In other hands her death throes became a less culturally charged comic device. That Bernhardt would die—and rise again for the next performance—seemed inevitable; yet because her intensely emotional depiction of death disrupted a comfortable complacency, satirists sought to distance the macabre by making it funny. *Puck*, which was otherwise appreciative, published "The Great French Dier," a parodic advertising circular aimed at a society heavily involved in business and advertising. Six "approved dies" were on the list, including "The Adrienne.—A rich and lasting die of strong solid color shot with poison streaks ..."; "The Donna Sol.—A

"Sara dies all over the place." *Chic*, 17 November 1880. President and Fellows of Harvard College.

sombre die of richly contortional nature. Has very dark shades of impropriety and high-lights of unhappy love...."; and "The Sphinx.—A crawly sensational die.... Has fine green lights and foamy variations.... Corkscrew convolutions can be thrown on any desired part of the surface" (1 Dec. 1880: 208).[9] These tongue-in-cheek comments suggested that the writer recognized and responded to Abbey's and Jarrett's flair for advertising, but also that he was, however humorously, treating Bernhardt as a product. The customarily serious *New York Times* joined in the absurdity in its own way, claiming to reprint a New York medical journal's review of her death throes, which included "an acute hyperpyrexia of the emotions": "There is generally some fiend in red tights or domino, who, by craft or violence, induces a solution in the continuity of previously happy *affaires du coeur*, the result being dismay, despair, suicidal frenzy, and finally the moribund condition now under discussion." Other notable effects were given as "vertigo, blanching of the face from vaso-motor, inhibition of the arterioles (and possibly face-powder), irregular cries, convulsions, both clonic and tonic, and finally syncope, the latter occurring generally on a soft Persian rug or sofa" (14 Jan. 1881: 4). In one case life imitated the stage: the *Philadelphia Bulletin* reported that a young Norwegian immigrant, depressed about a love affair and penniless after splurging on Bernhardt tickets, determined to die *à la Froufrou*. Poison proved too distasteful, so he shot himself, leaving a letter in which he quoted Gilberte's lines. To prevent another such tragedy, the editor turned it into a joke, recommending altered endings for Bernhardt's plays: Adrienne will be given an antidote or undergo the exigencies of a stomach-pump; Marguerite "must take cod-liver oil or pulmonic syrup"; and Gilberte "must be taken in hand by some good women" (19 Nov. 1880: 4).

These humorous responses occurred against a background of strident criticism based on a clash of moral sensibilities. *Adrienne Lecouvreur*, the story of an actress poisoned by her lover's mistress, was condemned as inappropriate for Bernhardt's American debut. Other plays elicited a similar response. In Basil Woon's account, the manager of Booth's wanted to pull *La Dame aux Camélias* from the boards for fear that the public would be offended. Faced with Bernhardt's stormy refusal, Abbey ingeniously rechristened the play *Camille* (272), a transparent deception that fooled no one, least of all the wildly enthusiastic audiences. Nonetheless, a series of preposterous claims surfaced: Bernhardt, it was said, "had seduced all the crowned heads of Europe including the Pope" and had borne four sons, two by Napoleon and two by the Russian Tsar (Skinner 155). The *Daily Graphic* proved to be one of her staunch defenders, albeit in spite of itself. Its review of *Froufrou*, which set up two personas—the tolerant "Amos Biggs, Butter and Eggs," and his disapproving wife of "granite countenance"—began as a typical piece of domestic humor and then broke down into genuine admiration: "I can only say that I was amazed, dazzled, spellbound. I never studied a word of French,[10] but I understood, or thought I understood, the whole plot and action of the piece.... [T]he magical presence of that wonderful Frenchwoman drove everything from my mind but the scene before me" (20 Nov. 1880: 157). *Puck*, too, was won over: "[s]he is not the menagerie, circus and brass-band combined that we had been led to expect.... she is an artist, quiet, delicate, pleasing, ... with ... polish and keen intelligence, and with a multitude of delicious little fascinating French ways and a voice like a nightingale" (17 Nov. 1880: 185). About the moral issue, *Puck* took a philosophical stand, admitting in its verse "The Play's the Thing" that *Camille* was *risqué*, but complaining that American drama was shallow and undistinguished:

> Such French plays as they give us here
>   Are made to cause our tears to gush,
> Or, when they show French morals queer,
>   To make our modest maidens blush;
> Most English plays, it seems quite clear,
>   Make from our lips loud laughter rush;

> The Germans deftly seem to steer
> 'Twixt laughter's noise and pathos' hush;
> While native plays, short-lived and drear,
> Are made—well, chiefly made of mush.
> [6 April 1881: 77].

Serious commentators struggled publicly with their own assumptions about foreign modalities. *Chic's* reviewer was uncomfortable, but not with the substance of the plays; after quoting a medley of comments, he objected to Bernhardt's mannerisms and to the weakness of her acting company, especially that of her leading man, Edouard Angelo (17 Nov. 1880: 4–5). Bernhardt suffered as well by comparison to Rachel,[11] the memorable French tragedienne whose interpretation of the title roles in *Phèdre* and *Adrienne Lecouvreur* set the standard. The *Atlantic's* Richard Grant White, for instance, admitted to being "thoroughly prejudiced" because of his memory of Rachel and because of the popular furor over Bernhardt's costumes, financial arrangements, and personal life. Like the public he tried to distance himself from, however, White suggested that Bernhardt's slenderness violated assumptions about natural womanliness: she looked "ignoble" and had

> a figure deplorably deficient in all womanly beauty.... Her drapery hung upon her like bunting on a flag-staff on a breezeless day. Such curves as she had curved all the wrong way; and as a mere physical phenomenon it is somewhat startling to find concavity where convexity is the order of nature.

Her performance in *Adrienne* somewhat modified White's assessment: although she is "not an artist in the grand style" and "her moral nature seems to be as thin and weak as her physique," her face was sensitive and expressive, and her purely "personal power" magnetic. Nonetheless, she could not ennoble Adrienne, and her other performance was like "Frou Frou playing Phèdre." In contradictory fashion he objected to Bernhardt's emotional intensity, which was also Rachel's trademark, and he complained that her death scenes appealed to "that sort of spectators to whom it was the crown of the evening's enjoyment to 'see Kirby wrap himself up in the American flag and die all over the stage' at the Bowery theatre."[12] Her *Adrienne* performance did, however, force a major concession from White, and it was an important one because it placed Bernhardt within prescribed gender boundaries: in that play, he said, she outdid Rachel in conveying the attributes of "womanliness"—that is, "of confiding love, of a sweet, tender joy, of purity, of all the little charms of woman's ways which minister so much to the daily delight" (*Atlantic*, Jan. 1881: 95–103). G. W. Curtis, occupying *Harper's* "Editor's Easy Chair," was less convinced. Although he agreed that Bernhardt had "winning, melting ways," she could not elevate *Adrienne* from a costuming spectacle to real tragedy. She was not Rachel's successor, Curtis decided; she was simply "an exceedingly clever woman of remarkable personal fascination" (*Harper's*, Jan. 1881: 306–7).

Both serious and comic reviewers agreed, however, that Bernhardt was indefatigable. She was a trooper, and a determined one at that: traveling long distances, and incessantly rehearsing and performing, she held to a grueling schedule. Such professional dedication nonetheless fell heir to the Populist prejudice[13] that although hard work was needed to build the nation, the Jews labored only for personal profit. Her dedication was also interpreted as a power play: like the immigrants' pride in their meteoric rise from rags to riches, Bernhardt sought to maintain her status at any cost, even by adopting the kind of brashness that the class-conscious New Yorker deplored (Higham, "Social Discrimination" 217). Among the first to recognize her hard work were the reporters who themselves were no strangers to long hours. When the *New York Sun* presented a review of a rehearsal (normally Bernhardt banned strangers), it stressed her good humor and her productivity. In a chatty column, the reporter praised her concern for minor details. She good-naturedly reproves two of her squabbling company—"'Goodness me!' she exclaims loudly, at the same time making a decided face; 'these New York bonbons are as sour as—as your tempers.'" Finally, as a postscript to demonstrating proper enunciation, gesture, and stance, she tells a story on herself:

> One day in London, to the many flattering utterances from a crowd of British admirers in the green room of the Gaiety Theatre, she said: "To act that part a person should be young and handsome." To which Lord ___, who had been warmest in his praise, replied: "Ah, madame, you are a complete proof of the contrary!"

In its typically breezy style, the *Clipper* praised her for her "grit" and her generosity: she "works right straight along like a hired man who is paid by the hour" and "she is not stingy—if she belonged to the gang, she would never renig [sic] when it came her turn to 'set 'em up again,' and she wouldn't call for beer—she'd give the boys brandy at forty cents a thimbleful; that's the kind of hairpin *she* is" (11 Dec. 1880: 302). The same paper paid her tribute in a ditty rife with poetic license:

2. Sarah and the Four Hundred

About Her

Of all the girls in New York town,
   There's none like Bernhardt Sarah:
She's blythe and gay most every day,
   And of complaints she's ne'er a;
She's up by daylight every morn,
   A-cutting stone so deftly,
And should her right hand fail her once,
   She tries it with her lefty.
O Sarah, sweet Sarah, much at thee we marvel—
   How one so slight and frail as thou
Can do so much hard work.
        [4 Dec. 1880: 294].

Hard work notwithstanding, complaints about price-gouging and profit-taking never completely disappeared, yet Bernhardt's energetic involvement in her profession fulfilled an egalitarian American promise that many satirists recognized. They capitalized on her professionalism, which bridged the foreign and the familiar, to domesticate her into a public icon, and they played on her complex position as a French woman of Jewish extraction to make her into a touchstone for any number of American religious and political controversies. In that role she was attacked by members of conservative groups who castigated her as a "harlot" and a "courtesan" (Gold and Fizdale 171). More often, however, she was depicted as a victim by the satirists, who used her vulnerability to pillory well-known public figures for their intolerance.

In *Chic*'s "Let Us Return To Our Muttons" (10 Nov. 1880: 8–9), for instance, the joke is turned away from Bernhardt, drawn as a lamb gamboling around outside a "pen for saved sinners," and directed against self-appointed guardians of public morality. In the drawing Henry Ward Beecher, a Congregational minister with a wide following, and De Witt Talmage, who attacked Bernhardt viciously from his Brooklyn Tabernacle pulpit, join in an attempt to brand the lamb; the freethinker and rationalist lawyer Robert Ingersoll looks on disapprovingly. The caption, "The Election being over, Evangelical Shepherds Should Look After Straying Sheep," suggests that pulpit orators were so occupied by political chicanery in the 1880 Garfield election that they neglected their duties. *Chic* was uniformly antagonistic to the three, whom it implicitly accused of fleecing their flocks. Coming so soon after a decade of renewed Christian religious fervor excited by the revivalism of evangelist Dwight L. Moody, among others, this caricature places *Chic* in the traditional role of satirist, turning a critical eye on those who supported such restrictive moral legislation as imposition of

"LET US RETURN TO OUR MUTTONS."
CHIC suggests that, Election being over, Evangelical Shepherds should look after Straying Sheep.

"Let Us Return to Our Muttons." Chic, 10 November 1880. President and Fellows of Harvard College.

blue laws and Constitutional amendment to include acknowledgment of God, scripture, and Jesus (see Cohen 270–71).

In this role *Chic* also attacked Anthony Comstock, organizer and secretary of the New York Society for the Suppression of Vice, in a labored but pointed editorial verse, "The Bernhardt Ballads." Bernhardt was a "sweet and seductive" danger, the writer suggested, but far more threatening were the "*Union League* fogy" and overzealous censors like Comstock,[14] who as a modern-day Samson should take up his cudgels against the "conventional shoddy":

> Oh, city of virtue transcendent,
>   Set free from superfluous sins,
> With preachers and purists resplendent,
>   Where Satan can set not his gins,
>
> Where Comstock, as Samson Accounted,
>   Is armed with the jaw of an ass,
> Has Cant from the high horse dismounted
>   That this comes to pass?

> Lo! Sarah, the fair, frail and fragile,
>   Has dared to alight on your shore,
> Where the eye of the puritan agile
>   Was skinned and alert heretofore;
> Oh, yet of immaculate virtue,
>   With matrons and maidens so chaste,
> Let not presence of—folly desert you,
>   Make haste, oh, make haste!
>
> She is made in no cut-and-dried fashion,
>   She is sweet and seductive, if thin,
> She runs the whole gamut of passion,
>   Which the prurient count as a sin.
> Let no Dona Sol lure or entice you,
>   Ye elders of "corners" and "rings,"
> Let conventional shoddy suffice you,
>   Nor long for new things.
>
> Shall genius absolve its possessor
>   From breach of society's laws?
> No *Union League* fogy can pause.
>   'Tis true you can all see the *diva*,
> With daughter, and sister, and wife,
>   But under your roof-tree receive her—
> Oh, not for your life!!!
>   [10 Nov. 1880: 10].

Time and again, *Chic* conveyed the message that although Bernhardt posed an attractive danger, native-born public figures were culpable. The magazine's 24 Nov. 1880 cover is explicit: there, Bernhardt appears as an alley cat on a New York rooftop, with Henry Ward Beecher and Senator Roscoe Conkling prowling behind. Although the feline iconography points to Bernhardt's promiscuity, the drawing more strongly indicts a powerful religious and political alliance that pursued in the dark of night what it railed against by day. Beecher's own sexual misconduct had been in the news in the late seventies, and Conkling, with his suspect support of political patronage and political career on the wane, was within months of resigning his Senate seat.[15] In "A Catwumpus," the accompanying jingle, Bernhardt maintains that Beecher and Conkling pose a greater danger than any she has so far faced:

> I am never in terror of evident danger;
>   In Paris I travelled up in a balloon.
> I could stare at a convict or criminal ranger,
>   Be caged with the craziest kind of baboon.

VOL. I.- No. 11   NOVEMBER 24, 1880.   Price 10 Cents.

CHIC

NEW YORK,   Copyright 1880, by the Chic Publishing Co.   OFFICE - No. 21 PARK PLACE.

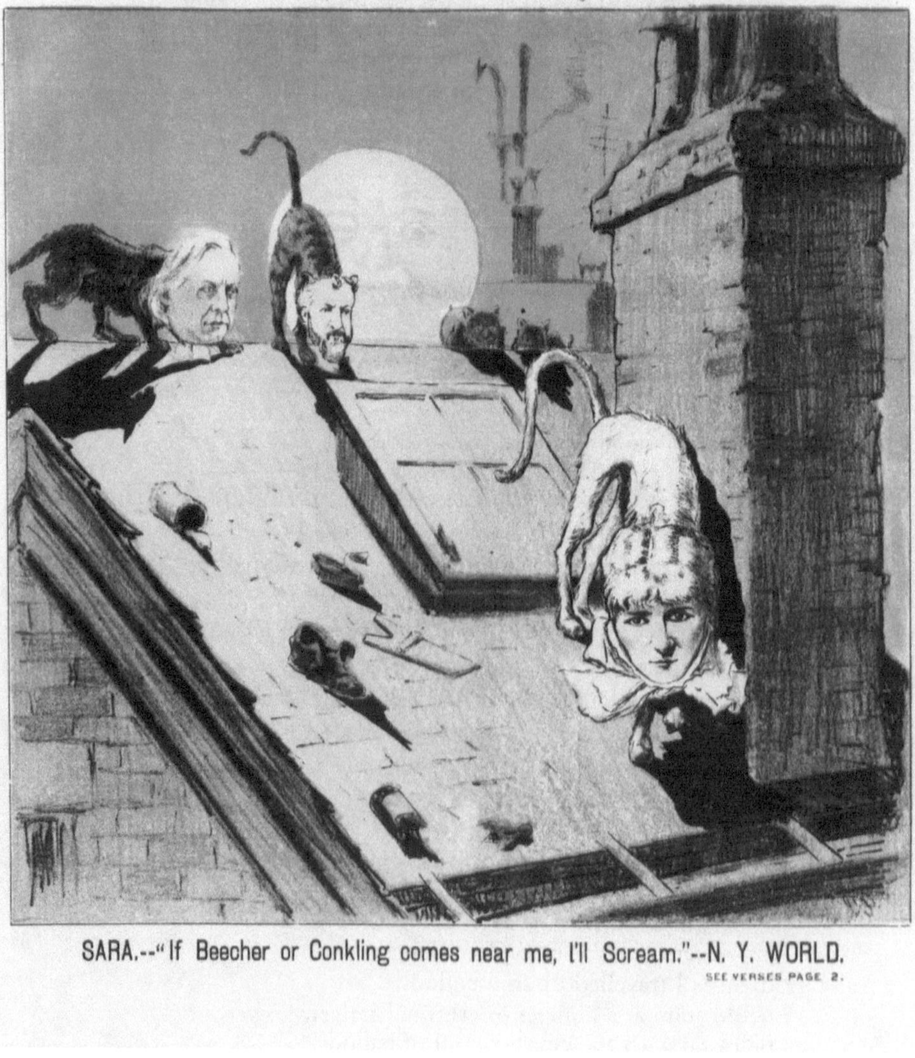

SARA.--"If Beecher or Conkling comes near me, I'll Scream."--N. Y. WORLD.

SEE VERSES PAGE 2.

> I shall visit old Nick in his regions infernal
>   As soon as they open a railroad with steam,
> But I swear by the gods and by peanuts eternal,
>   "If Beecher or Conkling comes near me, I'll scream!"
>
> I have sailed in a storm on the fickle Atlantic,
>   And never beseeched them to take in a reef.
> There are very few things that could render me frantic,
>   Not even a blood-thirsty Indian chief.
> I can lie in my coffin and peacefully slumber,
>   And flirt with a horrible ghost in my dream;
> Though of lovers I've scored in my time quite a number,
>   "If Beecher or Conkling comes near me, I'll scream!" ...
>   [24 Nov. 1880: 1].

By the end of Bernhardt's visit to New York, her image had changed in the press. No longer depicted exclusively as a threat, a profit-hungry foreigner importing dubious morality, she had become a yardstick for local problems. Her personal contact with the public secured her reputation for charm, and many seemed to agree with *Chic* and *Puck* that hypocrisy was behind some of the most offensive attacks. Those periodicals were the ones to defend her when some of her detractors deliberately blurred the line between the actress and the characters she played (Skinner 166) or embroidered allegations into anecdote, like the squib published in the *Norristown Herald*:

> Miss Bernhardt retired to her couch at eight P.M. yesterday, worn out with excitement.—*Ex.* Mrs. Bridget O'Flanigan retired to her couch at eight P.M. yesterday, worn out with scrubbing four rooms and doing a big family wash. But here the resemblance ends. Mrs. O'Flanigan has had four husbands and no children, and Miss Bernhardt has had four children and no husbands [qtd. in *Philadelphia Evening Bulletin* 3 Nov. 1880: 6].

Both *Chic* and *Puck*, generally supportive of family-oriented morality, avoided the question of Maurice's illegitimacy, choosing to concentrate instead on local religious hypocrisy. *Chic* pictures Talmage in fool's motley, forcing bitter medicine on the Bernhardt doll on his lap. The accompanying burlesque sermon, written as an exaggerated example of pulpit oratory peppered with flamboyant phrases and innuendoes, casts Talmage,

Opposite: "If Beecher or Conkling comes near me, I'll Scream." *Chic*, **24 November 1880. President and Fellows of Harvard College.**

Talmage, holding the Bernhardt doll: "He goeth after her straightway as an ox goeth to the slaughter...." *Chic*, 11 January 1881. President and Fellows of Harvard College.

Bernhardt as "The Modern Rizpah, Protecting her son from the Clerical Vultures." *Puck*, 29 December 1880. Harry Ransom Humanities Research Center, the University of Texas at Austin.

III.
The years rolled on, the stattoo never came;
Its light, like Edison's, still fails to flame.
Dost tumble, Sadie, to Our little game?
    We've cash to back it.
Be thou Our stattoo, ornament Our Bay,
Thy task were light; continue to portray
Thy most successful rôle, *la Libertê*.
    Wilt stand the racket?
                    FRANK I. CLARKE.

who controlled the Tabernacle collection plate, as the profiteer (11 Jan. 1881: 16). *Puck* joins the fray more directly by depicting Bernhardt as "The Modern Rizpah, Protecting her son from the Clerical Vultures," after the Old Testament mother in Samuel who sheltered the bodies of her two sons hanged by the Gibeonites. The commentary, also written in mock orator style, supports "virtuous marriage" and discusses the problems faced by young women who cannot make a match; yet it also distinguishes the artist from her personal life and takes the "professional censors" to task for using "strong language and vulgar censure ... for the purpose of advertising themselves" (29 Dec. 1880: 292). Other publications were quietly indignant. The *Times*, for instance, dismissed a denunciation of Bernhardt by the Roman Catholic Bishop of Montreal: "A more decided and unanimous disapproval of sixteenth century bigotry could not have been wished for" (24 Dec. 1880: 1). These later verbal and pictorial commentaries, without blinking at conservative standards, nonetheless shifted the focus from Bernhardt to her attackers, suggesting that their behavior makes them unable to judge her. As was the case with Bernhardt's shrewd business sense, her self-advertisement, and her independence, the Americans found in themselves the moral apostasy they criticized in her.

The satirical record of Bernhardt's first visit to New York is mixed. Bernhardt was an interloper, after all, bringing "foreign" values to American shores at a time when many began to complain that the entrepreneurial spirit was sapping the American endeavor to develop its own literature. And because she was so obviously successful and independent, she posed a new model for American women. What popular writing reveals in its rush to domesticate Bernhardt is both angst over differences and desire to tolerate

Bernhardt as the Statue of Liberty, holding aloft the flame. *Puck*, **12 January 1881. President and Fellows of Harvard College.**

them. The conjunction is well illustrated by a Frederick Opper sketch in *Puck* showing Bernhardt as the Statue of Liberty, holding aloft the flame. Frank I. Clarke's poem "Columbia to Sadie," written in a combination of slang and "poetic" language, asks that Bernhardt pose as the statue (which, given by France, was not assembled and dedicated until 28 Oct. 1886). The lines suggest that as Bernhardt became Americanized, the public attitude had mellowed:

> Sweet Sadie, when thy brief engagement ends,
> When on thy final act the drop descends,
> And hopeless agony our bosom rends
>   That we must sever,
> Do not desert Us in Our dire distress,
> Remain, We pray, to comfort and to bless,
> In all thine elongated loveliness,
>   And leave Us never.
>
> A century had crowned our hopes and fears—
> Old time had kissed away the many tears
> That marked the passage of a hundred years
>   Of our existence—
> When sister France, to prove her *amité*,
> Presented Us, on Our centennial day,
> A "stattoo," as Artemus Ward would say,
>   With sweet insistence.
>
> The years rolled on, the stattoo never came;
> Its light, like Edison's, still fails to flame.
> Dost tumble, Sadie, to Our little game?
>   We've cash to hack it.
> Be thou Our stattoo, ornament Our Bay,
> Thy task were light; continue to portray
> Thy most successful rôle, *la Liberté*.
>   Wilt stand the racket?
>   [12 Jan. 1881: 316].

The "racket," partly of Bernhardt's own making, continued until May 1881, when she completed the circuit that Abbey and Jarrett had agreed on. As she left New York for what the humorists called the city of "cultcha"—Boston—before she continued West, *Puck*, brash as ever, bewailed the neglect of "John Root" and "Peter Crow" and professed sadness to see "Sadie travel forth into the backwoods and wilds of America, and show the savage, as well as western, eastern and southern civilization how to die" (1 Dec. 1880: 205 and 209).

3

"Bust-on" Beans
and Other Delicacies

> Engelhardt says that he would not trade his whale for Sarah Bernhardt, especially as an object of curiosity for the West [*Boston Globe*, 15 Dec. 1880:2].

By the time Bernhardt arrived in Boston, her reputation had been largely constructed by the press. A powerfully emotive actress, she had been subject to criticism shaped by gender assumptions and anti–Semitic fears, both of which fostered visual iconography emphasizing her slenderness and economic rapacity. As her visit progressed, however, she became more assimilated into the American experience. Balancing the negative perspective of Bernhardt as artistic refugee was the icon of the actress as "*la Liberté*," thin and solitary against the New York skyline, representing the kind of feisty, independent force that had engendered the dream of a melting pot and redefined it as a mosaic of diversity.[1]

Bernhardt's domestication as an American cultural icon was in part accomplished by the series of caricatures and satires that shifted focus from her idiosyncrasies to American inadequacies, hypocrisies, and imperfections. That shift can be seen against the background of one of the tasteless pamphlets whose title greeted her on a billboard in Boston—*The Amours of Sarah Bernhardt. The Secrets of Her Life Revealed*. The pamphlet, supposedly written by Frank H. Sims, purports to be biographical; in fact, it is a clever compound of fact, fiction, and sensation. The subtitle, "Her Eccentric Freaks and Queer Fancies before and behind the Footlights. Society in Paris described in all its Phases," suggests the tone. The writer, who describes her "diaphanous" physique and "worldly" outlook, calls her a "christianized Jewess" and "Satanella," a "paradox" and a "monstrosity." After constructing a tissue of love affairs, trickeries, and scandals, he ends on an adulatory note, insisting that she cannot be judged by ordinary standards nor be subject "to the rules of womanly propriety":

> If we regard her ... as a sheaf of golden grains, fresh minted by the fickle fortune that gifts human beings at their birth, or as a mere casket or repository of all conceivable jewels of intellect, we may view her rightly and understandingly.
> To subject her to the rules of the world, or to bring down the soaring, irresponsible genius to the laws of ordinary every-day life would be like raiding the plateau at the summit of Mount Olympus, dragging the gods down to earth's level and judging them by the prim laws that are supported to control first society.... Who will speak of her as a woman when he knows of her as an artiste?

Sims tries to satisfy both a lust for scandalmongering and a desire for high-mindedness, but his exempting Bernhardt from "the rules of the world" puts him in league with the movement of public interest from Bernhardt's personal life to larger issues. In Boston, commentators embroiled her in the sometimes-friendly rivalry between that city and New York, a rivalry based on classism. If New York, faced with a quarter million immigrants in the middle of the century, was seen as a city with a changing and problematic class structure, Boston was equally defined as an educational center known for its smugness and starchiness. When Bernhardt visited, the area boasted a number of institutions, including Boston University, established in 1839; and across the river in Cambridge, Harvard University, 1636; Radcliffe College, 1879; and Massachusetts Institute of Technology, 1861. New York humorists, who deliberately ignored that aspect of Boston, sought through deflation to suggest that the city was less well known for its intelligentsia than for its purveyors of pork and beans.

Chic's approach to the standing joke was to present Bernhardt as an innocent tourist asking questions about Boston. She is faced with significant historical sites, which she fails to recognize, and she is regaled with Boston "delicacies" that wreak havoc on her digestive system. "Sara Bernhardt in Buston," published on December 8, continues the mock journal that appeared in conjunction with her visit to New York. She has, she maintains, been taken to visit the Boston Common—"There is Faneuil Hall; and also the Uncommon—it was formerly called the Common, but the

Committee of Prominent Citizens of Bus-ton.—"Now, Sara, give us your candid and unbiassed opinion, Isn't this Park the finest in the world?"

A "Committee of Prominent Citizens of Bus-ton" demand Bernhardt's opinion of Boston Common. *Chic*, 8 December 1880. President and Fellows of Harvard College.

name was felt not to be adequate to the importance of the place." And, asked whether she has seen Plymouth Rock,[2] she prevaricates:

> Being unwilling to reveal my ignorance, [I] replied diplomatically that M. Plymouth Rock had left his card on me, but I had not yet decided whether, as a single woman, it would be strictly proper for me to visit him. I added that I intended to make a bust of him. This announcement was received with manifestations of the most awe-stricken delight and admiration.

The accompanying drawing shows a group of gun-wielding "Prominent Citizens of Bus-ton" threatening a needle-thin Bernhardt to give her "candid and unbiassed opinion" that the Common is the "finest [park] in the world"; for proof, they point to a tiny fenced-in area in front of a collection of signs—"Unvarnished Beans"; "Beans stewed roasted and in the shell" (8 Dec. 1880: 10).

Taunting Boston about beans[3] was as popular an activity as referring to Bernhardt's weight. The December 8 *Chic* cover—"Bernhardt's

Opposite: "Bernhardt's Boston Boom—Sara's Bust-on Beans." *Chic*, 8 December 1880. President and Fellows of Harvard College.

3. "Bust-on" Beans and Other Delicacies 63

Boston Boom—Sara's Bust-on Beans"—reversed the expected visual idiom. In this drawing, she and her dog rise from the table with enormously distended bodies. "Mille Tonnères," she exclaims; "what have I swallow—a earthquake—a tornado?" The accompanying verse begins with her praising the "Hub" and goes on to extol the effect of beans on her acting:

I

Queen of histrionic queens
    Entered a saloon,
    And very soon
Was eating baked beans.
That night I played Frou Frou
With much more fire than u-
    Su-al,
And the people all shouted"
    "Go in, Sal,
    You bully old gal!"
And in reply,

I

Louder spouted;
My success I staked
In these sweet scenes
Upon old Boston's baked
    Beans!
These beans are making me fat,
Think of that!
And I'm glad
Soon I shan't have to pad.
I eat them every day
Two platefuls I put away,
And so I shall
As long as my name is Sal.
The bean is freedom's bird;
Its praises should be sung
By old and young
Throughout the world and heard.
Now, my true ambition, waked,
    Leans
Right unto Boston's famous baked
    Beans.

In the same issue of *Chic* (10), another versifier, who incorporates a variety of New York jokes against its rival, imagines that she begs Abbey to protect her from eating what represents Boston's civic pride:

> You say the Autocrat will scold
>   If I the Hub should slight[4];
> That Longfellow, so gray and old,
>   Awaits the opening night;
> That all the nation's intellect
>   There toward your Sara leans;
> But Abbey, master, oh, reflect!
>   The horrid pork and beans!
> And slapjacks, too, so I've heard say,
>   All dripping o'er with grease;
> And then the lingo, by the way,
>   The tongue called Bostonese;
> I ne'er could catch that nasal twang,
>   Though I were in my teens;
> I am not up in Yankee slang,
>   And don't like pork and beans.

The author goes on to employ the kind of urban humor that plays on cultural differences underlying distinctive ethnic stereotypes. The "heathen," are, of course, Christians, and so Bernhardt's persona seems to be Semitic, although the point is not stressed:

> They say my people eat the frog;
>   That Englishmen eat beef;
> That none save heathen like the hog,
>   Of dirty beasts the chief;
> But there 'tis sausage, shoulder, ham,
>   With bacon, too, and greens,
> And when the curtain drops, they slam
>   Before you pork and beans....

Satires like these created an imaginary world parallel to her actual visit to Boston, where she visited local industrial sites, met celebrated writers, and became an unwilling participant in furthering another stereotype—Boston as a whaling port. These adventures followed swiftly on the heels of an exhausting weekend that began when she left New York City's Grand Central Station at 10 P.M. on Sunday, December 5, and arrived at the Boston & Albany Depot the next morning at 8:05. Her railroad car, the "Manhattan," had been redecorated for the occasion and offered the comforts of a nineteenth-century mobile home. The accommodations for her entourage were less luxurious: they were billeted in sleeping berths or in the "Rip Van Winkle," regular New York and Boston Express cars pulled by the Boston & Albany railroad. She professed to be impressed by her surroundings, praising details like the "real ... brass bedstead," "basket tied up with ribbons for [her] dog," and flowers everywhere. Inside, the car was lined with walnut inlay; outside, it was painted olive and gold, with touches of crimson (*Globe* 6 Dec. 1880: 4; 8 Dec. 1880: 1). Although she was sensitive to the special care taken in furnishings and decoration, she nonetheless later commented that the train that took her across country from Philadelphia was superior (*Memories* 396), and she confides to a *Globe* reporter that even though the cars are "elegantly gotten up" and "very well appointed, ... yet there is something—well, they remind me strongly of a hospital" (8 Dec. 1880: 1).

Between New York and Boston, she left the comfort of her sleeper at 2 A.M. to pay a visit to Thomas Edison at Menlo Park. That the inventor should have agreed to open his house, offer a tour of his laboratories, and dine with her and her entourage at that hour suggests the strength of her reputation, or, as Gold and Fizdale maintain, the expertise of Jarrett's public relations skills. Robert Conot, Edison's biographer, makes a similar claim for Edison: Robert Cutting, Jarrett's friend and director of the Light Company, had arranged the meeting between the two divas from different walks of life to publicize Edison's incandescent lighting system. When Bernhardt arrived through the snow, Conot says, "across the fields the lights sprang up like budding flowers," and Bernhardt, delighted, took the rheostat in her own hands (180–81).

In her memoirs she paints an arresting verbal picture of the frigid weather, the jagged ice, and the darkness. It is, as she comments, like "a scene out of an operetta." And although she enjoyed dramatizing her life, as her accounts of her Atlantic voyage make clear, she admits that she is "confused and embarrassed" at imposing upon her host. To her dismay, Edison, who seemed "intensely bored," also seemed to have taken "a dislike to [her]" and apparently thought the visit due to "the idle curiosity of a foreigner, eager to court publicity" (*Memories* 395). She set herself to overcoming his coolness by resorting to fainting in his arms and was satisfied with her success when the "Napoleon"[5] of electricity gallantly carried her into his workshop. There, he demonstrated how to record a phonograph cylinder: two assistants sang "Le Cadavre de John Brown," Bernhardt recited from *Phèdre*, and Edison sang "Yankee Doodle" (Skinner 169). According to Conot, she was so delighted to hear her recorded voice that she wanted to buy the cylinder, but had to rely on Edison's promise to send it to her.

Once she returned home, she sent "the giver of light" two landscapes painted by her own hand (156).

After leaving Menlo Park at 4 A.M. on December 6 (*Memories* 396; Skinner puts the time an hour earlier), she arrived at the Boston & Albany Depot and was taken to the Vendome on Commonwealth Avenue and Dartmouth Street, a newly opened hotel whose rooms and service the management hoped to advertise by means of its illustrious guest (*Globe* 6 Dec. 1880: 1). Whereas in New York she was accused of self-advertisement, in Boston she was made to serve as advertising for others, although whether Jarrett fostered the marketing stratagems is unclear. Bernhardt did offer genuine praise for the accommodations, which were, as she said, "charming," "magnificent, very comfortable and warm, and furnished in European style with American taste." Her comments, published in the *Globe* on December 8, did scant justice to the entire arrangement, however. Her living quarters, decorated in pale tones of gold and green offset by ruby-colored drapes, included six rooms overlooking the avenue—a private dining room, two bedrooms, a parlor, and her secretary's bedroom and parlor. The maid and valet slept across the corridor, and Abbey had his own suite. For her receptions, she was given a smaller ladies' parlor on the ground floor, a room described by the *Globe* as being "both rich and chaste" (5 Dec. 1880: 5). In her bedroom the draperies were "billowing white muslin curtains festooned with blue taffeta ribbon," and the satin bedspread was embroidered with her motto "*Quand Même*."[6] The sitting room overflowed with Persian rugs, oil paintings, statuettes, and fine vases sent on loan from unknown local admirers (Skinner 171). Some of the "treasures" included, as the *New York Sun* reports, a pair of John Hancock's porcelain pitchers and a curious painting by Ball Hughes,[7] "burned on canvas with a poker" (6 Dec. 1880: 1).

As a pleased occupant of the Vendome, Bernhardt offered informal testimonials; she was less accommodating, however, when the owner of an enormous right whale displayed at the Boston Fort Hill dry dock tried to enlist her cooperation. In her memoirs Bernhardt pictures herself as alternately angry and amused by the machinations of Henry Smith, the proprietor of a small fleet of cod fishing boats whose fishermen had harpooned the whale. Smith, who had jumped uninvited into the coach taking her to the hotel and who "talked in a loud voice, laughed, coughed, spat, and addressed everyone," tried to persuade her to see the whale. How instrumental Jarrett was in arranging the encounter is unclear, but the next morning at 7, the former societaire of the Comédie Française climbed on the whale's slippery back, pulled a piece of whalebone from its mouth, and finally, "nervous and flustered," insisted on driving the coach furiously back to the hotel, endangering life and limb (*Memories* 398–401).[8]

This sideshow, which pursued Bernhardt across the country, offers a glimpse of the way in which popular figures were commodified; whether animal or human, both were seen as consumer goods, needing special handling and transport. Like Bernhardt, whose artistic manager was Edward Jarrett, the whale had its own manager, an entrepreneur named Fred Engelhardt; and like the French actress, the whale was a novelty, "a thousand miles away from his native element." Also like Bernhardt, who had her own salon car outfitted for her comfort and convenience, the whale was provided with a customized railroad car. Once the special mechanical apparatus was built—the *Globe* described it as a frame from which the floating giant was raised by "shears and derrick"—the whale was stuffed with ice and transported across the country, following Bernhardt to Hartford and then greeting her at the Chicago exposition building (15 Dec. 1880: 2). As they traveled across the country, reports show an almost indiscriminate popular appreciation of the two; both were mobbed, both needed Pinkerton guards, and both left viewers awestruck.

This tendency to treat Bernhardt as a sideshow was matched in Boston with a more serious and intelligent assessment of her acting, although her own love of luxury and spectacle off-stage seemed to validate the popular view. From her hotel suite, she drove out in a glassed-in Berlin landau leased to Abbey by C. Russ & Co.; designed especially for her, the carriage was lined with green velvet and outfitted with monogrammed antimacassars, a bison-skin mat, and a double fur lap-rug provided by Jordan, Marsh & Co. Her horses were a matched pair of black Knoxes, their heavy English harnesses appointed in silver (*Globe* 5 Dec. 1880: 5; *New York Sun* 6 Dec. 1880: 1). Recognized wherever she went, she patronized jewelry stores and other establishments; visited educational and historical sites; opened the exhibition of her art works; and met the Bostonians. And, of course, she presented her repertoire, with an increasingly enthusiastic response from the papers. To put Bernhardt's perspective together with that of her hosts reveals mutual courtesy and caution. Boston women, more confident of their status than their New York sisters, proved willing to meet her socially and to see her plays, although their initial response was reserved. Bernhardt viewed the crowd that met her at the railroad station as "more interested than friendly," more concerned with making up their own minds than listening to the gossip that had preceded her. It was, she decided, a "strange, courteous, and cold crowd," but one whose women she was moved to admire for their intelligent Puritanism and graceful independence, as much as for their ability to speak French (*Memories* 397).

The Bostonians' guarded, sometimes deliberately critical attitude is evident in the December 9 report of the Boston correspondent to the

Connecticut Courant. He comments that the "culture of the city is not to do homage to this French woman," who is "the most extensively advertised woman the world ever saw." She is ungraceful but understands "attitudinizing"; she is neither "magnetic" nor "sympathetic," but has perfect articulation; she is not a genius and lacks the "divine faculty" of influencing her audience, but her "educated cleverness" makes her "coldly artistic" (16 Dec. 1880: 1). The *Boston Evening Transcript* reported a similar reaction to Bernhardt's debut: at the December 6 opening night performance of *Hernani*, the audience was, the reviewer says, in an "inquiring, coolly, almost coldly critical frame of mind." He attributes the attitude in part to the stately, almost formal mien of Victor Hugo's drama. A different assessment in the *Connecticut Courant* suggests with some smugness that the audience was too mixed to depend upon for a critical response: because of the speculators' successful salesmanship, the "society" audience was "much mingled with those of less social prominence," and even Longfellow had "slighted" the actress by leaving the city (16 Dec. 1880: 1).

The oblique mention of Longfellow refers to Bernhardt's disappointing visit to the poet; arranged by Mrs. Lillie Moulton, a society woman of high repute on the Continent, the company included William Dean Howells and Oliver Wendell Holmes.[9] Bernhardt, who had wanted to sculpt a Longfellow bust, was put off by excuses, but did recite part of her favorite poem—"Ee-ah-vah-tah." The Boston Brahmins may have been secure enough in their first-family heritage and professional standing to be open-minded about receiving a French actress, but Longfellow was reportedly horrified at being kissed farewell by Bernhardt. He avoided her when she returned to the city in the spring and shared a private joke at her expense with G. W. Greene, to whom he wrote on 3 April 1881:

> The famous French actress, Sara Bernhardt, has been again in Boston, but I did not see her. The fame of her extreme thinness has reached far and wide. A common man, driving by here in a cart, with a poor lank horse, gave him a cut with his whip, crying, "Get up! Sara Bernhardt!" [*Letters* 299].

Bernhardt's frustrated attempt to sculpt Longfellow became current in the public satirical record, where the incident invoked the longstanding charge of self-advertisement. In the ongoing *Chic* journal of her adventures, "M. Long Fellow" refuses to allow Bernhardt to chisel his bust:

> The ruffian, thus to spoil an advertisement that would have forwarded the sacred cause of Art! Where is his sympathy for a sister artist...? I ask myself it! However, I triumph over him—fool

him. My announcement was that I would prepare a bust of *a long fellow*—not of M. Long Fellow. And I shall keep faith with the public. I have prepared one of the giant Chang![10]

The author of the *New York Mirror's* theatre gossip column is amused by the clash of moral stances and cultural assumptions posed by coupling the poet and actress in an artistic endeavor: on December 17 he writes, "I'd give an old shoe to see the French sinuosity pottering about with her clay and chisels, while the silver-haired poet poses gracefully before her, reciting the "Psalm of Life" (7)."[11]

The initial coolness displayed by Longfellow and Boston theatergoers is attributed by the *Globe* to general ignorance of French and distaste for public fervor engendered by "overwrought anticipation." This specious excitement was said to be fostered by a number of factors, including the "sensational" photographs exhibiting Bernhardt's "oddities of ultra-fashionable costume," her "freakish" poses as a sculptor, and other suggestions of "wild waywardness" (*Boston Evening Transcript* 7 Dec. 1880: 4). Her shopping excursions only increased the popular appetite to see her in person. When she went to Bigelow Brothers & Kennard, where she bought jewelry, the unfriendly *Connecticut Courant* correspondent commented that "Barnum himself could hardly be broader in his devices to draw a crowd." Pushing and shoving, some of the more determined forced their way into the store until it was locked against them; others, more athletic, climbed up to peer through the windows (16 Dec. 1880: 1).

The scene was repeated at Jordan, Marsh & Co., on December 16. There, she was escorted through the establishment by Eben Jordan and his son and preceded by mobs making "headlong rushes" in anticipation of her next move. Her guides, it is said, soothed her annoyance by suggesting that even a glimpse of her gratified those who could not afford tickets. Just as Edison's laboratory fascinated her, so did the steam sewing-machine room, where she was presented with several aprons made on the spot to demonstrate the speed and execution of the technology. A mistress of compliment, she exclaimed "American business men ... are *tres vivant*" and pointed out that no other establishment—the Louvre, the store Bon Marché—lived up to Jordan & Marsh in degree of hospitality. She paused to buy curtains for $37, but one commentator gave a better indication of her normal shopping habits when he advised female readers not to "go into the shops after some pink and gray brocade like that which Mlle. Bernhardt wore last evening [at *Adrienne Lecouvreur*]. The pattern was designed for her at Lyons, and the stuff cost $60 a yard" (*Boston Evening Transcript* 9 Dec. 1880: 4). Later the same day, Bernhardt visited Harvard University,

Berhnardt in costume for *Adrienne Lecouvreur*. Photograph by Carvalho, 1880 (?). Harry Ransom Humanities Research Center, the University of Texas at Austin.

where she was said to be impressed by the library cataloging system and manuscript storage. Harvard's educational method, she declared, was as good as, if not better than, the Continent's (*Globe* 16 Dec. 1880: 2).

Bernhardt's combination of vivacity and genuine interest in her surroundings pleased the Bostonians, who, in turn, received her artworks with politeness. In contrast to the earlier outpouring of parodic sketches and accusations of financial gouging in New York, Boston accepted Bernhardt's artistic endeavors with quiet seriousness, inviting her to visit the Museum of Fine Arts and putting her works on display without the expressions of social anguish that characterized the New York Union League reception. Surrounded by students at the museum, all of whom were endeavoring to sketch her, she was escorted by Jarrett and Professor Crowinshield, whose painting *Winter* she admired.[12] Her day of art, which, next to her visit to Edison she pronounced the most pleasant of her stay, concluded with viewings at other artists' galleries and a sitting from a client, Mme. Rudersdorff (*Globe Supplement* 15 Dec. 1880: 2). According to a report in *The Springfield Republican*, Bernhardt was an impulsive artist, setting up her studio in her subject's dining room and sending Jarrett foraging for more clay. Attired in "close-fitting brown velvet," she chattered incessantly to visitors as she worked and finished her bust in two days (qtd. in *Chicago Times* 26 Dec. 1880: 2).

Her own works of art were shown at a gallery in the Studio building on Tremont Street, with a free private viewing for a hundred guests on Thursday, December 9, and a public viewing for a twenty-five cent admission charge the following day.[13] She exhibited twenty-one of her works, some of which had been previously caricatured in *Chic*. The *Globe* critic was restrained, noting that although she exhibited "remarkable skill," viewers were interested in the works primarily because a dramatic artiste had created them. He praised the *Ophelia*, which Bernhardt expected to show at the 1881 Paris salon, called her bust of her sister Regina "creditable," and said that her sculpted self-portrait would be "noted with no little pleasure," although it was not a "marked" resemblance. It was the paintings, however, that even the kind critic of the *Globe* found difficult to countenance. *Une Jeune Fille et la Mort* was "unpleasant" and "incomplete"; the figure in *L'Espagnole au Repos* seemed to have no knees; and the scenes drawn for the plays in the American repertoire were "hastily executed" and "badly done" (10 Dec. 1880: 2). Despite that assessment, however, almost all the works were purchased by New York and Boston admirers for delivery after the American tour was completed.

The restrained journalistic response to Bernhardt's Boston adventures at retail stores and university, art museums, and whale exhibit suggested that Boston writers tried to focus interest on Bernhardt as actress, not as spectacle. Even so, trivial details found their way into the press. Manager Stetson of the Globe Theatre reportedly "transformed the star's dressing-room into a perfect boudoir" and clothed the ushers and himself in "dress-suits of the sombre hue" to rival the "swells" in the audience (*New York Clipper* 18 Dec. 1880: 307); and columnists described theater-goers dressed in full evening regalia, crowding two thousand strong into the Globe Theatre. Of all her venues, Boston was among those that drew the largest receipts, although the price of tickets also sparked unfavorable commentary. The *Norristown Herald* complained that "the philanthropists of Boston were so busy paying five dollars and upward to see Sarah Bernhardt" that the starvation death of an eighty-year-old woman was ignored (qtd. in *Puck* 5 Jan. 1881: 308), and the *Boston Post* published a rhyme bewailing the cost of an evening on the town: "Ten dollars. Quite a sum to pay / For one, who earns but four a day ..." (qtd. in *Puck* 5 Jan. 1881: 307). In actuality, patrons paid from four to eight dollars per seat, more if they bought from ticket speculators, who, the *Atlanta Constitution* reported, made well over $40,000 in Boston (16 Feb. 1881: 1).

The Boston audience for her December 6 debut in Hugo's verse drama *Hernani* was initially ambivalent. Since the female lead, Doña Sol, does not dominate the stage until the end, those eager to see the Bernhardt spectacle were vocal about their disappointment. Many were unaware that Bernhardt was repeating history in trying to introduce an unfamiliar style of acting to a New World audience. *Hernani* was unpopular when it was first performed in 1830; then, the proponents of Neoclassical artistic tenets did more than grumble—they rioted over the new Romanticism. For Bernhardt, however, the play was an auspicious way to begin her repertoire, because it represented a theatrical triumph. After her 1877 performance of Doña Sol, Hugo was so overwhelmed by her acting that he sent her a priceless mark of attention—a bracelet with a diamond drop pendant and a note including the words "This tear which you caused me to shed is yours. I place it at your feet" (Skinner 110). The *Globe* reviewer shared this assessment, ecstatically extolling Bernhardt "as unrivalled in the romantic drama as Ristori in tragedy" (8 Dec. 1880: 1) and agreeing with the general critical estimate that she successfully avoided the "grand manner" of the Italian tragedienne to follow a more natural style. The *Transcript* reporter was also a convert. Although he began his review in a coolly analytical way, he confessed to being electrified by Doña Sol's transformation from a loving bride to a vengeful fury, from ingénue to impassioned woman railing at the death of the brigand Hernani, who has poisoned himself: "[Bernhardt's] hair seems to stand on end as she shakes her head menacingly, her marvelously musical voice has grown as fierce and unhuman as the snarl of an enraged animal ..." (7 Dec 1880: 4). Bernhardt, routinely compared to actresses like Ristori, Rachel, Janauschek, and Modjeska,[14] eventually won over both critics and audience, whose enthusiastic applause and "Bravas" at the end of her first performance suggested that the sensational aspects of her advertised arrival were less important than her acting ability. In effect Bernhardt had challenged her audience and her critics on different levels, and had won.

As predicted by the *Transcript*, her performance in Meilhac and Halévy's *Froufrou* proved decidedly popular, partly because the work was familiar to the audience. The commentary dwelled on her originality of stage presence and on the naturalness of her expressions—her blushing and paling seemed real. On one count at least the reviewer objected to her lack of "womanliness": "her riding-habit's skirt was 'worn with a difference' so striking that it seemed as though a man were stalking about." Yet, her "intensity in volatility" is impressive, he says, although her brilliance makes the rest of her company "dull as paste" (8 Dec. 1880: 4). In breaking the ice with her Boston audience with *Hernani* and *Froufrou*, Bernhardt was alternating classical and contemporary drama. On the third night, she returned to the classical with Eugene Scribe and Ernest Legouvé's *Adrienne Lecouvreur*, again a piece in which the leading lady does not immediately appear. Perhaps the audience felt that it was getting a glimpse of the real Comédie Française as it watched the play's ingénue actress Adrienne learn her lines, achieve success, and then find herself the object of surreptitious plots by her rival in love, the Princess. And perhaps Bernhardt herself identified with Adrienne, remembering the anguish of her own first audition at the Conservatoire, when dressed in torn black silk and unable to perform Molière as planned, she recited La Fontaine's *Les Deux Pigeons*[15] (Gold and Fizdale 43).

December 10, her fourth performance, provided a respite for Bernhardt in *The Sphinx*, a drama complete with jealous wife, philandering husband, and the beautiful Blanche de Chelles, who wears a ring that contains poison. "[W]e wish that this drama, morbid in much of its character, and serving no good end, had not found favor with Mlle. Bernhardt," commented the *Globe* reporter (10 Dec. 1880: 2), who echoed the *Herald's* assessment that the work is "morbidly sensational" (qtd. in *Globe* 28 Nov. 1880: 10). The *Evening Transcript* reviewer, however, found her "thrilling and beautiful" in the part, especially at the crisis when, having emptied the poison in the wife's water glass, she decides to drink it herself. Even though the New York periodicals satirized her death scenes, her throes were said to be more restrained than Sophie Croizette's, her rival at the Comédie Française,

Bernhardt in costume for *Froufrou*. Photograph by Napoleon Sarony, 1880 (?). Harry Ransom Humanities Research Center, the University of Texas at Austin.

whose study of death by poisoning allowed her to give an "intensely vivid and painfully realistic portraiture."[16] Few seemed to agree with the *New York World* that Bernhardt's intensity was a sham, mere "mannerist acting," or that she earned the audience's approval in the dying scene "by a mere trick" (qtd. *Globe* 28 Nov. 1880: 10). Rather, most felt that Bernhardt's death agonies were "terribly realistic, especially when she called for a veil to conceal her face (*Transcript* 10 Dec. 1880: 4; *Globe* 10 Dec. 1880: 2).

In keeping with her attempt to alternate classical and modern, sensational and realistic dramas, on Friday, December 11, Bernhardt performed Racine's *Phèdre* for a large audience that had braved the exigencies of a storm to compare "the reserved power of this fragile woman" with Rachel, the "grandest of Phèdres." The *Globe* gave warning that the modern audience might find the story of a woman's love for her own stepson repulsive; yet Bernhardt, in essaying the Enlightenment version of the powerful Greek tragedy, again succeeded in a drama whose moment of crisis is an internal one made visible through the actress's expressiveness. After her first week in Boston, critics gave generally strong praise for her realistic and evocative handling of the high dramatic points of the dramas she presented, although opinion was somewhat divided about her ability as a tragedienne. The joke of the New York *Chic* writer, that "to conciliate the severely classical tastes of the Athens of America" she played *Phèdre* "dressed in a mackintosh cloak, blue stockings, shoes of gum and spectacles" (8 Dec. 1880: 10), pales in comparison to the actual, careful assessment accorded her performance in Boston. The *Transcript* marveled at the "piquancy of zest" with which she "dashes at the very summits of art in that cold, serene atmosphere that is the farthest possible removed from the madding nether world of Paris"; nonetheless, it felt that at the most intense moments, she lacked "strength and voice" (11 Dec. 1880: 4). On the other hand, the *Globe* reporter discerned no such weakness; for him, the performance, characterized by her "magnificent delivery," was a "signal success" (11 Dec. 1880: 3).

Of her remaining performances in Boston, *Camille* was the one major newspapers agreed broke box-office records and removed the last vestige of audience reserve. It was also the one in which Bernhardt narrowly escaped serious injury when a sideboard holding a burning oil lamp toppled over on stage. Reportedly, one of the actresses on the other side of the scenery had lost her balance while bending over to button her boots (*Globe* 16 Dec. 1880: 1; *Clipper* 25 Dec. 1880: 319). Wiseacres treated the situation humorously: "Sadie is now proved to be the queen of the stage," said one: "Not only the audience but the scenery tumbles to her acting." And another made fun of her slenderness: "T'was a remarkable escape of Sadie in Boston. A little more, and a whole cupboard of pasteboard bric-à-brac would have fallen upon her, injuring it seriously against her many angles" (*New Haven Register*; qtd. in *Puck* 5 Jan. 1881: 307). Bernhardt later commented gratefully on the sympathy of the audience but confessed that her first thought was a cynical one: "How unhappy some of the clergymen will be to think that the theatre was not set on fire and destroyed by the falling lamp" (*Globe* 20 Dec. 1880: 1). The play itself received rave reviews. The *Transcript* reporter, for instance, lauded her ability "to make nature and art one," to engage in "complete self-surrender and absorption in her role," and to convey the "subtle flavor" of womanhood: these, he suggested, were what commingled to create a "higher, more artistic, more intellectual" performance of *Camille* than had hitherto been presented (14 Dec. 1880: 4). The *Globe*, almost always friendly to Bernhardt, commented that because earlier audiences had expected an actress who combined the talents of earlier divas, they were unwilling to perceive "the delicate charm and artistic instinct of the great French actress" (14 Dec. 1880: 1); in recreating Bernhardt as a less awkward but equally forceful Janauschek or a more realistic Clara Morris, they overlooked Bernhardt's own "perfect" diction, her breadth of talent, and her "lack of affectation" (*Globe* 19 Dec. 1880: 3). This analysis lays the blame for the audience's early reluctance to accept Bernhardt dramatically on its overriding curiosity to see the cause of the "absurd fables" circulated about her.

On the whole, Boston reviewers liked her combination of artistry and naturalism. She was praised for her talent in conveying emotion through a range of realistic physical representations, from the effects of taking poison to seeing a lover for the first time; but taken to task for her eccentric dress and for her intensity, which outclassed the less sustained attempts of her company. Nonetheless, as the *Commonwealth* reporter noted, she is without "artificiality" and has no "tricks.... Everything she says and does belongs to the legitimate stage" (11 Dec. 1880: 3). Out of town papers sometimes commented more on Bostonian *sang-froid* than on Bernhardt: the *New York Sun*, for instance, blamed her opening-night audience for its "frigid aesthetics" and "self-satisfaction," all of which had "a somewhat depressing effect upon Mlle. Bernhardt" (7 Dec. 1880: 1). The *New York Mirror*, however, maintained focus on the actress's exceptional "individuality" and "originality" as well as on her fine elocution and consistent, coherent interpretations. In the long run, however, Jarrett's advance publicity about her idiosyncrasies and temperamental lifestyle attracted public attention but did Bernhardt a disservice with serious reviewers. As one *Globe* writer concluded after making an intelligent assessment of her strengths and weaknesses, although he expected to see a spectacle, "one of transcendent abilities," he saw instead "a most talented and artistic performer, whose talents are not superior to many actresses that I could mention" (19 Dec. 1880: 3).

No tinge of disappointment colored the *Globe*'s assessment of her on a personal level; in fact, that newspaper was her most friendly advocate. The reporter's quiet admiration of her "bewitching grace" won him both introductory and farewell interviews. Cordial and hospitable, she was pleased with her reception but noted that European audiences were more likely to be conversant with French language and repertoire. She laughed at the rumor of her performing with the great Italian tragedian Salvini[17]: "Ca serait pis que la tour de Babilone! [That would be like the tower of Babylon]," she exclaimed. Her own reception was not a laughing matter, however. She confided that had she not triumphed in New York, she would have returned to France (8 Dec. 1880: 1). Three weeks later, she met with the *Globe* reporter again, after a 1:30 P.M. breakfast. By then, her tone had changed, and she roundly denounced the religious diatribes that had been directed at her from the pulpit. Earlier, she defended her choice of secular dramas by saying that she did "not approve of the dramatization of religious history in any form" (8 Dec. 1880: 1); in this interview she went on the attack, complaining especially about the religious oratory of De Witt Talmage:

> A comparison of the morals of the clerical fraternity with those of actors and actresses would be by no means unfavorable to the latter. A great many occupants of pulpits are simple showmen. What, for instance, is the essential difference between the calling of an actress like myself and that of the mountebank Talmage, always on the scent for the freshest bit of scandal?

Bernhardt threatened to hire stenographers to produce verbatim records of pulpit libel so that she could sue the ministers who inveigh against her publicly, and she lamented that despite their censure, church leaders across the country besieged her with letters begging for contributions.

That interview proved to be a popular one: picked up by the *Hartford Daily Times* on Christmas day, it became the excuse for a refrain. "Good for Sarah!" said the reporter after repeating each of her points about Talmage. *Puck* also came quietly to her defense by publishing a twin cartoon. "Money in the Theatre—they get their money's worth" pictures a couple buying tickets at the box office; "Money in the Tabernacle—do they get their money's worth?" shows a self-satisfied usher taking up a collection in front of signs like "No Free List" and "Private Pews—No Strangers Admitted" (12 Jan. 1881: 321).

Marie Colombier proved to be another champion, an unexpected gesture in light of the 1883 publication of her scurrilous *Les Mémoires de Sarah Barnum*, a *roman á clef*, reminiscent of the earlier *Les Voyages de Sarah Bernhardt en Amérique* (see Ch. 1, endnote 5). In a letter to *The Parisian* about the Boston repertoire, Colombier defends Bernhardt against "ignoble libels" by making fun of American misrepresentations. To compensate for their lack of children, Colombier says, American women have more than one husband; yet

> All the sovereigns of Europe, even those who are dead, are attributed to Sarah as the fathers of her imaginary children. Yesterday a lady wanted to find the address of Sarah's dentist, saying that her false teeth were admirable. Another asked the address of her hair-dresser, saying that she wished to have her head shaved, in order to have a wig like that of Doña Sol. Two newspapers have endeavored to prove that our Sarah was not the true Sarah, but a false, simili–Sarah. To support their case, they added: "You see, this one is not so thin as people say!" [qtd. in *St. Louis Globe-Democrat* 23 Jan. 1881: 9].

Colombier's defense is probably an appropriate coda for Bernhardt's visit to the Northeast. Reviled on the one hand and worshipped on the other, "The Bernhardt" presented the many faces of Eve. As her repertoire suggests, she was versed in classical and romantic drama, yet the personality she allowed reporters and critics to see was the stuff of soap opera. A mixture of paradox and sensation, she was intrepid in climbing whales and facing down allegations about her "amours"; she was curious about sewing machine workers and Boston Brahmins; and, although spendthrift by nature, she was financially shrewd enough to collaborate with Jarrett, a mastermind of advertising. In New York and Boston, she could hope that the audiences had at least marginal familiarity with the French language and repertoire and could be confident that her very real talent would be recognized. In smaller, less sophisticated towns and cities, however, she came face to face with the popular specter of herself. Her created reputation preceded her, and scandal took up residence not only in legitimate theatres but also in the minds of her audiences.

4

"Ehue, Jaques! How frail we are!": Bernhardt and the Sympathetic Barbarians

> She was for the moment also indifferent to her part, threw pecuniary glances over the house, and then deliberately studied the audience, returning the provincial interest that was felt in her [*Connecticut Courant* 23 Dec. 1880: 4].

Although Bernhardt's reception was warmer in Boston than in New York, less furor attended her departure. This more reserved attitude suggested that Bernhardt had been valued more as dramatic professional than as cultural phenomenon, shaped principally by ticket-brokers and gossip-columnists. It also implied a weariness of scandal and a sense of cultural elitism: after the Four Hundred and the Brahmins had spoken, speculation about her acceptance in the far reaches of the West and South was irrelevant. As her entourage moved out of the Northeast, however, two cities—New Haven and Hartford—became the bridge between the reactions of East Coast metropolitan areas and those of more isolated regions. Together they prefigure the ambivalent responses of other cities to spectacle and to commodification.

Both were close enough to their larger sister cities to be influenced by complaints about spectacle and rapacity. Bernhardt's receipts—in New York $98,942, an average of $3,958 per performance; and in Boston $49,158, an average of $3,781 per performance—raised the specter of artificially inflated ticket prices and foreign political influence. Her vocal French claque was half-jokingly said to be spreading the rumor that she will be "proclaimed president of the United States" because of her unprecedented popularity and because of the Americans' willingness to support her financially (*New Haven Palladium* 6 Dec. 1880: 2; 20 Dec. 1880: 2). Such rumors, even as vehicles for humor, would have been likely to put reviewers on their mettle in these two cities with deep historical and literary roots (both were settled in the 1660s; Hartford was the home of Mark Twain, Noah Webster, and Harriet Beecher Stowe).

Prospective audiences were also influenced by newspaper columns reprinted from urban publications, some of which provided guidelines from a fashionable if not discriminating perspective. In the *New Haven Palladium*, for instance, the Boston correspondent "Templeton" preserved a cynical tone, downplaying Bernhardt's abilities and popularity and insisting that she was a social detriment and an aesthetic sham: she was too thin, had prominent nose and teeth, and walked with an ungainly, bent-backwards gait (12 Dec. 1880: 4). Such sideshow freakishness removed her from the social norm, he said, as did her commodification—she can be bought, and cheaply so: imperial photographs (23" x 31") of Bernhardt cost 5 cents. Ignoring the actual record on behalf of his society readership, he maintained that she had been a "disappointment" in Boston and that aside from a few quiet receptions, "ladies" ignored her (*Palladium* 18 Dec. 1880: 4; 23 Dec. 1880: 1).

"Templeton's" focus was on seeing: either "being seen" with Bernhardt or "seeing" her was incompatible with maintaining one's status. Here the gaze becomes a speculum, a device for examining the actress as a social body and determining her "health" in accord with a social norm; the gaze is, however, also a mirror, reflecting the viewer's preconceptions. In New Haven, such a judgmental gaze was typical of the kind of Boston elitism ridiculed by New York humorists. Hartford readers, however, were interested in history, an approach perhaps fostered by a latent sense of social and academic inferiority: although Hartford could boast Trinity College (1823), Hartford Seminary (1834), Hartford College for Women (1839), the Hartford Graduate Center (1855), and the University of Hartford (1877), New Haven had Yale. As serious critics, then, Hartford reviewers sought to contextualize Bernhardt in such articles as "The *Camilles* of Our Stage." This exhaustive survey on the front page of the December 11 *Hartford Times Supplement* systematically compared Bernhardt to her predecessors, including Eugénie Doche, who played the original role in 1852 opposite Charles Fechter at the Théâtre du Vaudeville in Paris. Fanny Davenport, Matilda

Heron, Laura Keene, Clara Morris, Mme. Modjeska:[1] all these were banked against Bernhardt and found wanting. She was "the greatest of '*Camilles*,' like the lace she twines round her slender neck—light, exquisite, elaborately wrought." This graceful, witty, and tactful French actress knew

> How all the various emotions of the soul, brain, and heart have to be wound into fireworks, to be delicately touched and sent forth only when the spectator's mind is so laden with eager anxiety that the match is never laid without starting the firework, and the firework never breaks but in a shower of stars.

Despite these plaudits, it was New Haven, not Hartford, that experienced a roaring trade in ticket sales. "Templeton's" effort to blacklist Bernhardt socially had the opposite effect of making her into a desirable spectacle. American profit motives also came into play. Almost two weeks before *Camille* opened at Carll's New Haven Opera House on December 20, scalpers staged a performance complete with suspense and sensation. As a prologue, many queued up for over twenty-four hours; fought to be at the head of the line; successfully bought their tickets; began the two-week process of selling them; and, in the epilogue, discounted the remainders.

As customers and scalpers' representatives crowded the doorstep at Loomis's Temple of Music at 7 A.M. on December 9, the day before the sale,

> Each comer was numbered in the order of his arrival, and then took the freedom of the room and ranged around as he pleased, all on the qui vive for customers. About 150 Yale students were –represented. These ticket office crowds are made up of errand boys, bootblacks, anybody who can be hired to undertake the job [*Palladium* 10 Dec. 1880: 2].

The published details give a glimpse into practices of the time: thirty-two buyers waited overnight. By the time the box office opened, the line had swelled to fifty, including six "ladies." In a wildly fluctuating market, some standees sold their places, earning up to five dollars apiece; within minutes of each other, one received twenty-five cents for the twenty-ninth place and another five dollars for the thirty-first place. Others bought batches of tickets, hoping for an average resale return of two dollars on each. Notwithstanding an individual quota of twenty tickets, along with special premium fees, sales were brisk. By 2 P.M. receipts totaled at least $2000.

Despite the flurry of sales, Bernhardt herself was relatively ignored.

She arrived at 3:30 P.M. on December 20 and was driven to New Haven House, although a "leading citizen," unafraid of "Templeton's" disapproval, had reportedly offered her hospitality (*Palladium* 9 Dec. 1880: 4). A day later, the situation reversed itself. In Hartford, her welcome was enthusiastic, but rumors of ticket profiteering dampened the market. Sales beginning eleven days before her December 21 booking proved so disappointing that three- and five-dollar tickets changed hands for half price the day of performance (*Hartford Daily Times* 22 Dec. 1880: 2). As details of her Hartford itinerary attest, she was sharing headlines with the whale. Even at this early date, although featured as "a mouth with a smile that is entrancing," it seemed no more than a sad carcass, bound with twelve iron hoops and boxed in its railroad cars with wooden planks (*Connecticut Courant* 20 Dec. 1880: 4). Bernhardt apparently ignored the whale, but was invited to pay extensive visits elsewhere. After traveling by Rustemeyer's omnibus from the depot to Allyn House (her company was accommodated at the United States Hotel), she was escorted to see Hartford sights. Visits to Colt's Armory, the Capitol, the envelope works, and Trinity College were all on her agenda by December 18. Two days later, other sites—the church of the Good Shepherd and the Charter Oak Life Insurance Company headquarters—were added (*Hartford Daily Times* 18 and 20 Dec. 1880: 2). The schedule was trimmed for practical reasons, but she enjoyed a local experience: Hartford Alderman Samuel Walker guided her "through the mazes" of the armory, where she received a demonstration of the Gatling gun (22 Dec. 1880: 2).

The *Hartford Daily Times* drew an observant and friendly picture of the tour, and finally, like its predecessors, abandoned high critical ground for spectacle. Her dress was described in detail as was her dolman of green velvet, silver fox, and sable, newsworthy for its $4000 value. Her trademark gloves, a symbol of elegant excess, were almost three feet long and worn crushed from wrist to elbow to distract attention from her thin arms. Reporters found her very foreign. Although she asked to have unfamiliar words spelled, she quickly made herself at home by taking her troupe to a restaurant, where they all "turned cooks, and very shortly prepared a good dinner of soups, fried onions, sausage and macaroni" (2). Bernhardt, in short, appeared to her Hartford hosts as a mixture of opposites. Flamboyant and down-to-earth, formal and spontaneous, she exhibited a mercurial temperament that made her off-stage media performances a sellout, even if, as in Hartford, ticket sales were not stellar.

Her temperament helped foster the mixed reception that became typical as she moved away from New York and Boston. In New Haven she faced unfriendly reviews, high ticket sales, and a restrained welcome; in Hartford she was treated like an honored guest, but ticket sales were slow.

These characteristic responses were complicated by religious issues. In both cities conservative forces related her financial success to her Jewish ancestry, perpetuating an anti–Semitic stereotype accentuated by the Christmas season. The *New Haven Palladium*, which reprinted and cheered her rebuff to De Witt Talmage's "outrageous" attacks, also cynically noted the free advertising such "pulpit denunciations" provided (22 Dec. 1880: 2). And in "Bernhardt Chat," appearing in the *Hartford Daily Times* two weeks before her arrival, the accusatory tone was barely tempered with appreciation. "It is good to have her off our minds," the writer declared, since Bernhardt was "an Old Testament character ... [who] means to gather her 'loss and her profits' before the jingling of the Christmas bells." Since that jingling put money in the merchants' pockets, the writer's complaint about her was disingenuous; however, his real appreciation of her "frail, graceful body," her repartee, and her underlying seriousness prompted his grudging admission that there was "fine metal in the blade, although not much of it" (11 Dec. 1880: 2).

Countercharges of religious hypocrisy revealed local tensions. A New Haven letter-writer, for instance, pointed out that churches in the area had themselves sponsored a series of amusements from "Little Red Riding Hood" to "Undine" (*Palladium* 18 Dec. 1880: 2), and the *Hartford Daily Times* weighed in on Christmas Day with a complaint about gender bias. Like the *Puck* critic who compared Bernhardt to Rizpah and refused to let her personal life color his theatrical assessment, the Hartford reporter defended her, arguing against the double standard that vilified Bernhardt but not Salvini:

> Clergymen have not from their stronghold of faith, hope and charity denounced him to their followers. Would-be newspaper wits have produced no abortions like this, that "the ladies admire his costumes, but do not approve of his kids [a pun on 'gloves']," though he has two (one more than Sarah), and lived with a woman whom he could not marry because she had a husband. Is it because he is a man, and his sins are forgiven him of men? [2].[2]

Lingering religious caveats, along with social ones, may have dissuaded some from going to the theater in New Haven, but doubts vanished for those inveterate lovers of spectacle who saw Bernhardt perform. The previously unfriendly *Palladium* praised her "gifted" and "distinguished" acting in *Camille* and complained that the audience was "making up their estimate of the woman herself" rather than empathizing with Marguerite, a distorted focus the paper had done much to encourage. The aftermath of the play was quiet, the reverse of what the box-office bustle had foretokened: "no marked demonstration" occurred, and "only a few students" followed her to the hotel after her performance, the reporter noted with some surprise (21 Dec. 1880: 2–3).

In Hartford, as the contradiction between the poor box-office showing and warm welcome might suggest, a medley of reviews appeared after she performed Gilberte in *Froufrou* on December 21. On one hand, the *Courant* writer was suspicious, not least of all about the modernity of modern drama. Bernhardt's entrance in *Froufrou* was "disappointing"; her costume—the notorious riding habit—was ungraceful; and her stage manner smacked of economic interest. The rest of the review was a backhanded compliment. Since the play was "light, ... an affair of shallow emotions and fine wardrobe," it was "perfect" for Bernhardt, who would not shine in high tragedy (23 Dec. 1880: 4). On the other hand, the *Daily Times* was impressed by the "close and devoted attention of the audience" to *Camille* despite the language barrier. Noting that only the "cream of social, commercial, political, and literary circles" comprised the audience, the reviewer commented that Bernhardt's portrayal of Gilberte possesses "firmness of outline" and "magnificence of detail." Without handsomeness, grace, or presence, "she is a great intellect, and she is a superb *artiste*" (22 Dec. 1880: 2).

Although in Hartford the religious argument became sublimated to theatrical concerns, in Montreal, where she appeared during the Christmas holiday, the newspaper reaction was particularly bitter. In *Our Lady of the Snows*, Ramon Hathorn provides a perspective on the French Canadian response from her appearance in New York to her arrival in Montreal. He finds the earliest mention of the actress in Anthony Ralph's column in *L'Opinion publique* on Oct. 28, where the poem "À Sarah Bernhardt" appeared. Hathorn implies that Louis Frechette, considered to be the *poète national* by the French Canadians, plagiarized Ralph's work:

> Poet dedicated to the fine arts
> You spread the sacred fire
> In salons and on the stage
> You have crowns of gold
> But New York proclaims you
> Once again
>   Queen! [9].

Hathorn's coverage of Bernhardt's Canadian visit provides a corrective to both Skinner's account and the one-sided version in the memoirs. In his account the disagreement between the public on one side and the Bishop and clergy on the other was not as clear-cut as Bernhardt suggested, since religious arguments were complicated by politics. To be sure, her visit was made more problematic by what seems to have been a last-minute arrangement for the performances during the Christmas holidays. Nonetheless, when she reached St. Albans, Vermont, a special Canadian deputation boarded her train to welcome her. With a senator, several lawyers, the founder of the liberal publication *La Patrie*, and the Academy of Music manager looking on, Frechette read his entire eulogistic poem.[3] Her public welcome in Montreal was at odds with her welcome by the religious establishment: in one report, the night of her arrival was so cold that her bouquet "crystallized" as she stood shivering "in the light of a hundred lanterns held by a hundred students to hear an ode of welcome in eight stanzas" until she finally "collapsed with cold" (Richardson 96). Her other welcome, a letter from Bishop Fabre, was more guarded. The Roman Catholic prelate promulgated an analysis of *Adrienne Lecouvreur* and a commentary on the inappropriateness of the play to the Christmas season, but contrary to the implication in her memoirs, did not mention Bernhardt by name. This letter, which some observers called restrained and carefully phrased, exhorted faithful Roman Catholics to abstain from going to the theatre during the holiday. Many ignored the letter, and, as *Chic* gleefully commented on Jan. 5, 1881, the Bishop's remarks proved to be good advertising:

> A Bishop—this is no canard—
> His parishioners put on their guard;
> Said he, "if you go
> To Sara B.'s show,
> In the world that's to come you'll burn hard."
>
> His flock at the prospect was sad
> For a moment, but then it got mad,
> And when Sara did act,
> The hall was so packed
> That standing-room couldn't be had...
>   [qtd. in Hathorn, *Our Lady* 34–35].

The religious objections to Bernhardt's presenting *Adrienne Lecouvreur*, *Froufrou*, and, on Christmas day, *La Dame aux Camélias* and *Hernani* were complicated by anti–Semitic overtones and by political allegiances, both local and international. The signed commentary in *Le Canadien* by the reviewer Tardivel, for instance, followed the lead of the New Haven and Hartford commentators: Tardivel, eventually editor of the ultra-conservative publication *La Verité*, suggests that "as a good Jewess" Bernhardt naturally sought wealth. Others more slyly attacked her mother, complaining equally about her many love affairs and Dutch Jewish ancestry. On the political front, city council members were advised by their lawyers that although the city charter gave them the power to limit disturbances on Sundays, they could not impose the law on a weekday holiday to ban Bernhardt's performances. Such advice may have been welcome news for those members who had already bought tickets, but the existence of such a law indicated the power of the church in secular matters. In Bernhardt's case, as Hathorn points out, the church was in part reacting to the danger of importing liberal and anti-clerical plays and ideas from France, which was "expelling by force long-established Roman Catholic religious communities from its cities and provinces" (*Our Lady* 13).

The audiences and reviewers thus tiptoed around a host of patriotic modalities. The reviews for *Adrienne Lecouvreur* and *Froufrou* in *La Tribune* illustrated the complexities of the situation: there, the writer first praised Bernhardt's delivery, at the same time loyally maintaining the superiority of Rachel, and then censured Abbey for choosing a repertory at odds with local values. Given the box office receipts, however, ordinary French Canadians were enthusiastic about hearing the visiting prima donna perform in their native tongue. Although she had been accosted by a gang of hooligans at the station and at the Windsor Hotel, her performances were met with heartfelt nationalistic fervor: Laval University students built a two- by four-foot floral replica of the French flag and lowered it onto the stage, and the audiences who braved conservative displeasure to attend the Christmas day performances responded warmly to her acting and gave her high praise for the melodiousness and power of her voice (*Our Lady* 19–20; Gold and Fizdale 180–81).

Once Bernhardt left the charged atmosphere of Montreal, she traveled to Springfield, Massachusetts. There the highlight of her visit was purchasing a lady's pistol (in her own account, a hunting rifle) and then, upon invitation, demonstrating the *canon-mitrailleuse*, an experience that she found "amusing" but, as she says, "not one which affected me emotionally" (*My Double Life* 275). Gold and Fizdale suggest that she feared the perils of her projected visit to the Wild West (181), yet the contretemps in Montreal may have awakened her to possible dangers, both political and physical. In fact, her mixed welcome in Montreal prepared her for what she called the "icy welcome" in Springfield, where the population seemed to confuse the fictional Marguerite with Bernhardt.

Accounts of her performance itinerary over the Christmas weekend are unclear. The *Baltimore-American* says authoritatively that she performed in Springfield the evening of the 25th and spent Monday the 27th in New York. Bernhardt herself remembered the more exciting scenario that followed Springfield's "chilly reception"; she writes in *My Double Life* of leaving for Baltimore "at a dizzy pace," with two locomotives pulling her three cars in a wild chase to catch up with the Baltimore express (275–6). When she arrived in Baltimore late on Tuesday, December 28, she disappointed her fans by being driving immediately to a "splendid suite" at the Carrollton Hotel, where she ate dinner and went to bed. As the *Baltimore American* complained tongue-in-cheek, "[T]he newspaper men who had provided themselves with an unlimited supply of Ollendorf's and Fasquelle's French grammars, and were prepared to paralyze Mlle. Bernhardt with such questions as 'Have you the shoes of the oblivious tailor?' or 'Have you the long vase or the unreliable flintlock of your ancestors?' were entirely disappointed" (29 Dec. 1880: 4).

Baltimore, however, seemed to promise audiences that were both sophisticated and welcoming; with that expectation, Abbey had made special arrangements for a Bernhardt Washington night at the Baltimore Academy of Music on New Year's Eve, restricting ticket sales of *Camille* to Washington residents and reserving special cars on the Baltimore & Ohio railroad (*Boston Globe* 10 Dec. 1880: 2). In actuality, most of her audiences were small. Since Baltimoreans had restricted access to tickets, the Washington night was not a financial success, albeit a theatrical one—"Camille" was given five curtain calls, "amid a rapture of bravas." For Bernhardt, too, New Year's Eve was sad, and although she celebrated with two appreciative guests from the French embassy, she wept with homesickness (Gold and Fizdale 181). Notably absent was any question about the immorality of the plays, which must have been a welcome relief after Bernhardt's difficult Montreal experience. *Froufrou*, for instance, was presented as a lesson against spoiling young women instead of correcting their caprice and frivolity so that they develop independence and self-control; it was praised for showcasing "the whole gamut of passion" and allowing "the widest range of dramatic expression" (31 Dec. 1881: 4).

The *Baltimore American* reviewer was lyrical in his praise for all of her performances. Her debut in *Adrienne Lecouvreur* was before an audience restrained in demeanor, he suggested, because advertising had prepared them for "weird or bizarre" acting instead of the "naturalness and simplicity" she conveyed. For this reviewer, her "art" was melodically displayed in an expressive voice and her "attenuation" was not thinness but "lithe and marvelous grace"; lacking the force of Clara Morris and the "tragic genius" of Modjeska, she nonetheless found inspiration in "an innate sense of beauty, that is like a conscience to her" (30 Dec. 1881: 4). Her experience had perhaps taught her that opening with *Hernani* was a deterrent to good reviews; in Baltimore, the play was presented as her farewell performance, but even then it was dogged with ill-luck. The restless audience, unwilling to wait, developed the "strange caprice" of forcing a curtain call after the fourth act,[4] which by rights belonged to Don Carlos, whose performance was "ineffective." Bernhardt seemed "annoyed," and "Don Carlos, whom she led in by the hand, seemed dumbfounded." The reviewer, who had critical reservations about the dramatic worth of the play, found Hugo's "tissue of exaggerated sentiments, ... hysterical heroisms, and downright idiocies in the way of motive" more appropriate to the *Pirates of Penzance*; but just as Hugo's "splendor of language" redeemed the plot, so Bernhardt's acting transformed the play with "such magical force that one los[t] sight of its inherent absurdity." This "peerless and wonderful woman" similarly impressed the audience, who gave her a tumultuous send-off (2 Jan. 1881:4).

At the start of the new year, much of her tour lay before her, and as she traveled, the character of her audiences changed according to the flavor of the region, but few of the audiences were so isolated that they failed to be influenced by the outpouring of satire and reviews from other cities.

By the time she performed in Philadelphia (on January 3) and in Chicago (on January 10), she experienced increased tension between the image she wished to present and the image created for her by the press. Religious, ethnic, and class issues resurfaced, as well as complaints about her rapacity. Yet despite the protests about American dollars going into foreign pockets, Bernhardt was in actuality supporting American profiteers. As the newest and most volatile stock in town, she became hot commercial property. Philadelphia ticket scalpers, like their brothers in other cities, intensified the buying frenzy. Writing in the *Philadelphia Evening Bulletin*, a reporter gave a vivid picture of the Chestnut Street Theatre on a rainy November 4. Through the gaslight in the gloom, eight boys uniformed in the blue and brass of the American District Telegraph Company marched up and took their places for an all-night wait. Their employer arrived after they had spent the night whistling and joking to keep awake, and, because of the ticket quota, paid each boy in turn to buy ten seats for him, spending a total of $1460 on tickets alone. In the meantime, preferred places in line were sold to the highest bidder, and after only an hour, almost all the parquet and half the balcony seats were filled (7).

Only a large city like Chicago could restrict the practice of scalping, but in doing so, it guaranteed that the purchase price went to fund Bernhardt and not to enrich American speculators. This economic intervention also operated negatively against an open market. Fewer seats were sold, and both Bernhardt and the speculators earned less. At McVicker's Theatre, for instance, where advance sales started on December 27, the Chicago managers refused to offer a reduction for bulk purchases and limited tickets to four per person, unless shown proof that larger families would suffer. Less money consequently changed hands than in Philadelphia the previous week, where $100 bills were reported to be common currency. The five-day sales figure in Chicago amounted to $10,000, one third of which was for single-seat purchases. Although it was a record for advance sales in that city, it still did not match earlier receipts in Boston and New York. *The Chicago Tribune* was proud of the lower figure, however, attributing it to strict regulation. The dealers were less happy: after the "speculative gentlemen retired disgusted," one grumbled that the managers "should be stuffed, put into a glass case, and sent to the British Museum as a pair of extraordinary men who wouldn't make an honest dollar when they got such a chance" (2 Jan. 1881: 11).

Unlike Chicago, which prided itself on its economic morality, the Philadelphia press was more concerned with Bernhardt's marital status. The *Inquirer's* practice was to call attention to the confusion by using both titles—"Miss—or Madam—Bernhardt"—or a blank in place of the honorific—"M___ Bernhardt." This persistent carping about her private life affected her reception, as did the pervasive sense that the Bernhardt image was a compound of puffery and fashion: posing as sympathetic, the *Philadelphia Evening Bulletin* concluded nastily that Bernhardt's supposed New York "failure" was her manager's fault: "Mr. Abbey or his great French star has failed ... owing to the circumstance that Mr. Abbey has failed to pay first-class prices for first-class newspaper notices. The chief artistic successes thus far seem to belong to the Bernhardt's dress-makers ..." (10 Nov. 1880: 4). Once the performances began, Bernhardt and the press agreed on their mutual dislike. "That handsome city I do not care for," she wrote (*Memories* 416), and Philadelphians returned the sentiment with interest.

When Bernhardt had performed in Hartford, the audiences were small but appreciative; in Philadelphia they were small and hypercritical, in part echoing the vocal furor in Montreal. The hue and cry began when the *Philadelphia Evening Bulletin* lashed out on Christmas Eve against "free" pulpit advertising: "The clergy have been persuaded to preach against her.... When it becomes thoroughly understood that it is wicked to go to see Bernhardt her managers can safely take her to larger theatres and put up the price of tickets." Like the earlier "Bernhardt Chat" writer in Hartford, the Philadelphia reviewer warned local ministers against "gratuitous advertising" and suggested that their parishioners would be unlikely to see her "under any circumstances" (24 Dec. 1880: 4). Some of the Philadelphia clergy followed the lead of Talmage, who reportedly claimed that "all actors, play-actors, and actresses were dissolute without exception" (Talmage 122). Edwin G. Sweetser, the pastor of the Philadelphia Unitarian church, began moderately by conceding that "Human nature needs both religion and amusement" and by trying to differentiate between "good" and "bad" theatre, but he concluded, with Talmage, that "notoriously immoral performers who dared to flaunt their vice in the public eye" should be driven from stage and that "plays that appealed to the wrong instead of the right in the human heart—and among them were classed many of the modern French society plays—should be left to be acted to a beggarly array of empty boxes..." (*Inquirer* 10 Jan. 1881: 3).

Her debut in the City of Brotherly Love was thus inauspicious. Viewed as a moral danger and as a commodity subject to fair trading practices, she began her repertory with what seemed to be a dishonest business tactic. Because Marie Colombier had been detained by a train accident on a shopping spree in New York, *Adrienne Lecouvreur* could not be staged as advertised, and *Phèdre* was substituted. Colombier writes that when she finally arrived, Bernhardt was furious: "You're not even dead.... You can't even show me a broken arm or leg. You are ... unforgivable!" (qtd. in Gold and Fizdale 182). Everyone was angry about the attendant woes, especially the audience. The managers, who had allowed librettos and tickets for the cancelled performance to be sold up to the opening curtain, refunded only one-third of the $9 ticket price. According to the *Philadelphia Press*, the entrepreneur Fred Schwab[5] offered a free libretto to every lady in the house, but he was virtually drowned out by hisses from the "gallery gods." The reviewer maintained spitefully that what was left of the audience—some of whom persisted in consulting the incorrect libretto—"sat it out, relieving the awful tedium with abundant yawns, grievously disappointed" (4 Jan. 1881: 8).

Given such an unpromising beginning, the Philadelphia visit seemed foredoomed. Yet Bernhardt's personal motto was "*Quand même*": despite all, no matter what, she would be a success. Even though the initial debacle put her on her mettle, the battle to win over audiences and reviewers was difficult. The *Inquirer* systematically explained away any hint of success. Although the reviewer admitted to liking Bernhardt's "exquisite voice" and "magnificent posing" in *Phèdre*, he complained about her "hopeless lack of feeling, magnetism, soul, or whatever else it is which in dramatic art is called genius." At the January 5 performance of *Camille*, the applause was attributed to a claque, the ticket-holders' presence to "curiosity," and their boredom to the "dull monotony" of the play (5 Jan. 1881: 8; 6 Jan.1881: 4).

No one was satisfied with her choice of repertory. According to the *Bulletin*, *Hernani* was unsuited to Bernhardt's talents, and the *Philadelphia Press* agreed that the play was "insufferably dull and dreary." Finally, with *Le Sphinx* at the end of the first week, the *Bulletin's* reviewer was partly won

Bernhardt, advertised and advertisement. The prompt book is translated by Fred Schwab. Harry Ransom Humanities Research Center, the University of Texas at Austin.

Bernhardt in costume for *Phèdre*. Photograph by Napoleon Sarony, 1880. Harry Ransom Humanities Research Center, the University of Texas at Austin.

over. Like the Montreal reviewers, he grumbled about the subject matter and the "moral perversity" of modern times, but was enthusiastic about her "subtlety," emotive strength, and control. There was "no doubt," he concluded, that she "ranked among the foremost of the members of her profession" (8 Jan. 1881: 5). Similarly, the normally discontented *Press* noted the "profound" effect of Bernhardt's "artistic naturalness" and praised Jeanne Bernhardt for her acting and beauty (8 Jan. 1881: 5).

One measure of Bernhardt's eventual success in Philadelphia was the hard-won approbation of the critics; another, more lighthearted, was the full-scale theatrical parody *Sarah Heartburn* that ran concurrently. Performed at the Arch Street Opera House, it featured the well-known female impersonator William Henry Rice, who began his career as a boy singer in Pittsburgh in 1856 and who eventually joined Thatcher & Ryman's Minstrels[6] for the Bernhardt burlesque. From the time of its New York opening on November 14, *Sarah Heartburn* attracted notice for its inspired comedy and unobjectionable humor.

Bernhardt, invited to a private performance on January 7 with Jarrett, her company, and the press, would have agreed with *The New York Clipper*'s comment that Rice "did mock heroics in a style that would have made even Niobe laugh" (15 Jan. 1881: 339). Earlier, she had been furious about the hostile caricatures published in the magazines, but now her "hearty applause and heartier laughter" at the spectacle of Rice dressed as Bernhardt, coupled with the other absurdities of the show, displayed her generous sense of humor. Reviewers were surprised at her naïve enjoyment: she was as "unaffected ... as that of the most unsophistocated [sic] child" (*Inquirer* 8 Jan. 1881: 8). When confronted by Rice as a "cork female" surveying her from stage through a large pair of glass bottles in lieu of opera glasses, she tried to control her laughter, but

> She abandoned all attempts, however, when the death scene ensued and Heartburn threw herself upon the sofa, after the manner in which a diver starts for the bottom of the sea. Sarah gave vent to her sense of the ludicrous until her eyes were full of tears. There might have been danger of hysterics had not an attack of coughing interfered and had not George Thatcher made himself known as Victor, Heartburn's son, blowing a horn and crying lustily [qtd. in Rice 166].

Bernhardt took the burlesque as a comic compliment, and other, more serious accolades poured in at the end of her visit. The *Inquirer* conceded handsomely: with the exception of *Phèdre*, she conveyed "refined sentiment ... splendid talents ... ripest and most delicious fruits of the noblest intellect" and "rose to heights of excellence never before attained." The reporter's spleen, which had first been directed at the Bernhardt spectacle, was redirected at the Chestnut Street Theatre, which did not live up to the dramatic spectacle: "old, dirty, inappropriate" scenery, "tawdry" furniture," worn carpets, and poor ventilation were among the complaints. This catchpenny venue, however, did not curb the growing enthusiasm of the Philadelphia audiences. By the end of her stay, she had amassed over $200,000, and the receipts on her last Saturday were the highest she had taken in a single day (10 Jan. 1881: 7, 8).

Like her stage performances, her Philadelphia art exhibit received mixed reviews. In the theater she could win over her audience by the dynamic nature of her acting and her personal appeal; she could adjust her acting to her venue. In the gallery, however, each work, a completed performative event, stood on its own merits. She used the Boston model, in which the public was invited to a viewing for a twenty-five cent admission charge. The reporters who flocked to the Haseltine Galleries at 1516 Chestnut Street, from January 5 to 8 had little praise for her artistic technique. The *Philadelphia Press* was one of the few to defend her artistic endeavors, noting that other celebrities, including Sarah Siddons, Joseph Jefferson, and Henry Irving,[7] had enjoyed similar avocations. At the same time, the newspaper objected to her amateurism. Not only was her sculpture "buttery," the reviewer complained, but in *The Young Girl and Death*, "although her arm and neck are well and carefully painted, they are not joined together, unless by some slat or wire" (5 Jan. 1881: 5). The *Inquirer* conceded less to her artwork than to her acting, its tone similar to that of *Chic*. One of the birds in *Parrots*, for instance, "has been so well brushed in that he looks as if he had been on a prolonged debauch"; the *Little Breton Girl, Standing* seems "to be suffering from colic"; and *The Young Girl and Death* features drapery reminiscent of a pink snowstorm. That aside, the reviewer compliments the "decidedly good" sculpture, from the sphinx inkstand to Ophelia, but ends with the ambiguous suggestion that "the stage could well afford to lose her to let another field of art be the gainer" (5 Jan. 1881: 3).

Disgruntled pastors, reviewers, and art critics notwithstanding, the *Inquirer* sent Bernhardt off to Chicago by reprinting Frank Clarke's *Puck* poem:

> Be thou Our stattoo, ornament Our Bay,
> Thy task were light; continue to portray
> Thy most successful role, la Liberté!

Bernhardt's reputation as "la Liberté" and her success as a good businesswoman fostered the public's confusion, since her unconventional lifestyle and dubious genealogy had not prevented her from holding high professional standards or from receiving professional acclaim. The comfortable Puritan assumption that financial success blesses the obedient, to say nothing of the wellborn, was invalidated as she overcame her severest Philadelphia critics with a display of talent and verve. Perhaps because Philadelphians so strongly believed in their historical role in developing an American ethos, their caution was understandable; yet Boston, with equal if not greater claim, had been surer of its stance, exercising a bluestocking broadmindedness to welcome her on aesthetic and intellectual grounds. Chicago, her next stop, posed a different problem. A relatively new city with a diverse ethnic population, it was known for manufacturing and shipping, not culture. Its mixture of discomfort and excitement over Bernhardt may well have reflected the realization that in crucial ways she was like those who, in this gateway city to the West, had risen from commonplace backgrounds and had by sheer force of will carved out secure business and social niches. The discussion about how warmly to welcome her was a very public one that continued much longer than the similar discussions elsewhere, as in New Haven. It forced Chicago preachers to negotiate the relationship between the theatre and the pulpit, and their parishioners, already sensitized by social aspirations, to decide how to participate in the sensation without becoming party to it.

Although the French community in Chicago was cordial, reports about her chilly reception by church and society alike suggest that the two groups had shared rationales. One common assumption was that Bernhardt, an outsider from an indeterminate class, held values identical with those of the heterodox characters she played; the "proof" was her public and unremorseful acknowledgment of her illegitimate son. The free publicity afforded by the discussion delighted Abbey so much that when the Bishop of Chicago fervently denounced Bernhardt *ex cathedra*, he pointedly contributed $200 to the city's poor to match the savings in advertising (Richardson 97–8). The *Inter-Ocean* entered the fray on Bernhardt's side by commenting acidly that the stage was preferable "to find[ing] the pulpit converted into the box of a mountebank where sensational worldliness takes the place of devout piety." Either because Christmas had passed or because the city was less imbued with a sense of historical identity than those on the East coast, the response to Bernhardt evoked fewer anti–Semitic stereotypes. In fact, some preachers and ministers pleaded ignorance of the theater, invited Bernhardt to attend their services, and, while condemning her lifestyle privately, publicly left their parishioners to reconcile theater going with their consciences (*Inter-Ocean* 8 Jan. 1881: 9).

Of course, no member of high society could see Bernhardt perform and remain anonymous, since the newspapers listed fashionable theater attendees and detailed their costumes—a nicely ironic theatricalization of those who planned to cold-shoulder the actress socially. The Chicago smart set was thus caught between two obligations, being seen at the theatre and not being seen with Bernhardt. The exclusive "Bohemian" Owl Club solved the problem by excluding her from private club activities (2 Jan. 1881: 10). That move prompted the *Chicago Times* to remind the club members that the Boston Artists' Guild had greeted her with "fervency of recognition" and that in Boston, "many society ladies were noticed among the guests." "There is a very distinct line to be drawn between Mlle. Bernhardt and immorality," the article instructed its readers: "She is a woman of intellect, fine mental culture, artistic feeling, and delicately refined—one whose acquaintance, whose friendship, no lady need hesitate to enjoy" (27 Dec. 1881: 5). By their particularity and social uncertainty, Chicago women had shown themselves to be more like the mothers of Orange, New Jersey, than like their aesthetic and blue-blooded urban sisters.

Such fears had little effect upon the general public, which was as inquisitive about Bernhardt as about her shadow spectacle the whale. Crowds flocked to see the whale, which had arrived before her on January 3 and was booked into the Chicago Exposition Building for ten days. Ghoulish spectators who tried to enter its jaws were prevented from doing so by a Pinkerton man, who reportedly served as an informal exhibitor, stirring the behemoth's whiskers with his club and pointing out, "'them is what he strains his food through'" (*Inter-Ocean* 4 Jan. 1881: 6).

In the same way the public thronged the railroad station to wait for Bernhardt, who left West Philadelphia at 9 A.M. on January 9 and arrived three hours late in Chicago the next day. By courtesy of Jerome Marble, the President of the Worcester Excursion Car Company, she—like the whale—traveled in her own car (*Cincinnati Daily Enquirer* 31 Jan. 1881: 4). Contracted for use until April 20, "The City of Worcester" car was equipped with modern kitchen, dining tables, and a "cozy little couch" curtained off by heavy damask drapes. Reporters who met her eagerly cataloged her furniture and costumes, and waxed eloquent over her lack of cosmetics and good health: if she "makes it fashionable for ladies to be well and be proud of it, she will set a fashion even more beautiful," they said. She escaped the hullabaloo by riding to Palmer House in style: drawn by a pair of matched bays with silver harnesses, her carriage sported her monogram and was lined with dark green velvet. As on her first day in New York, she retired to her suite, a set of rooms that faced State Street. Besieged by reporters and in need of rest, she refused to see anyone, even a messenger from the French Consul M. Edmond Carrey, who delivered an enormous floral arrangement in the shape of an anchor and chalice, with "Sarah" spelled out in red roses (*Inter-Ocean* 10 Jan. 1881: 4). Whether reporters in the Midwest were less rapacious than those in New York or better acquainted with her need for privacy, they did not object to their exclusion by drawing vicious caricatures of a balding Sarah.

Although the cool welcome envisioned by the social set was sidetracked, Bernhardt's theatrical debut in Chicago was not a resounding financial success. To what extent that resulted from the enthusiasm of those who could not afford tickets and boycott by those who could is difficult to judge. The *Times* maintained that Chicagoans "liberally" bought tickets and that Bernhardt would "find in that shining American gold a more than ample reward for social ostracism," yet the receipts of second week's performance were so low that her managers refused to release the data (23 Jan. 1881: 11). The order of her repertory may well have affected her theatrical popularity, even though the Philadelphia opening night debacle was not repeated and the *Adrienne Lecouvreur* performance went smoothly. As in New York and Montreal, however, the delay of her most intense scene frustrated the audience's desire to see her immediately. Applause at McVicker's was therefore "perfunctory," "patriotic," and only sometimes "involuntary," and both the critical *Times* and the more moderate *Inter-Ocean*, which cautioned about the unfairness of a snap judgment, agreed that the actress was "consummately an artificer" and lacked genius. "Finesse" and eloquence, intelligence and attention to detail: these she had, but because of her poor supporting cast, the performance was "at the mercy of incompetent coadjutors" (*Times* 11 Jan. 1881: 10; *Inter-Ocean* 11 Jan. 1881: 4). Although the play's rhythm assuaged her stage fright and preserved her energy after a tiring journey, the audiences' manifest discontent in city after city was bad public relations and may have influenced her to change the repertory order: she opened with *Adrienne Lecouvreur* only two more times, in Cincinnati and on her return to Philadelphia.

The record of disappointment continued in Chicago as the *Times* and *Tribune* reacted to later performances with headlines like "Sarah to Satiation" and "Sarah the Bizarre." *Froufrou*, a winner in New York and Boston, failed to please in Chicago. There, the play was taken as a symptom of the demise of French drama, whose "atmosphere is morbidly bad and ... rationale both perverted and limited." The same papers that had praised her naturalness and health complained about the artificiality of her acting; her part, polished to perfection, was "as accurately put together as the works of a watch and quite as mechanical." In *Le Sphinx*, when she did succeed in winning over her audience, the *Times* took exception to her harrowing death scene as "meretricious and essentially base," yet it equally disliked

Le Passant, "an elegant trifle" that broke the morbidity (13 Jan. 1881: 5). When praise came, it was backhanded. According to the same day's *Tribune*, Bernhardt, unlike her rival Sophie Croizette, whose "repulsively horrible" death throes were famous, died in an "eminently lady-like" manner. The reviewers' complaints that the plays were immoral and not didactic enough echo the kind of criticism that came from the Bishop of Chicago, but they also point to the naïveté of an audience unused to continental plays. Her performance of Marguerite in *Camille* was roundly denounced because it added "pulmonary disease" to "moral incontinence" and created "an apotheosis ... of bawdry." The *Inter-Ocean* liked the performance but was quick to say that emotional intensity had colored its objectivity and that it too feared Bernhardt's lack of "moral force." (*Times* 14 Jan. 1881: 5; *Inter-Ocean* 15 Jan. 1881: 8).

The struggle against the weight of constant disapproval added another measure of stress. At the performance of *Phèdre* on January 14, Bernhardt created a sensation by fainting on stage. The *Inter-Ocean* and *Tribune* agreed that she had been tired out by the effort of interpreting "the heavy lines of this uninviting drama," its "lofty classicism" failing to consort with her talents (15 Jan. 1881: 8; 15 Jan. 1881: 8). Indeed, the overall response to her indisposition was unfriendly rather than sympathetic. The *Philadelphia Bulletin* reacted with a tasteless pun—"And yet she has been accustomed to act syn-copiously" (qtd. in *Puck* 2 Feb. 1881: 372)—and the *New York Commercial Advertiser*, unwittingly nearest the truth, commented snidely, "Chicago wickedness has been too overpowering for Bernhardt. She closed the performance last evening with a faint." Despite her illness, she honored her next day's special engagement, a gesture that should have mollified even those members of the social set determined to snub her: she appeared at a memorial benefit for George B. Carpenter, the founder of Central Music Hall, whose funeral was held on January 9. Although the benefit was primarily a musical event, Bernhardt, who arrived very late from a sickbed, did a series of readings "with tears in her voice," including "Beruria"; "Christine," from "Poèmes barbares," by Leconte de Lisle; and "Un peu de musique," by Victor Hugo (*Inter-Ocean* 17 Jan. 1881: 10).

Bernhardt's other nonrepertory performance was a debut of Alexandre Dumas's *L'Étrangère* on Tuesday, January 18. This offering was criticized for its tedious monologues, for the "impassive and informal" role forced on Bernhardt, and, finally, for the "flaming red necktie" that the actor playing Clarkson, the American character, adopted to demonstrate his national pride (*Inter-Ocean* 19 Jan. 1881: 4). On more serious grounds, the *Tribune* reacted to the "peculiarly French" nature of the play's radical modern theories—"household as a prison, marriage as a warfare, woman as a rebel, and adultery as the result looked for." The unlooked-for feminism and the length of the four-hour performance prompted almost a quarter—or, as the *Times* maintained, almost half—of the audience to walk out before the end. Chicago critics were difficult to please. They blamed her equally for popularizing French *opéra bouffe* and for introducing modern issues on stage; yet they disliked *Hernani*, judging it "out of tune with the times," despite its history of revolutionizing the theatre with a melodramatic blow against classicism. And, undercutting their own criticism, they praised her for her delicate conveyance of "pure love" and "poetic fragrance" (*Inter-Ocean* 21 Jan. 1881: 2; *Tribune* 21 Jan. 1881: 5).

What, then, went wrong in Chicago? Treated as a social pariah by a bourgeoisie too newly shaped by industrial wealth to be confident in its position, Bernhardt played to lukewarm audiences and captious critics. The Chicago community seemed to be more Puritan than the Puritans—extraordinarily intolerant, narrow-minded, and insensitive to the theatrical nuances highly praised on the East coast and on the Continent. The response was partly attributable to insecurity, partly to class-consciousness. One defensive reviewer pointed to a linguistic problem that went far beyond learning another tongue. Bernhardt *was* foreign: she spoke a different moral, political, and social language. American dissatisfaction with Bernhardt's acting and lifestyle became, then, not so much ignorance of adequate aesthetic discourse, but rather the lack of a "Parisian implement"—a pen that could produce the "illusive reality" of the costumes and performances. Likewise, the dissatisfaction was attributable to the lack of a French vocabulary, "unlearned and unlearnable by heathenish Saxon organs of articulation," that could adequately describe the details (*Inter-Ocean* 15 Jan. 1881: 8). The *Inter-Ocean* reporter sought to have it both ways, asserting the purity of American taste and making fun of American pronunciation. Bernhardt's name was pronounced "in every conceivable and inconceivable way," he complained:

> It ranged from Burnhard, with a prolonged and guttural roll of the arbitrary "r," to Barnhart, with the most delicate slurring of that same "r:" It slid from Bairnahrdt to Beernhairt, and descended from the pathos of Burnhurt to the bathos of Bernherdt, with the most finical hypercritical and learned pronunciation of the "tildae" ... [11 Jan. 1881: 8].

Such self-deprecation suggests another facet to the vinegary reviews: Chicagoans approached cultural convergence suspecting that they would be victimized financially and also judged wanting in sophistication. In the light of denunciations from pulpit and high society, it took a clear-sighted writer to exclaim, "Ehue, Jaques! How frail we are!" (*Times* 2 Jan. 1881: 10).

The problems associated with clashing foreign and domestic assumptions appeared even before the theatre critics had made their final judgment. Her art exhibit at O'Brien's Art Gallery on January 12 created a double set of questions about class and economic considerations; many believed they were being "had" by an advertising ploy. Not surprisingly, Chicago matrons who dithered over receiving Bernhardt were outclassed by the performing Frenchwoman who sent out five hundred invitations, printed on beveled satin paper, to "a private view" of her work. Again, anonymity was impossible, and the showing became *de rigueur*. The *Chicago Times* viewed with amusement the society ladies who, scathingly labeling Bernhardt "Mlle.-Mme.," nonetheless crowded around, as they had in New York, to meet or view "the naughty Sara" as if she were "an interesting but highly dangerous wild beast" (13 Jan. 1881: 5).

Some columnists reviewed Bernhardt as if she herself were a piece of art, describing the texture, draping, and accessorizing of her royal purple costume as carefully as an aesthetic composition; at the same time, they praised her for her natural complexion and manners. About her artwork, others expressed the reverse of their theatrical assessments. The inimical *Times* liked her impressionistic style; the friendly *Inter-Ocean* was disappointed in her attempt to master more than one artistic form, since she lacked a "divine spark" in both of them. The *Inter-Ocean* critic preferred her sculpture to her paintings, but legitimately objected that the subject matter should not rely on the work's title for explanation, as was the case with her bronze *Ophelia* (15 Jan. 1881: 8). Not all the commentary was directed against her artworks, however. Just as in New York and Boston, Bernhardt was made the vehicle for social commentary, Chicago *Play* transformed the reception into a sly dig at the intelligence of city officials. According to the anecdote, an Alderman, incensed as much by not receiving free tickets, threatened to arrest her for running a sideshow without a license. "When Mr. Barnum was here last season," he grumbled, "he paid his little extra on the side-shows where the wax figgers and snaix was, and give me a whole hatfull of deadheads besides. Fact is, Miss Bernhardt haint sent a single ticket to the Council yet." Moreover, he complained, "she has a wax figger of christ in her shebang, which she's trying to rope in the sucker on as one of her own pieces of work. I hain't seen it, but I'm willin' to bet that it's the same one that I saw in a side-show last summer that had a putty nose on it" (qtd. in *Cincinnati Daily Enquirer* 4 Feb. 1881: 7).

What the responses to the art show suggest is that reviewer and reviewed, alderman and society matron alike, were struggling with problematic translations of language and culture. The motto imprinted on the frame of *The Young Girl and Death*—"*La mort glisse en son rêve a tout bas, viens, dit-elle amour est l'éphémère en je suis l'immortelle*"—might stand as Bernhardt's own life motto, a coda to "*Quand même*"; but the puzzled reviewer would need to look beneath her well-publicized eccentricities and grande dame façade to understand the hardiness of spirit that declared, "Despite everything, in spite of the ephemeral nature of love and the inevitability of death, I will persevere." Her very toughness and invincibility may have exacerbated Chicagoans' fears and caused them to prefer to view her as a commodity, a creature wound up and set moving by her managers. These fears were especially evident in the wrap-up discussion upon her departure for St. Louis after her last performance on January 22. The reviewers were disturbed by her chameleon-like ability to express and recreate herself in a plastic way, in both appearance and behavior. That very ability, the core of her acting, defined her for the *Times* and its readers as the embodiment of "French decadence" and opened her to the charge that she was "artificial," not "artistic." Her body was thus said to reflect the "mechanical" nature of her performances, her large mouth "filled with the most brilliant and best-made set of teeth that modern dentistry could possibly manufacture." Trained to the peak of artifice in body, behavior, and clothing, she herself was ultimately exonerated from having a role in her success, which was said to owe everything to her agent's cleverness and the power of the press, not to her own ambition and hard work. She emerged, then, from her Chicago experience as a commodity, packaged by her managers and sold to the public on her private life rather than on her theatrical ability. But because the Chicagoans were good business people, used to speculating and making money, and because they were very concerned about their own social standing, they would not "buy" that private life; and they could not "buy" her aesthetic product, since they did not understand it.

Once Bernhardt arrived in St. Louis, which had been settled as a French trading post in the 1760s, she was given an enthusiastic welcome from the French community; but as in Chicago economic entrepreneurship occupied public attention. The *Post Dispatch*, for instance, determined not to allow Bernhardt's theatrical successes affect its judgment, spitefully argued that every unsold $3 ticket was a vote against chicanery. It estimated early box-office receipts at a poor $2000 or so and expressed cynical pleasure at an opening night house almost one-third empty (the competing *Globe-Democrat*, whose French sympathies were clear—it had published Marie Colombier's first review in her native tongue—maintained that the house was full). On the street interest in Bernhardt's artistic achievements and lifestyle ran high, and ticket sales flourished. Theatre managers, however, were less successful than in Chicago in containing the speculators.

One clever operator gained a $600 profit by using a shill, someone who pretended to bargain the ticket price down: the real customer, overhearing the fracas and believing that he might get good seats at a bargain, would step in and pay an inflated price. A host of other scams were reported, even against Jarrett—someone posing as an Associated Press agent promised international coverage of the St. Louis visit, someone else purportedly representing the Western Bureau of correspondence sent in a fraudulent bill. Trading on Bernhardt's worth on the open market in St. Louis turned out to be brisker than in Chicago, whose citizens were busy weighing their social status. Despite the intercultural antagonism that fueled some reviews, the public, no matter its extraction, was eager to make and spend a dollar on the exotic visitor.

Despite her profits and warm welcome, Bernhardt disliked St. Louis as much as she had disliked Philadelphia. She found the streets "repulsively dirty" and was bored enough to consider breaking her contract but for Jarrett's resolute refusal (Bernhardt, *Memoirs* 181). The reporters, unconcerned about being tainted with scandal, happily wrote about what they found— politeness, aesthetic appreciation, and a trainload of "ladies and gentlemen of refinement." They were amazed by the company's towering pile of luggage,[8] described by a *Cincinnati Enquirer* writer as "rather on the grain-elevator order, ... covered with coarse reddish water-proof duck canvas cases, provided with innumerable straps, buckles, hooks...." It also caught the attention of a St. Louis *Globe-Democrat* journalist—a Mr. Coulter—who had met the train between Chicago and St. Louis. Clearly charmed by Bernhardt, he paid whimsical attention to counting the suitcases—106 bags, 30 belonging to Bernhardt alone, requiring four baggage wagons to take all to the hotel. The *Spectator*, envious of Coulter's oneupmanship, suggested that the Bernhardt party had "the impression ... that he was some kind of a custom-house officer, and they do say that Miss Bernhardt herself insisted on unpacking her valise for his vision."

Her warm welcome continued at the Lindell Hotel, where she and her sister occupied a three-room suite, refurbished with new furniture, *objects d'art*, freshly painted walls and wood, and lace and rose damask drapery. For her, the stay was a theatrical success, but the tone of the public accounts shows that she had moved into a different sphere both culturally and geographically. Newspaper accounts in the smaller towns of the Midwest and South proved to be more anecdotal, more likely to weave personal incidents into stories. These accounts, which replaced the satire that appeared in larger Northeastern publications, catered to the same desire to domesticate Bernhardt that the *Chic* diary and other burlesques did. They also granted a moment of fame to local interviewees who would otherwise not have been noticed. In St. Louis, for instance, the *Post Dispatch* published a lengthy discussion of the poor impression left at Lindell's by the troupe. Jarrett was rude to the porter, and Bernhardt not only failed to tip the chambermaid but also refused to eat most of the chef's special creations. "[S]he was fond of curry of chicken and rice," William Downey, the veteran waiter, noted sadly, but "she was rather disappointing" (31 Jan. 1881: 3).

Perhaps in actuality Bernhardt made more effort to bridge the cultural gap than her hosts suspected. As the *St. Louis Republican* reports on January 29, the French were bemused to discover that she had adopted American dining habits—10 A.M. breakfast, 1 P.M. lunch, 5 P.M. dinner, and midnight supper—and that instead of drinking *eau rouge*, a mixture of water and Bordeaux, she drank water plain and iced, or, when homesick, added drops of Chateau-Yquem, "a means of marrying the king of wines with the queen of waters," as she claimed diplomatically. When she returned to France in May, however, she convulsed her friends with descriptions of how Americans used fingers and knives to eat:

> "Mon ami ... you would not believe it—the Americans never take more than a quarter of an hour to dine, and they eat in whichever order the cook has prepared the dishes. If the fruit is ready, then they eat that first! Ugh! It was terrible!" [qtd. in Woon 279].

At the end of her life, she found the phrase to describe the Americans: "sympathetic barbarians" who were only at that point "catching up in refinement and in courtesy" (*Art of the Theatre* 16).

As Bernhardt moved farther West and South, her hosts were more honest about enjoying her as spectacle. Without understanding French, they flocked to see her on stage, they crowded into her art shows, and, in St. Louis, they admired her jewelry, a very tangible reminder of her success. Despite the "bible bangers," as one headline put it, they engaged enthusiastically in a complex form of off-stage interactive performance in which Bernhardt assumed a variety of roles. In St. Louis, her art reception was organized, as earlier ones had been, with works on sale and Bernhardt on display, ready to act the gracious hostess. Held at Pettes & Leathe's Art Gallery on January 25, the evening was a social vindication, if not an artistic one. "Fully 1000 leading ladies and gentlemen" appeared at the soirée, according to the *Memphis Daily Appeal*, including the governor and mayor and their wives. The turnout was so high that the *Spectator*, generally cautious about Bernhardt's "bull-dozing" character, took its readers to task for crashing the reception uninvited, staring at Bernhardt while audibly refusing to be introduced, and keeping their hats on—in short, for acting like social barbarians. Commentators noted that at the "private" showings, the crush was too great to see the works (on the average, a mailing of 300 invitations yielded 1200 visitors; in St. Louis, 400 yielded 2000, presumably a combination of "leading ladies and gentlemen" and others). Everyone wanted to see the dangerous woman, including one minister who, interviewed by the *Spectator*, "considered he shook just as clean a hand as those given him in six out of sixty every week."

The reception—or sideshow, as the *Spectator* grumbled—evoked more commentary about Bernhardt than about her artwork, including a mawkish tribute by John J. Jennings, who hailed her as "painter, sculptress, actress ... / A living trinity of art."[9] The shade of blue velvet she wore at the reception became fashionable, and everyone marveled at her hat, a huge blue velvet creation with bows and strings lined in sprigged blush satin. In comparison to the vibrant actress, her sketches seemed unhappy productions and her paintings full of "weird fancy." Her sculptures, on the other hand, were so good that the *Globe-Democrat*, like its big-city counterparts, doubted their authenticity, suggesting that "the defective modeling in the pictures ... could not produce the perfect modeling of the Girardin head" (30 Jan. 1881: 8). Even so, her critics praised her for pursuing so difficult a hobby, the *Spectator* reviewer "W.R.H." finding in her sculpture the "intuition of genius." Of all the critics, however, the *Republican* reviewer was most astute: "It is very apparent that Mlle. Bernhardt is well acquainted with herself, for with few exceptions she appears in most of [her paintings and statuary]." Bernhardt was aware of herself as spectacle, whether as actress, artist, grande dame, or work of art, and the receptions allowed her to play all roles at once.

As an aesthetic commodity, she was marketable in many ways. On January 28, by prearrangement between Jarrett and Speyer's, her jewelry was cleaned, repaired, and put on exhibition. Whether she agreed to the display to increase ticket sales (Gold and Fizdale 185) or whether, as she maintained in her memoirs, the display was the brainchild of Abbey and Jarrett, the ornaments attracted much attention. Catalogued and valued at over $75,000, the collection included many irreplaceable pieces, including a six-hundred-year-old belt of rubies, turquoise, emeralds, diamonds, and sapphires sent by the Prince of Wales to adorn her costume in *Adrienne Lecouvreur*. Despite her small stature, the jewelry seemed designed to emphasize the magnitude of her success: a four-inch diamond horseshoe pendant, a ten-inch butterfly hair ornament with movable wings. Other animals, icons of her living menagerie, included wasp and serpent bracelets (*Globe-Democrat* and *Post-Dispatch* 28 Jan. 1881: 9 and 8). As she complained in her memoirs, the jeweler added a number of outré items to the collection, including a sapphire-covered toothpick, a gold and turquoise cigarette holder, a pipe with diamonds set in its amber mouthpiece, and a pair of gold spectacles decorated with pearl acorns. She was especially angry about the spectacles. Jarrett, however, was undisturbed, and the jeweler was ecstatic about the additions: the exhibit had attracted five orders for similar pipes (Bernhardt, *Memoirs* 183).

Whether Bernhardt overcompensated after her Chicago experience or whether audiences were really more interested in her than in themselves, her St. Louis visit was theatrically successful. To be sure, the *Post-Dispatch* exercised its spleen on audience and actress alike, noting that society belles who prided themselves on understanding French ended by reaching for librettos and that Bernhardt was "greatly overrated," superficial, and entirely too artful. Yet for the *Globe-Democrat* and *Republican*, the opening *Froufrou* on January 26 was a masterpiece: Bernhardt's elocution was "polished and perfect," her voice like an "Aeolian harp," and her acting expressive. Even when the more critical *Spectator* placed her between Clara Morris and Rachel, it praised her for her realistic use of realistic details.

By the next performance, the few remaining cynics recognized Bernhardt's "marvelous quality ... of giving voiceless but unmistakable expression to a wide range of differing emotions." Her carefully modulated death scene in *Le Sphinx* evoked both humor and serious meditations on death and on the theater. One writer laughed at a Boston journalist who applied to Massachusetts General Hospital to determine whether Bernhardt's death throes were not only aesthetic but accurate; but the same writer also made fun of common American stage practices, noting that even death was class-conscious, since heroes take longer to die on stage than supernumeraries. Death was relative to weight and poison, he pointed out: "[A] thin heroine dies harder than a stout woman, and ... a lady who has been poisoned is apt to crawl over more of the stage than a lady who has been stabbed" (*Globe-Democrat* 23 Jan. 1881: 4).

After seeing *Camille*, one *Globe-Democrat* reviewer made an important point, so important that it accounts for some of the negative commentary Bernhardt received in other cities. Natural, low-key, and conversational, French acting was simply different from American acting, he emphasized; for an audience whose command of French was non-existent or sketchy, the long speeches in the plays may well have proved unbearable. American audiences seemed to have a "morbid craving for tableaux, catastrophes, stage effects and other sensational developments of the cheap and nasty drama." Like the audiences in St. Louis, this reviewer was able to come to terms with the monologic and dialogic propensities of French art and so could gleefully object to the American preference for the "Angliloquent pirate" whose "shrieks, gasps, stamps, screams and other soap-chewing devices" were better received than Bernhardt's heart-rending death scenes (30 Jan. 1881: n.p.). For those who expected sensationalism, then, she failed: eschewing bombast and gesticulation, she found other ways to express her emotions. For Continental viewers who were accustomed to realism, she was transcendent.

Other reporters gradually adopted this perceptive attitude. As the performance week progressed in St. Louis, the reviews grew shorter and more adulatory, full of praise for her "wonderful attention to detail [and] marvelous naturalness, ease and grace" in *Camille*, *Hernani*, and *Adrienne Lecouvreur* (*Post Dispatch* 27 Jan. 1881: 3; *Globe-Democrat* 28 and 29 Jan. 1881: 6). By Thursday, audiences were so large that the orchestra had to be moved under the Grand Opera House stage to provide more seats. Of all her roles, Doña Sol in *Hernani* was the least popular, not only because of her delayed entrance but because the company was not strong enough to maintain dramatic interest throughout. Nonetheless, the troupe was commended for costumes, natural behavior, and perfection of elocution and delivery. The cultural difference was remarkable, one *Globe-Democrat* editorial concluded humorously: in Bernhardt's troupe, ease and understatement prevail and spotlight-hogging was nonexistent, in contrast to an American performance, in which "The leading juvenile gives us the counterfeit presentment of a howling swell with renovated pants and obsolete hair oil" (30 Jan. 1881: n.p.).

This self-critical attitude, combined with broad-minded appreciation for modern, continental theatre, showed a measure of dramatic sophistication that Chicagoans on the whole were unable to achieve. The stance was particularly noteworthy, since De Witt Talmage had given another of his long-threatened diatribes against actors the day before Bernhardt opened in St. Louis. Some members of the clergy anticipated his attack, but those who attempted to police morality from the pulpit had little influence on the critics. Talmage, who denied that he had ever pilloried a "celebrated foreign actress," suggested that the innate dramatic impulse in all people needed to be controlled and purified: "The very fact that the drama has been dragged through the sewers of iniquity is a reason why we should endeavor to elevate it" (qtd. in *Globe-Democrat* 24 Jan. 1881: 5).

In St. Louis the religious response was divided between Catholic and High-Church Episcopalians, and other Protestant sects. The first two argued for freedom of choice, exonerating both actors and members of their parishes who went to "wholesome" plays and who nonetheless fulfilled their religious duties. The others, "news-gleaning scavengers and moral ragpickers," as the St. Louis *Republican* styled them, followed Talmage's lead.

They were represented by the Rev. James H. Brook, editor of *The Truth* and pastor of the St. Louis Walnut Street Presbyterian Church. Brook held to the hard line that became identified with Talmage: "Theatrical plays are popular precisely in proportion to their coarseness and lewdness, and the fashionable world is prepared to welcome an actress who is a notorious prostitute" (*Republican* 13 Jan. 1881: 5). Although the "Town Talker" in the *Spectator* maintained that Bernhardt and her managers desired such "open war" for advertising purposes, Jarrett publicly objected to the Rev. Brook's statement. Instead of an apology, he received a letter in which Brook, like Talmage, denied speaking directly about Bernhardt, but acknowledged that in *The Truth*, he had indeed commented "without reserve" about the depravity of stage and actors.

Despite the zealousness of popular preachers, the charge of depravity seemed to have little effect on the audiences, who were more likely to be concerned about social rather than moral issues. An upstart with indeterminate parentage and questionable upbringing, Bernhardt was, for all her enjoyment of spectacle, a serious actress who had been recognized by the best society abroad and who was hailed as the new Rachel. Indeed, she occupied a parallel universe, one in which Mrs. Grundy and the old rules of genealogy no longer held sway. New York was brash, Philadelphia cold, and Chicago uncertain. But Boston, which prided itself on aesthetic discrimination, welcomed her; and St. Louis, whose French population had made a place for themselves in the New World, perhaps saw its own success figured metaphorically on stage in Bernhardt's slender shape.

5

"We are hardly good colonists": Bernhardt's Southern Odyssey

> Two slugs on the tickut, if yer buy as many as eight, and if yer only buys one, fifty pur cnt. On de dollar.... I've got a gang here, Cockey, and don't you forget..." [*Louisville Courier* 15 Feb. 1881: 3].

Once Bernhardt had passed halfway through her hegira, her traveling gathered momentum and its nature changed. She had played to self-styled sophisticates in New York, Boston, and Philadelphia; she had braved the abattoirs of Chicago; and she had been courteous to French scions in St. Louis. After a week in Cincinnati, she would face almost two months of one- and two-night stands in front of inquisitive, theatrically naïve audiences. Like those in St. Louis, they were honest about valuing her as spectacle and therefore wrote more about her than about her dramatic performances. Their rhetoric, too, was different, their humor and colloquialisms broader than those of urban journalists. On this leg of her journey, Bernhardt was treated to down-home drollery and reporting of a peculiarly American sort; she had more to fear from man-made and natural disasters than from critical acumen. Indefatigable as ever, she confronted thieves, laughed at collapsing scenery, performed in spite of illness, waded streets running with water, and braved a railroad washout.

From Cincinnati to Louisville, then, her hosts cordially welcomed an actress who offered modern French drama to the South. They were also less finicky about the social implications of entertaining and being entertained by a woman of the world, whether because of Bernhardt's sense of *noblesse oblige* or their own business acumen. The members of the local *beau monde* were just as eager to show off their finery at each performance and the crowds just as eager to buy tickets as in the larger cities, although the scams were somewhat less polished. Like their more sophisticated counterparts in Montreal, however, these folks were worried about the moral implications of Bernhardt's repertory and larded their praise with caveats and explanations. At the same time, small-town Americans, unlike their cosmopolitan Philadelphia cousins, were willing to separate Bernhardt the woman from Bernhardt the actress and enjoy the spectacle of both performances. What Bernhardt benefited from was the spirit of American independence, insistent on judging for itself and unwilling to be awed by foreignness.

A less generous and more self-serving version of that independence, however, took shape as theft, both actual and virtual. Controlling the first was the easier task: Jarrett hired plainclothesmen from Pinkerton's National Detective Agency to discourage the gang of sneak thieves and pickpockets that followed the troupe and preyed upon gullible theatre crowds. The situation was serious enough that William Pinkerton himself announced publicly that New York, Philadelphia, and Chicago detectives would be part of the entourage (*Courier* 24 Feb. 1881: 4). His action came too late, however, to prevent jewel thieves from an attempt on her railroad car on the way to Cincinnati, and he was powerless to protect her from Olive Logan, a writer who basked in the actress's reflected glory and who laid hands on her privacy and her personality in a way earlier reporters had failed to do. In truth, Bernhardt was surrounded by Artful Dodgers, whether they were called managers or scalpers, gossip columnists or gawkers. All had a vested personal or business interest in something that belonged to her, be it the proceeds from her jewelry, her performances, or her image.

Typically, Bernhardt dramatized the attempted jewel theft incident in her memoirs, where her account is a testament not only to her spirit of adventure but also to American entrepreneurship run amok. On January 30, after leaving St. Louis for Cincinnati, she settled down in the observation car to enjoy the view from the back of the train through her binoculars, her artistic eye transforming the natural scenery into a theatrical backdrop "like a continually changing living panorama" (*Memories* 422). Suddenly, the train stopped; someone fired a pistol; and a would-be armed robber, strapped to the underside of her car with strong leather thongs, was dragged aboard. The troupe returned to St. Louis, and a decoy baggage train, with eight detectives as passengers, was sent ahead to bait the gang members waiting at Little Incline. As expected, the gang ran the baggage train off the tracks, but all were apprehended. Bernhardt ends her account with divided sympathies. Melancholy about the fate of the gang's chief, hanged at the young age of twenty-five, she blamed the St. Louis jeweler for making his display so tempting to thieves. Yet she also created a melodramatic tableau out of the situation, as she had on *L'Amérique* when the émigré's child was born:

> Perhaps when [the poor fellow] stopped and looked at the jeweler's window, he said to himself: "There is jewelry there worth 1,000,000 francs. If it were all mine I would sell it and go back to Belgium. What joy I could give to my poor mother who is blinding herself with work by gaslight..." [*Memories* 427].

While Bernhardt was romantically sympathizing with the jewel thief, another less threatening admirer sneaked onto the City of Worcester, hoping for a private interview. Expected to greet fans at the St. Louis Plum Street Depot at 7:30 P.M. on Sunday, January 30, the troupe was delayed in Indianapolis because of a broken baggage car wheel; there, a youthful lawyer bribed the conductor to part with badge and hat so that he could pass disguised into Bernhardt's car. For all his efforts, she was sound asleep (*Cincinnati Daily Enquirer* 31 Jan. 1881: 4; *Atlanta Constitution* 13 Feb. 1881: 2). A more insidious intrusion occurred in Cincinnati, as much a gateway to Bernhardt's Southern odyssey as Hartford and New Haven were to the West. There, she was joined by a traveling reporter-companion, a white-gloved *Enquirer* journalist eager to reflect Bernhardt's glory and interpret her to the public. Olive Logan's mannered style and labored rhetoric stands in contrast to the purely American vernacular that relied on bromides, shaggy-dog stories, and rib-ticklers to get its results.

Once Bernhardt arrived in Cincinnati, she was driven to the Burnet Hotel, along with Abbey, Jarrett, her three servants, her sister, two Paris reporters (J. H. Haynie of the *Gaulois* and Jehan Soudan of the *Voltaire*), Mme. Guérard,[1] Marie Colombier, and Edouard Angelo. There, the party went immediately to bed, a far cry from what the December 6 *Hartford Daily Times* had predicted in an acid comment buried in a column about auctions, poultry sales, and liver complaint cures: "They now talk of having the Bernhardt visit Cincinnati. She is, on arriving there, to take a drive about the city and remark: 'Mon dieu! Zis ees so mooch like Paris! Eet seems as eef I was at home!' And then, the price of tickets will be shoved up to $25. Sara and her managers know how to work these things" (2). From the considerably more prosaic beginning to her Cincinnati tour, the

Enquirer reporter wove his stories. No detail was too small: he described the elevator (a mark of the hotel's status), dissected her costumes, and reprinted the invitation card to be issued for her art reception on January 31. Unlike New Haven and Chicago newspapermen, who focused on social issues, he spun a tongue-in-cheek human interest story about what the cultured Parisian might have seen and heard on her visit to a provincial American hotel in the late nineteenth century:

> Tom Zimmerman, looking just too sweet to live, stood behind the desk, with a pen behind both ears. Clerk Bainford, with his Burnside whiskers curled and perfumed, showed decided trepidation at times. Lev Steele dropped in, disguised under a new set of pinkish whiskers, and bantered the boys to buy a few of his choice seats.... Phelps Neff pretended to be just upon the point of retiring, but it took him nearly three hours to get started. Johnny Drummond, the serio-tragical clerk of the Grand Hotel, called in just to see, you know. A row of bald-headed boarders were strung along the office ... pretending to talk but all dreadfully on the *qui vive* [31 Jan. 1884: 4].

Jarrett's actual publicity ploy was more effective than driving Bernhardt around Cincinnati. Given the local interest in spectacle and diminished concern about social standing, he took a calculated risk and held the art reception before Bernhardt's theatrical debut, thereby generating ticket sales where she was relatively unknown. His gamble paid off, as it might not have in a larger venue: the receipts for the first performance, while lower than those for the second, were well within a reasonable range. Some reception and theatergoers were deterred by the torrential rain, which also delayed Bernhardt. Her 4:30 P.M. arrival at Room 9 of Pike's Opera House was itself theatrical: a red curtain opened, and the actress suddenly emerged—"Her appearance did not cause a ripple of applause.... The closed lip and eager gaze were greater plaudits than cheers and huzzas." The report entirely omits a critique of the artwork—Bernhardt herself was on display, as was the audience, not quite half the article taken up by their names—but the homespun reviewer admits what his more sophisticated colleagues hid under satire: "The pictures and art works of this most industrious of all women were greatly admired, but *the* woman, *the* artist, *the* creator of the works of art was the center of attraction—the object of all eyes" (*Enquirer* 1 Feb. 1881: 4). Cincinnati citizens enjoyed the spectacle in blissful ignorance of a more cynical reaction, like that of the Parisian writer who complained equally about the artistic "insensibility ... [of] the hard-hearted Republicans across the seas" and about the Prince of Wales's friendship with Bernhardt as "the abyss of ... social or artistic absurdity" (*Enquirer* 6 Jan. 1881: 2).

In actuality, the Republicans were not hard-hearted—rather, they focused on the main chance. They were also hospitable in their own way. After Bernhardt's full day of rain, reception, interviews, and performance of *Adrienne Lecouvreur*, they surprised her with a midnight serenade at her hotel. Organized by Grand Opera manager Bob Miles and conducted by Professor Alexander Haig, the double orchestral program was arranged as a compliment to French tastes. Exhausted, Bernhardt retired after a single bow, leaving Jarrett to make her excuses and to listen to "Fleur de Joie Waltz," "Tout a la Joie," and the "Marseillaise" (*Enquirer* 1 Feb. 1881: 2).

In Cincinnati the voice of the serious press was manifestly shaped by Olive Logan, Bernhardt's self-styled "warm friend and companion in London and Paris and throughout Europe" (*Enquirer* 1 Feb. 1881: 4). Logan led a busy public life as actress, writer, theatre critic, playwright, and lecturer for women's rights.[2] The cheeky *Enquirer* reporter and the overly fine-spun Logan presented two poles of Cincinnati response: the Yankee wisecracker and the proponent of belles-lettres journalism, "one of the boys" and the New Woman. Both were poseurs. The first exaggerated the local vernacular as a form of bravado, thereby protecting himself from Bernhardt's possible condescension; the second adopted a form of sophisticated patter, thereby identifying herself with Bernhardt as a member of fashionable society.

The difference appears markedly in reviews of the art exhibit. The *Enquirer* reporter emphasized Bernhardt as spectacle; Logan paid attention to the attendees, "six hundred ladies of the elite." Her care, at this late stage of her career, was more to establish her *bona fides* than to critique Bernhardt's artistic output, and so she was careful to point out that although she knew the "exact position" of European aristocrats or financiers, she was unfamiliar with Cincinnati social ranks. Yet, from the standpoint of amateur ethnologist, she advised her readers that to miss opening night is "to confess oneself a set star, a lost pleiad on the firmament of fashion." As a putative member of society writing for a newspaper, she became the public's voyeur, a stand-in for the curious bystander, yet one "in the know." At the same time, she was an actress, posing as a lady, and so she identified herself as a member of Bernhardt's cortège.

A spokesman apparently in the confidence of manager and actress alike, she provided a jumble of gossipy tidbits, all of which magnified her privileged position. She humanized the businessman Jarrett by printing a grab bag of anecdotes about his personal and professional life. He expected to receive £2000 from Chapman & Hall for his memoirs; he owned eighteen chairs embroidered by the likes of Patti and Grisi;[3] and in his early years he engaged in drinking bouts with his American hosts (*Enquirer* 1 Feb. 1881: 4; 3 Feb. 1881: 4). Faced with describing his run-in with an Indianapolis lawyer, she was unable to resist the local patois: the lawyer, riding on the same train, persisted in thinking that Jarrett was going to Indianapolis for a divorce. "Incompatterbility is sufficient. Hain't seen for two weeks more than enough. Ship you off a free man in no time," the lawyer promised, pressing his card on the dumbfounded manager (3 Feb. 1881: 4).

When she conveyed her impression of Bernhardt, however, Logan avoided jokes in order to present a potpourri of disconnected, if charming, details or to create scenarios that complemented the actress. The kind of whimsicality published by the *Cincinnati Star*—

> "How slim is Sarah Bernhardt, pa,
> That shadow of a shade?"
> "My boy, she's just about as thin
> As picnic lemonade."
> [Qtd. in *New Haven Palladium* 12 Dec. 1880: 4].

—was supplanted by Logan's domestic trifles, like her engaging sketch of Bernhardt wearing the almost-stolen diamond lizard, its mouth full of roses. Bernhardt carelessly uses an India shawl as a fire screen; she prefers landscapes of the Dutch school. She cannot make herself understood to the waiter, who ignores her request for bread; and she complains that her mail is cluttered with tracts and requests for loans. For all their triviality, many of Bernhardt's reported comments seem in accord with others she made elsewhere. She complained, for instance, that American men were "too practical ... [and] chew too much tobacco," but she admired their moral qualities. She admitted to difficulty in playing a convincing *Adrienne Lecouvreur* because the role was low key, and she acknowledged a near-defeat from New York critics. Despite Logan's lavish praise, she found the first Cincinnati audience "the coldest" possible and speculated that Americans were used to "rolling ... eyes" and actresses who "goggle and mouth"—that is why they like Mary Anderson, she said cattily (4 Feb. 1881: 4). As Jarrett put it, "Americans will have it hot"; in Fanny Davenport's words, "What an actress Bernhardt would be ... if, with her naturalness and polish, she had the magnetic and emotional power of Clara Morris!" (4 Feb. 1881: 4).

Logan's stated goal in these "intimate" interview letters was to invalidate the "human interrogation points" that doubted Bernhardt's talent and criticized her troupe. While down-home reporters shuffled their librettos and focused on the audience, Logan engaged in purple prose to provide the melodrama that many American audiences seemed to expect in the plays. "Such physical throes are awful! What terrific nervous power it must require to keep them up!" she exclaimed (*Enquirer* 1 Feb. 1881: 4). In the midst of these verbal pyrotechnics, one reviewer signing himself "an Old Stager" quietly offered a serious critique: in *Camille*, Bernhardt showed "ease and naturalness," recognizing her mortality with "utter hopelessness" instead of a "convulsive gasp, as from the bite of a snake" (*Enquirer* 4 Feb. 1881: 4). Logan's adulatory and gossipy reviews rarely escaped hyperbole, yet some of her observations were astute. One of the few to articulate the actress's culture shock, she gave a sympathetic and humorous picture of the foreigner's misconceptions about America: "Fenimore Cooper still lays on the warpaint...; the buffalo bounds about ... the Alleghenies; and ... the unhappy hunting-ground is popularly supposed to be Kentucky." When she engaged in serious criticism, she followed the lead of her St. Louis *Globe-Democrat* colleague in dealing with the audience's untenable assumptions about drama. Especially in *Froufrou*, she maintained, Bernhardt observed the fourth-wall convention naturally, in contrast to some American actors, about whom "you would think Heaven had made [them] differently from other men, and that only their front views were intended to be seen." Finally, adopting an argument that reviewers would later use in Memphis, she saw in Bernhardt's plays a "terrible moral" that may have swayed "some young being wavering betwixt the knowledge of wrong and the petulant yielding of youth to that which tempts it to diversion" (*Enquirer* 3 Feb. 1884: 3).

Logan had preconceptions of her own, and while Cincinnati reporters used down-home wit to satisfy their readers, she used bombast to flatter them, perhaps in hopes that they would return the favor. She recreated blue-collar workers as "hard-handed sons of toil" or "fairy maids of the wash-tub" and envisioned a scenario for the solid middle-class Thursday night audiences peppered with visitors "from tropic lagoons of languid Louisiana." On a riff about "these traveled Darwinians" who saw "The Bernhardt," she imagines that they return to tell their tales to "girls swinging themselves in rocking-chairs, mother and Aunt Sue chewing a little snuff, the Ex-confederate officer who is said to have belonged to the Klu-Klux [sic], ... while the argent moon swirls through the distant sky, and perfumes arise from the sweet dank earth...." (*Enquirer* 4 Feb. 1881: 4). The emergence of this kind of voice in the Cincinnati reviews tended to mask other kinds of criticism; presented as the voice of society, however, it also tended to drown out by its verbosity and preciousness the doubts of Chicago matrons about Bernhardt's social acceptability.

Once Bernhardt left Cincinnati and moved away from the linguistic hot-house, the two rhetorics reversed themselves: Logan observed inelegantly that the "*Charmeuse*" had "captured the pork-packers" (*Enquirer* 4 Feb. 1881: 4), and the *Cincinnati Saturday Night* tried to be delicate about Bernhardt's proposed memoirs—"We hope she will remember that we have always spoken of her in the highest terms as a woman, an actress and a mother" (qtd. in *Puck* 2 Feb. 1881: 376). As she proceeded through New Orleans, Bernhardt generally received the genuine, unpretentious welcome due a trooper who had overcome—or at least battled—some very real difficulties in weather and personal health. In Atlanta, sympathetic reviewers sometimes lapsed into Logan-like outbursts; in Nashville, Memphis, and Louisville, however, local variations of colloquial rhetoric appeared, sometimes with a patriotic flavor, suggesting that a "plain" American style accords with morality, while a French "high" style reflects dissoluteness and promiscuity.

Her early February journey to New Orleans—the real Paris of the South—was by no means as simple or as safe as her approach to St. Louis had been the previous month. While she experienced as warm a welcome, her accommodations were considerably worse, and rather than simply disliking the city, as she had St. Louis, she was unquestionably distressed at the poverty and disrepair she found. Her adventurous entrée into New Orleans recalls her voyage over a rough sea to the New World, when she reacted to the emigrants' suffering with a combination of despair and theatricality; it also recalls the attempted train robbery, when her bravery gave way to a melodramatic recreation of an impoverished thief and his old mother. Depending on the account, her determination to cross a crumbling bridge over St. Louis Bay seems either courageous or opportunistic. Probably both are true: a good businesswoman, she wanted to avoid disappointing sold-out houses in New Orleans; but she also wanted to move to a warmer climate, since she suffered bitterly from the cold American weather.

Typically, she began the adventure bravely, and then succumbed to guilt and self-blame as she envisioned the plight of those traveling with her. When the engineer refused to move the train over a railroad bridge crossing the bay, Bernhardt offered him a $2500 indemnity (in coins—she distrusted checking accounts and kept her funds in an old chamois bag guarded by Mme. Guérard) to send to his new bride and father in Oklahoma. How much choice her company had is debatable. In her memoirs she claims that she told only four of her companions of the risk; in Skinner's account she presented a short exhortation, and all but two of the "*chers et braves enfants*" elected to stay. Granted the privilege of smoking, Jarrett stoically puffed away on a cigar; Angelo was "ashen"; and Marie Colombier furiously brushed Hamlet III, Bernhardt's pet griffin (Skinner 192). As the engineer hurtled across the bridge, Bernhardt watched it crash to pieces behind them. From then on, she confessed, she was troubled by nightmares at her temerity at risking the lives of so many people.

The culture shock she experienced on her arrival in New Orleans was exacerbated by her high expectations of a Francophone welcome. At 2:30 A.M. the troupe arrived at the St. Charles Hotel "in a somewhat perturbed state of mind." Whether the accommodations were palatial or dilapidated depends on the account. The *Daily Picayune* proudly announced that Abbey and the rest of the troupe were quartered at John's Restaurant and Victor's, but that Bernhardt occupied the "finest room" at the St. Charles, a bridal chamber replete with damask and other adornments, (6 Feb. 1881: 12). What for New Orleans was the "best," however, for her was "squalid—dirty, uncomfortable, black with cockroaches, and ... filled with large mosquitoes that buzzed around and fell on one's shoulders, sticking in one's hair." Her only happy surprise was that the food was the "most satisfactory" yet (*Picayune* 7 Feb. 1881: 1).

Adding to the misery, incessant rains put five states on flood alert, and New Orleans, built below sea level, was seriously threatened. Her own company suffered, the hairdresser apparently worst of all. Insisting on sleeping in the trunk with his wigs to prevent theft, he awoke screaming to find that he was sharing his accommodations with two large water snakes (*Memories* 432). Bernhardt herself was uncomfortable but undaunted. Crossing the flooded streets on small, mobile bridges to survey the damage, she visited the poorer section of town and was appalled to find cabins floating in the water, "hundreds squatting on these moving wrecks, with eyes burning from fever, their white teeth chattering. Right and left, everywhere, were dead bodies floating about, knocking up against the wooden piles." As on the *L'Amérique*, she was swept by a combination of egalitarianism and *noblesse oblige*. She took her own country to task, noting that everywhere the French were, the "country was poor.... Ah, we are hardly good colonists!" she lamented (*Memories* 430–31).

Poor colonists, perhaps, but politely eager hosts: in this racially divided city, society welcomed Bernhardt and winked at her antecedents. The social vindication she received in St. Louis and in Cincinnati continued, as did the acknowledgement that she was valued principally as spectacle. In Chicago, treating her as a work of art meant anatomizing and dehumanizing her; in New Orleans, when her art exhibit failed to arrive in time, it meant displaying a capacity for polite aesthetic appreciation. While she herself was the primary exhibit at Grunewald's music store on Monday, February 7, her guests comported themselves *as* guests rather than as spectators. To be sure, the *Picayune* reporters paid attention to her costume—blue velvet dress with lace and matching bonnet, and long fawn gloves—but they also gave personal, generally flattering glimpses of her personality and manners. She is tired of the rain; she wishes to understand English, but cannot when it is spoken quickly. She is "very agreeable," "the perfection of French politeness and winning grace."

Even with no Olive Logan to smooth over possible discourtesies, she was surrounded by vocal admirers. Unlike the judgmental smart set in Chicago, New Orleans society women accompanying the city's "best known business men" were "particularly demonstrative" at the reception (*Picayune* 8 and 13 Feb. 1881: 2 and 8). In this city of French extraction, the visit of an internationally known *societaire* would be a welcomed event. Perhaps, too, some took to heart Robert Ingersoll's comments about Bernhardt, reprinted in the *Picayune* on February 8. In his attack on the double standard, the "Great Agnostic" complained about the "moral mirage" fostered by those who excuse men for breaking the commandments but hold in "utter contempt a common girl who has broken only one" (2). The measure of polite regard Bernhardt received prompted the *New York Express* to comment spitefully that "The swell society of New Orleans has decided that Sarah Bernhardt is not quite wicked enough to be interesting off the stage." In return, the *New Orleans Picayune* retorted, "Guess not. New Orleans swell society is not troubling itself about the private affairs of an artiste who is certainly admired on the stage. The gush and meddle business is left for the swell heads of New York" (qtd. in *Puck* 26 Feb. 1881: 426).

Agreeing with the social set about Bernhardt's importance, New Orleans reviewers gave a perfunctory nod to the idea that her wild popularity was the result of her being "the subject of America's peculiar style of advertising" and insisted rather that her renown lay in her dramatic strength. The economic returns disappointed Bernhardt, however. Although other events in town "did a very poor business and we did not do excellently, either," she says in her memoirs (430), the New Orleans newspapers spoke of full houses and disappointed speculators. Some seats were available privately, as *Picayune* advertisements indicate. Overall, reporters in New Orleans agreed with their St. Louis brethren—Bernhardt's talent was exhibited by the naturalness of her acting. In *Froufrou*, they felt, her interpretation of Gilberte presents a believable character, a weak woman who neither loves strongly nor thinks carefully. *Phèdre* had the distinct disadvantage of being staged opposite *Aida* at the French Opera House; the result was that Francophones flocked to *Aida*, so that few in Bernhardt's audience were bilingual. Nonetheless, her acting moved one reviewer to adopt a Logan-like tone: using the conceit of a letter "To My Dear Old Lady" and posing as a bee "nestled among [Bernhardt's] jewels," he points out that many there, while ignorant of French, were entranced by her musical voice and physical grace (*Picayune* 13 Feb. 1881: 8).

That tone is mildly countered by the *Picayune*'s flippancy. Hardly sensuous enough to attract Armand's love, "she is best fitted for the last, consumptive act"; "Her death scene is as near to real death as one can approach in health and live" (8 Feb. 1881: 4; 9 Feb. 1881: 4). While self-styled *cognoscenti* dubbed her "Queen of the Bohemians" and placed her second in tragic force to Rachel, *Camille* drew a larger audience than any performance ever at the Grand Opera House. Whether from weather or strain, by the end of the week, Bernhardt was reported as ill, her death scene in *Le Sphinx* entirely too realistic—"glazed eyes, a rigid face, blanched cheeks and convulsive movements" (*Picayune* 30 Jan. 1881: 2; 11 Feb. 1881: 4). She was unable to perform the next day in *L'Étrangère*, the first interruption in her tour. D. C. Halliday, a local physician, diagnosed a "nervous attack," and theater treasurer Donning returned over $2300 in tickets (*Memphis Daily Appeal* 15 Feb. 1881: 1). After a night's rest, she was ready to finish her gig—a Saturday matinée of *Camille*, thronged despite the special "night" ticket prices; *Froufrou* in the evening; and *Adrienne Lecouvreur* as a close on Sunday, Feb. 13. This last was thought the "best" of the eight performances. "Emotional drama is her forte," the *Picayune* reviewer pronounced before adding a lone note of approval for her lucrative contract: she "deserves her world-wide reputation in her special line of acting, and fairly earns the financial success that follows her performances" (14 Feb. 1881: 2).

Moving from her insect-infested hotel and transported by boat over flooded streets to the City of Worcester, Bernhardt began on Valentine's Day what she called the "dizzying round" of smaller cities. The uncomfortable juxtaposition of two kinds of reportorial magniloquence continued, as if her hosts were unsure of how to treat her. In fact, insecurity is at the heart of both the attempt to sound over-sophisticated and the adoption of exaggerated provincialisms. Yet in the next phase of her journey, Bernhardt had little time to consider the sensitivities of her reviewers. Pausing at each venue for only a few performances, if that, she was rarely able to identify the regional peculiarities of her audiences or to discern their eccentricities. Nonetheless, plagued by mishaps and illness in Mobile and Atlanta, she was perhaps relieved to move on quickly to other venues.

Mobile again proved a place of misadventure. She had already established her reputation earlier in the month, when she dumped water on importunate fans trying to peer through the windows as her train paused on the siding. On this visit she arrived too late for the scheduled February 14 performance. The next day, the only available theatre was so small that the scenery had to be dismantled to make room for the supper scene in *Camille*. The audience, swept by merriment as the crew wrestled ineffectually with an unwieldy dining room table, broke into gales of laughter when the scenery collapsed over the actors. Heads and necks impaled by the paper backdrop, Bernhardt and her troupe abandoned the effort, and the audience received a refund (*Memories* 432–3).

News of the debacle did not dampen her reception in Atlanta or in Nashville, where her February 16 and 17 performances of *Camille* were heralded as an economic boon. "Bernhardt plays and McCalla Bros work, that is how they both get crowds" sounds like an obscure pun—rather, it is one note in the advertising cacophony: "The rush for Bernhardt tickets was something like the rush for fine Shoes, Hats and Shirts at McCalla Bros, 3 Whitehall"; "Bernhardt may come and go, but Neuralgine is the constant friend that will relieve your Neuralgia and Headache." More enterprising retailers boasted of her patronage: "Quite a number of the Bernhardt troupe patronized Thompson's restaurant last night" and "Sarah called in and left her measure for a spring outfit at W. M. Scott's." A similar welcome awaited her in Nashville, where the *Daily American's* snide remark about the "weakly twaddle" of *Camille's* morality was drowned out by a local grocery store's enthusiasm: "A large lot of Bernhardt kisses just received by Rannie & Milne," the advertisement proclaimed (*Nashville Daily American* 20 Feb. 1881: 4).

While small-town entrepreneurs mimicked their big-city cousins by trying to ride Bernhardt's popularity, reporters bombarded readers with anecdotes and anxious reports about scalpers, sometimes employing the kind of down-home rhetoric made familiar by Cincinnati columnists. The *Atlanta Constitution's* serio-comic stance was maintained by a self-styled "knight of the quill" who interviewed Bernhardt aboard the train, while the *hoi polloi* climbed the depot gates and tried to peer through the blinds. At this point Bernhardt had a bad cold, but was not so ill as to lose her sense of fun. "I am agreeably surprised at your city," she said; "It is so different from all the other southern cities. You have such an appearance of thrift here." Only a few uncomplimentary squibs appeared: the *Constitution*, for instance, pointed to "a suspicion on the part of the ladies that Miss Sallie Bernhardt rubs snuff," an idea traceable to the lady's pipe exhibited with Bernhardt's jewelry in Chicago (17 Feb. 1881: 2). Rather, the biographical material and personal interviews were expressed in a popularization of Olive Logan's style. Bernhardt is an actress "who secured her bread at the sacrifice of her virtue in the haunts of poverty"; her choice between starving in an attic or living in "gilded sin" is made much of, as is her life with her son and lover. She possesses a "life sullied with but a single spot, and a heart sealed to all save her first and only love," the readers are told, under a headline that mixes the sensational with the satirical: "Sara's Survival—to Astonish the Cracker City" (*Constitution* 16 Feb. 1881: 1).

Atlantans accepted her at face value, with little apparent concern for the social implications of "gilded sin"; Nashvillians were more critical, but after registering a distinction between French and American mores, happily forgot their scruples. In both cities, seats were at a premium. Perhaps because Atlanta was smaller than New York or Chicago, the management was able to control speculation by holding back over 200 cheaper seats in the family circle and gallery until the day of performance, so that the tickets could not be bought in advance and resold. Some operators tried to frustrate the system, but buyers were warned to examine tickets carefully for alterations, since no "scratched coupons" would be honored. Despite the care, a number of private classified advertisements offering Bernhardt tickets appeared on the front page of the *Constitution* before her arrival. In Nashville, the theater ran an auction for the tickets (Maiden 345), and while control was looser, speculation failed in an unusually public way. On the night of the performance, the audience enjoyed the downfall of entrepreneurs Dennis McCarthy and Henry Langford, who had invested $60 each in private boxes. After the first act, when they tried to recoup some of their loss by selling to "twelve of the boys" at two dollars per seat, the audience, "who knew and appreciated the turn of affairs, loudly applauded and ... [were] convulsed with laughter" as the substitute buyers filed in (*Louisville Courier* 18 Feb. 1881: 1; *Cleveland Plain Dealer* 12 March 1881: 4).

Although *Camille* was a success for the Atlanta audience, for Bernhardt it was a trial. So ill that she had to be carried into DeGive's Opera House, where a doctor was discretely stationed behind the scenes, she cut the final act short. Her death scene was nonetheless judged remarkably fine—"no living person could hardly represent the last moments of a consumptive's life with more truth"—yet she may well have been happy to sink quietly into Armand's arms. As she made her way out of the theatre, she reportedly fell twice; and as the carriage drove away, "every step of the horses was accompanied by a groan." Mr. Marble, President of the railroad company sponsoring the City of Worcester, confided to a *Constitution* reporter, "You have no idea how intensely she is suffering" (17 Feb. 1881: 2). Her illness was a performance in its own right; as the *Constitution* concluded, "Truly, in the eventful life of Bernhardt there is material for a most thrilling romance" (qtd. in *Boston Commonwealth* 26 Feb. 1881: 3).

One day later in Nashville, sympathy turned to criticism. A *Louisville Courier* reviewer pointed out frankly that librettos were of little help in understanding the play, and another attempted to impose a moral distance between himself and the audience, and the French demimondaine. Nothing in English corresponds to French ideas, he maintains—to call an "illicit connection" by the name of "love" is impossible in America. In France, however, "they live, in a fevered, wild, delirious dream":

> The best of growths from that hotbed [*Camille*] are toadstool growths, sentiments from the dung heap—the most unselfish, the best actions poisoned by the fermenting, festering source are poison-fungus actions, possessing more of the cold gleam of the phosphorescent light from putrescence than of the warmth and glow of the actions sprung from virtue which they thus palely simulate.

Recognizing that language masked naughtiness, he was nonetheless won over artistically, declaring Bernhardt "inimitable," the "love scenes ... simply delicious," her reading of Armand's letter a revelation of naturalness, and the death scene an invocation of the spiritual" (*Nashville Daily American* 18 Feb. 1881: 4). If anything, the moralistic objections helped ticket sales: receipts were $3,362 in Atlanta and $3,200 in Nashville, where two days later the actress Kate Claxton[4] practiced the sincerest form of flattery by presenting *Froufrou*, advertised as "Bernhardt's Great Success" (*Constitution* 18 Feb. 1881: 4; *Nashville Daily American* 17 Feb. 1881: 1).

Bernhardt's reception—generally polite, if not adoring—grew boisterous when she moved on to Memphis and Louisville, where she was welcomed with an outpouring of commercial glee and avid curiosity. She proved such a sensation that riots broke out in both cities. In concert with the clamorous demand for tickets, squibs and jokes abounded, many reprinted from other cities' newspapers, and readers were regaled with advertisements and with biographical and theatrical summaries. Together, the newspapers accomplished what Olive Logan had single-handedly done in conveying a wealth of unconnected detail, along with apocryphal anecdotes and jokes. Readers learned indiscriminately of Bernhardt's illness in New Orleans and her habit of eating like "a dainty little canary picking its food and holding its little head on one side enjoying with keen relish every morsel taken" (qtd. in *Memphis Daily Appeal* 15 Feb. 1881: 2). Once again they heard about her thinness, courtesy of "Father Lickshingle":

> One day, Sarah kem in from a trip over the Rhine, an' when she got to her room she found that she didn't have the key to her door.
> "An' have yez lost your key?" said the chambermaid.
> "*Oui! Oui!*" exclaimed Sarah, in her own delicious tongue; "*Oui! Oui!* But no mattaire," and drawin' her skirts about her she passed in through the keyhole [Qtd. in *Appeal* 15 Feb. 1881: 2].

Although the jokes about her slenderness seemed to devalue her as a person, they had little effect on her value as a commodity. Even her name was at a premium: merchants like M. & E. G. Kremer & Co. entitled their advertisements simply "Sara!" and offered Bernhardt gloves, fans, collarettes, bonnets, hats, mantles, and costumes. Even those who had to brave the "miserable, muddy streets" of Memphis to see her were offered succor—"snow shoes and rubbers," available at J. M. Hill & Co., for those who needed to wait in line for tickets.

When trouble erupted, as it did in Memphis, it portended good box office receipts. In the abridged account that reached Atlanta, scalpers muscled in on a line that had formed four days before tickets were to go on sale at 9 A.M. on Friday, February 11. The police were ineffective, and theatrical agent Marcus Mayer postponed the sale until the next Wednesday rather than resorting to an auction, as had happened in Nashville (*Atlanta Constitution* 15 Feb. 1881: 1). Memphis papers were considerably more explicit about the affair, which presented serious racial overtones. Speculators had employed day laborers to wait in line in front of Kirkland's Hat Store, where the tickets were to be sold; the *Appeal* described them as a "row of burly negroes, faithful as the old dog Tray," perched on little chairs for days at a time. On the day of sale, after another ticket-buyer pushed to the front and refused to release the doorknob, a second line formed. In the midst of the chaos, the police chief and theatre manager were accused of generating ill-will among the private buyers, who believed that the postponement was made "in the interest of disappointed managers of the colored campaign" (12 Feb. 1881: 2).

Eventually, ticket sales took place in front of the theatre, with a contingent of policemen, a gangplank to shepherd the crowds, and two new rules: no exchanging places, and only twelve tickets allowed at a time (six in the front row, six in the second). "The Rush for the Front Row of Seats Almost Equal to the charge at Balaklava" proved reasonably peaceful, although the *Appeal* reporter was amused at the way in which the all-nighters passed the time, their employers having supplied them with whisky, cigars, tobacco, and food. Some literally fell out of line because of "fatigue, weariness, or drunkenness." Bernhardt's agent Mayer sat at a table with Treasurer Frank Gray and another theater employee to manage the money and seating diagram. The new rules were strictly followed, and while most of the first twenty-six ticket purchasers were able to show lists of names and verification of personal ticket use, many speculators got through and immediately returned to the front of the house, where they sold $3 tickets for double and treble the price. Nearly $4000 changed hands on the first day. "It is a purely business matter," the *Appeal* insisted, ignoring the racial aspects: "If the attractive Sarah Bernhardt only knew what an excitement her advent in Memphis was creating in society among the belles and beaux, she would no doubt feel gratified and give utterance to some charming French exclamation of delight" (17 Feb. 1881: 4; 13 Feb. 1881: 4; 15 Feb. 1881: 1).

A battle royal similar to the one in Memphis took place in Louisville between a group of "young society men" and the speculators, who were well organized despite their motley appearance. With the number of tickets limited to eight per person, well-known traders like Leonidas Fleishaker and others (Hemming and Speed, Col. George Flemming, and Watts & Hughes were named publicly) had hired a crew of helpers. The inquisitive *Louisville Courier* reporter, interviewing the cold but determined crowd in front of Macauley's Theatre at 1 A.M. on February 14, received a variety of answers to his question about commissions. One of the intermediaries, waiting in line for tickets to "Milly Bernhard's" performance, announced, "I gits five dollars, on de squar', boss—five whole dollars—an' don't you forget it. Dat's wuth stayin' up fo', if it is cold"; "Two slugs on the tickut, if yer buy as many as eight, and if yer only buys one, fifty pur cnt. On de dollar.... I've got a gang here, Cockey, and don't you forget," responded another, whom the reporter calls a "modern Wm. Sikes" (3). The first twenty-eight in line, many of whom had waited all night, were admitted peaceably, with other buyers lining up along a fence; these were pushed aside by another crowd that broke through the iron gates and forced open the theatre doors. Faced with the "howling mob," Eugene Elrod, a musician doubling as box-office attendant, proved himself "a warrior as well as a civilian." The General Manager John Macauley, a "scientific boxer," squared off against a large opponent whose "pretty rough language" he disliked; but suddenly "overcome with the ludicrous aspects of the affair ... burst into a hearty laugh," which the crowd echoed, and peace was restored (15 Feb. 1881: 2).

While the crowds were rambunctious, Bernhardt was tiring. Her arrivals in both Memphis and Louisville were characterized by her increased annoyance with the general public's insensitivity. In Memphis, for instance, when the troupe arrived at the Louisville and Nashville Railroad Depot at 5:20 P.M. on February 18, the crowd vocally preferred Jeanne Bernhardt's "pleasant and jolly French face" to a glimpse of the diva's nose and pale face swathed in furs. Nonetheless, once he met her, the *Appeal* reporter wrote of Bernhardt's "magnetism" and declared that "stories of her attenuation are moonshine." He praised her simple lifestyle—meals are taken family style in her room, where she "eats daintily of solid, plain food, ignoring ... rich viands or confectionery" (20 Feb. 1881: 4). Bernhardt was equally

Jeanne Bernhardt. Photograph by Napoleon Sarony, 1880. Harry Ransom Humanities Research Center, the University of Texas at Austin.

exhausted upon her arrival in Louisville, where she reached the depot at 1 A.M. on February 21. Accosted by the ubiquitous *Courier* reporter about Bernhardt's whereabouts, one "fiery-looking little Frenchman" on the platform retorted, "Zounds, monsieur! zounds, by gar, sir! What ze hell is ze matter, sir, by gar, sir? ... I am no ze slave of ze party. Aske ze porteer, sir, by gar." When the reporter did catch a glimpse of her, Bernhardt was being whisked away by a Louisville Transfer Company carriage to Galt House, where she occupied first floor rooms #204 and #208, "beautifully decorated with floral wreaths and hung with cut flowers." Abbey asked that she not be put on the register to protect her sleep, and Galt House accordingly denied that she had arrived. The reporter was thus left to interview her train porter, who provided a coda for the whole trip: "De gents dey drinked wine and played keards, and de ladies, dey played keards and drinked wine. Miss Sally, she slept de most of de way" (3).

Of the two cities, Memphis, short on racial tolerance, proved long on moral tolerance; Louisville, despite its French roots, seemed less certain about Bernhardt's pernicious influence. To be sure, the Memphis *Herald* presented a garbled report that made her mother the Marquise de la Herlig and Bernhardt herself the victim of a "technically void" marriage "to a scion of the *vielle noblesse*" (16 Feb. 1881: 1); yet other Memphis reports echoed Robert Ingersoll's complaint about the double standard—"why toast and feast men for the same offenses?" The *Herald* presented Bernhardt as a reformed Magdalene, whose "struggles to redeem the errors of the past" made her a model for all fallen women. Even more, the reporter maintained, she gave "heart and hope to the debased [who] ... could ... be reclaimed ... from a life of shame and sorrow by treating them as the world is treating Sarah Bernhardt" (16 Feb. 1881: 1).

Less broad-minded Louisville citizens professed theatrical ennui to disguise their moral qualms, thereby emphasizing her value as spectacle. One unnamed "gentleman" claimed that he would pay to see Bernhardt just once, as he would pay to see "the woman in Indiana whose arms were petrified"; others wished to see her because she was a "curiosity," because it was "fashionable," and "because it would not be the correct thing to stay away." The popular press dwelt on the same themes of thinness and expense found in big-city publications but expressed them in local patois. The February 15 Louisville *Courier* included Bernhardt in its Valentine's Day tribute, claiming that it had received a verse enclosed in a "lean and hungry-looking package ... contain[ing] four gum drops and three caramels ... mailed by a plump and fashionable damsel":

5. "We are hardly good colonists"   127

> Dear Sally, they say you are slim,
>   While I am so *awfully* fat!
> And they say you *can't* cast a shadow,
>   While I can do *much more* than that.
> Perhaps if you showed up in *tights*, dear,
>   You *couldn't* make much sunlight fade;
> But when you have piled on nine [?]
>   You'd throw *all of us* into the shade.

A far more pointed attack came from the pulpit when Talmage's sermon on amusements was reprinted in the *Louisville Courier* on February 7. While he failed to name Bernhardt, he did paint a vivid picture of the fruits of theatrical dissipation: "The champagne has cheated the children's wardrobe. The carousing party has burned up the boy's primer. The tablecloth of the corner saloon is in debt to the wife's faded dress." A local minister, the Rev. Mr. Detweiler, followed with a direct attack on "lewd performers, who before a promiscuous audience, by dress, gesture and language, exert a vicious influence." He instead recommended "dramas from real life, dramas in which persons legally married and the parents of legitimate children take part," and ended by giving his congregation a choice: "Will your going to see Sarah Bernhardt, and such as she, prepare you for a successful part in the drama of life? Which will be the better—Macauley's or Calvary?" (*Courier* 21 Feb. 1881: 3).

Despite such expressions of moral outrage, many in Memphis chose Leubrie's Theatre, as in Louisville they chose Macauley's. In both cities, however, everyone was concerned about economic issues. Scattered references, while phrased as jokes, suggest reluctance or inability to buy tickets, as this retrospective verse in the February 23 *Courier* indicates (2):

> Alas, sweet Sara B.!
>   You're the costliest female woman
> That ever eyes did see;
>   You're the costliest female woman
> That ever got aboard
>   Of the lightning ex-pre-ess tri-ain
> And through the meadows roared.
>
> O why, sweet Sara B.,
>   Do the tick-i-ets to your playin'
> Hang up so far from me?
>   I'm so mad I could be a-slayin'.
> Think you I'm made of wealth
>   And have nothin' to do but countin'?
> Sweet Sal, you mar my health.

> And what's that furrin talk?
>   Do you call that a conversation?
> I don't know clay from chalk
>   If in such there is information.
> Alas, sweet Sara B.!

In Memphis, discomfited speculators were selling *Froufrou* seats at a loss before the performance, and Bernhardt reportedly received a note from a fan that suggested a black market in unofficial seats: "Mille. S. Bernhardt—*Dear Darling*: May I sit on the curbstone and see you go by, as I have not got twenty-five cents to peep at you through the skylight?" Those whose seats were closer than curbstone or skylight reacted with "kindly humor" to *Froufrou*, despite the "meager stage" and their own ignorance of the language. The reviewer praised her depiction of a "child-woman," whose frivolity and waywardness are relieved by "occasional flashes of introspective power." Echoing more sophisticated critics in St. Louis, he applauded Bernhardt's natural approach, so different from the "artificiality and extravagance" of the American style of declamation. The February 19 performance of *Lecouvreur* in Memphis received perhaps the best reception anywhere: the dignity with which she invested the character, the growing intensity of her performance until the final, tragic moment—all prompted the reviewer to compliment the audience for its intelligent appreciation and to assert that Bernhardt was indeed the new Rachel (*Appeal* 20 Feb. 1881: 1).

In Memphis, too, Bernhardt's matinée performance of *Camille* transcended moral reservations and made her a model heroine. Nowhere else were women complimented on their theatre-going: "It is creditable to the cultivated women of Memphis that they ... came together in such number to witness, perhaps, the greatest performance of *Camille* ever given on our stage," raved the reviewer. He went on to suggest that the play's sexual permissiveness serves a moral purpose, since the "gay and glittering daughters of sin" may feel "in their hearts, too, there is the possibility of redemption by love." Too, Bernhardt's interpretation emphasized Marguerite's redeeming features, which existed "among those women who, every day, are sacrificed for the safety of their sisters" (*Memphis Daily Appeal* 20 Feb. 1881: 1). In Louisville, however, the reviewer was somewhat more cautious. After a prefatory defense of staging "delicate" subjects, he submits that adultery is as "legitimate" as other commonplace theatrical topics like murder and forgery, and concludes that despite Marguerite's fall from virtue, "the play is not at all immodest, and it most assurdedly [*sic*] is not immoral." Unlike earlier reviewers, who praised Froufrou as Bernhardt's best role, this reviewer praised Bernhardt as "marvellous," "magnetic," and "spiritualized" in *Camille* (2).

From Cincinnati to Louisville, Bernhardt's month-long progress was marked by the press's careful evaluation of her acting and a forthright attempt to come to terms with moral equivocation. She began this southern portion of her trip interpreted and defined by Olive Logan and ended it in her own right. Because she changed venues so frequently, she had little time to gauge her audiences, and so it is perhaps the greater triumph that she was so successful. Her public relations baggage included a paradoxical reputation: she was money-hungry and generous; promiscuous and ladylike; artificial and natural. This down-to-earth, charming, and hardworking *grande dame* was denounced in the pulpit and praised in the pit. She often moved her admirers and critics alike to speak in tongues, as it were—to adopt rhetorical strategies that were foreign to their natural idiom. As they attempted to come to grips with cultural differences, some commentators sought to understand her by glossing her artistic performances in the local vernacular. Others tried to demonstrate their sophistication by extravagant affectation; in so doing, they revealed themselves to have the same penchant for melodramatic overstatement that American audiences had been trained to prefer. With remarkably few exceptions, however, Bernhardt was accorded a serious consideration of her acting as an aesthetic event in its own right. One factor that worked in her favor was that many small-town reviewers took their responsibility as theatrical pundits seriously; lacking the steady stream of performers that visited the cities, these reviewers made the most of their opportunities. While New York had its own reputation to keep up and so engaged in the luxury of satire, St. Louis seriously considered the cultural clash and the effect of realism on the American theater. While larger cities sought to domesticate Bernhardt, smaller ones celebrated her difference.

6

"We be men of little wit": Audiences in the Midwest

> The idea of payin' six dollars to hear a lot of monkeys talkin' French or Dutch or somethin' an' to see a livin' skellington die standin' up, in a bedroom with no bed to it [*Toledo Blade* 12 March 1881: 5].

After finishing her southern tour in Louisville, Bernhardt embarked on a wide geographical arc through the Midwest before she returned to the East Coast. She left behind sympathetic audiences that were earnest and hospitable, often adulatory, and rarely rude. Their negative responses were clear-cut: in some cases based on moral grounds, in others on social uncertainty, audiences nonetheless were won over by her aesthetic appeal and theatrical talent. On the next leg of her journey, however, she faced practical-minded folk who well knew the value of a dollar and whose welcome was tinged with suspicion. More concerned about investment than entertainment, they begrudged paying for tickets and felt personal outrage at the speculators' profits. Attracting as much attention for her foreignness as for her acting, she encountered less dramatic *savoir-faire* in her audience: orchestra, gallery, and critic alike expected melodramatic, sensational acting from their exotic visitor.

Bernhardt's tour in Ohio was characterized by a popular focus on her earnings, disregard for her comfort, and a mixture of discourtesy and indifference. In Columbus, for instance, her last-minute decision to spend the night in a local hotel created more resentment than appreciation for the added revenue; and when she moved on to Dayton, she and her troupe roamed the streets unrecognized. The Columbus visit was fraught with misunderstandings that were exacerbated by the *Dispatch* reporter's determination not to be imposed upon. "It is customary to give timely notice," the reporter grumbled in an ill-natured way about Jarrett's telegraphed request for rooms at Neil House. To be sure, some of the friction may have been due to Jarrett's high-handedness: once the hotel proprietor had made special arrangements by moving occupants to accommodate Bernhardt's need for a parlor, four bedrooms, and two servants' rooms, Jarrett offended him by assuming that he was a servant. Learning of his mistake, he gracelessly observed that the proprietor need "not apologize for want of time to reserve apartments, as these were good enough for anybody" (24 Feb. 1881: 4).

On February 24, at the Columbus depot, another misunderstanding took place: when the "special" arrived at 12:50 A.M. attached to the Little Miami train, the hapless carriage driver tried to take the Russia-leather bags that contained Bernhardt's jewels, but "The ladies resisted, talking French, and holding the valises in a style that made the driver feel as though he stepped into the wrong pew." In this case a prickly sensitivity about status was complicated by the language barrier and by conflicting assumptions. Once the reporter vents his spleen against Bernhardt, however—"there are ladies in [Neil House] of the same height who are more attenuated in form"—and meets the troupe firsthand, he capitulates. He is impressed with their good-natured talking and joking, despite the lateness of the hour; and he likes Bernhardt's equanimity—"A third or forth rate actress ... would have walked the floor in tragic style, and wanted to know why in Hail Columbia the landlord didn't have things in his house that a decent hotel ought to have." Her satisfaction with Columbus's offerings showed, he said, "a true type of greatness" (*Dispatch* 24 Feb. 1881: 4). His own commentary showed an awareness that the accommodations were not of the best.

In Dayton, too, where she next performed, her schedule was again changed so that she stayed the night. The crowd that met her on February 25 at Union Depot was friendly, and although the town itself was not overtly hostile as Columbus was, it was innocently unprepared for foreign visitors. The leading members of the troupe who ventured out to look for a restaurant were turned away three times by clerks who could not understand French. At their fourth attempt, they were rescued by an itinerant Francophone worker who had earned his lunch by carrying in coal. Overjoyed at this *deus ex machina*, the party rewarded their interpreter with a full meal and a free pass to *Froufrou*. Later, when Bernhardt and her companions paid an unannounced visit to the Soldiers' Home, they were ignored; finally, after viewing the hospital and driving through the grounds and the city, they took refuge from a singularly insular city by withdrawing to their own City of Worcester.

For Bernhardt Dayton's ignorance may have been more palatable and easier to overcome than Columbus's resentment. Columbus citizens were as annoyed at the attempt to curtail speculation as they were at speculation itself, and they were vocally upset that she brought so little revenue to the city. One reason for the lack of "Bernhardt dollars" may have been the cautious approach of the theatre management, which feared the spate of disruptions that had accompanied ticket sales elsewhere, most recently in Memphis. It was, however, an orderly line that formed at Comstock's Opera House on February 24, well before the 2 P.M. opening sale for *Camille* tickets. Like many other small-town venues, the "box office" was makeshift, simply a table in a room, on which was displayed the seating plan. Suspicious Columbians posted a number of safeguards. General Manager Theodore Comstock walked back and forth; Treasurer Frank Comstock kept an eye on finances; Bernhardt's agent took care of the box sheet; and a special guard was assigned to keep order. Seats sold briskly at first, with $80–$100 changing hands rapidly. Acting on the rumor that speculators planned to corner the best 600 seats and so take them out of public circulation, the agent limited multiple purchases to ten; even so, many speculators over-invested and were left to recoup by selling high-priced seats for $1.00 after the first act, and fifty cents thereafter.

The limitation successfully stymied *sub rosa* entrepreneurs, but it also inconvenienced legitimate ticket-buyers, who were further outraged when the agent, in an attempt to guarantee the sale of expensive seats, refused to sell advertised standing room places. The decision raised such a universal outcry about theatrical profiteering that the *Columbus Dispatch* encouraged those standing in the lobby to follow the "Continental custom" of claiming unoccupied reserved seats, normally held open until the end of the first act (*Dispatch* 18 Feb. 1881: 4; 22 Feb. 1881: 4). The public's annoyance at the agent's overzealousness was more than matched by its displeasure at Bernhardt's earnings. After Abbey insisted on providing his own pictures and posters instead of making use of local services, newspapers made much of the disparity between the $4000 box office take and the reported expense of barely $100. That amount funded only a minimal advertising effort, even though businessmen, intent on profit, unwittingly took up the slack: in the *Evening Dispatch*, the advertisement for Osborn & Company's kid gloves for "Bernhardt Night" was graced with a sketch of Bernhardt's head. Popularity, concluded one reporter, "is good for a gigantic strain on the purse strings of the American people any time" (*Dispatch* 25 Feb. 1881: 4).

6. "We be men of little wit": Audiences in the Midwest   133

Once the members of the troupe moved on to Dayton, leaving the business community to its grievances, they took revenge by giving their own review of Columbus's food and hospitality and tolerating Dayton's naïveté good-naturedly. Jeanne Bernhardt, who happened upon a French-speaking gentleman, made him the conduit for some plainspoken commentary in the *Dayton Daily Journal* about the wearisomeness of the tour: "You see, Monsieur, we start in our palace car; we never know where we are going; we travel, we arrive, and we play. Then again, we go, go, go until we arrive again. Very tiresome life indeed." She grumbled about being besieged by the "book-venders, peddlers, ... beggars, loafers in fine clothes," and those who come to see Bernhardt out of curiosity—"very disagreeable and ill-bred and inquisitive." New Orleans was her and Angelo's least favorite city—"The most dirty, disgusting streets we ever saw"—and they returned Columbus's disdain with good measure. "The hotel and the eating are positively bad," she complained; "The fare in Columbus was horrible ... pepper in great quantities." Angelo, for his part, made a perceptive remark about Americans—and about himself: "To get rich in America, you must work very hard and fast, and that kills me." Bernhardt would have agreed that earning money in America meant hard work, but she fit into the ethos without missing a beat. Her leading man had to break off his protest to attend a rehearsal that she had called for that afternoon (26 Feb. 1881).

Whatever the conditions, Bernhardt pushed her troupe to perfect their technique, even when the audiences' ignorance of French and narcissistic focus posed problems that might have been daunting in her early days at the Comédie Française. The Dayton reviewers tried to engage in theatrical criticism, even though they were dismayed at the audiences' divided attention. To see the "greatest living actress," the "successor of the great Rachel," one who has passed through "a long and severe training of the most rigid character" perform in *Froufrou*, residents of nearby towns—Miamisburg, Springfield, Xenia—traveled to Dayton in their best *toilettes* and thereby gained fame in a newspaper column. The *Ohio State Journal* recognized that the onlookers were more interested in admiring their own clothing and Bernhardt's diamonds than her "extraordinary" acting, "which went on as if no one was looking ... with ease and trueness to nature, and this is perfection ..." (25 Feb. 1881: 4). The *Columbus Dispatch* joined in with a judicious appraisal of her performance in *Camille*, commenting that hampered by a language barrier and patriotic preconceptions, Americans cannot always assess the excellence of a visiting artist. While the reviewer is unhappy with the speed and volume of the troupe's delivery, which made the first two acts "very tedious," he praises a number of highly emotive scenes and concludes, although with some measure of *noblesse oblige*, that

Bernhardt "must be considered as a gifted woman, worthy of the sympathy of the American public" (24 Feb. 1881: 4).

In the dizzying succession of small towns that followed Columbus and Dayton, the schizophrenia involving economic chauvinism and naïve aestheticism persisted. St. Joseph, Leavenworth, Quincy, Springfield, and Milwaukee reviewers offered a sop to Mrs. Grundy while rejoicing in the opportunity of seeing Bernhardt, but the medley of tongues was greatest in Indianapolis, where she appeared on Feb. 26. Perhaps, as state capital, the city felt a responsibility to assert its prerogative; in its own way, it represented the entire spectrum of complaints and kudos in that section of the country.

Overall, Indianapolis papers adopted a marginally defensive attitude. Fearing that readers would succumb unquestioningly to the "Bernhardt Craze," the *Indianapolis Journal* writer claimed that most audiences would be unable to judge how good the actress really was; they were "innocents" who did not understand the language, the play, or even dramatic conventions. Country cousins to the French, they were easily fooled by appearances, just "as a dilapidated ice-house serves for many a pilgrim to Mt. Vernon on which to pour the offerings and the tears intended for the tomb of the Father of his Country." The writer, concerned at being taken advantage of, inveighed against "our semi-barbarous simplicity, upon which shrewd foreigners play with assurance and confidence"; rather than "humbugging the old country into an astonishment at our appreciation of art," he claimed, the unwitting Bernhardt worshippers were really being humbugged themselves (27 Feb. 1881: 4).

The fear of economic chicanery was key to much of the discomfort. That fear, coupled with self-consciousness about social status, expressed itself through critical and satirical disparagement. At the same time businessmen were complaining about Bernhardt's profits, however, they appropriated her presence and name for advertising. The clothier J. A. McKenzie, for instance, published several advertising anecdotes in the *Indianapolis News* that displayed the Midwesterners' distrust. In one, McKenzie essays a double-edged story about buying foreign goods:

> "Mr. McKenzie, do you speak French?"
> "Yes sir; but I don't understand what I say. Why do you ask?"
> "I want to buy a suit of French clothes."
> "We have the French goods; but you can buy them in English or Indiana language."
> "If you don't speak French, I will look at a German cloth suit, if you speak German."
> "Mr. ____, please excuse me; I don't understand German."

6. "We be men of little wit": Audiences in the Midwest

"Well, then, show me an English suit, if you speak the English correctly."

"Stranger, you will have to excuse me; I don't know a man in the city that can do that."

"Mr. McKenzie, if you can talk Hoosier, show me a Kentucky Jane suit you can sell for about $3.75, and I'll let up on you."

"Stranger, here, take the money, for I rather donate this amount to you than keep that class of goods."

"All right; but I can't use that $2 bill; it has a corner torn off; give me the silver" [3 March 1881: 4].

Among the multiplicity of interpretations the joke suggests is that Hoosiers, who are too clever to be taken in, have the "French goods"—they have outwitted Bernhardt, the greatest sharper of all.

Rumor magnified her earnings as much as it belittled her talent, but to McKenzie, whose success depended on his merchandising, Bernhardt was selling her notoriety, not her acting:

> Who was Sarah Bernhardt, pa?
>   The people call her great,
> Was she as large as J. A. McKenzie,
>   Her feet a number 8?
> Was she so tall that she could span
>   The largest waist of any man?
>
> Oh no; 'tis not her stature, child,
>   That caused so great commotion
> And made the people all run wild—
>   'Twas people's foolish notion.
> Her name so great, I know 'tis long,
>   And very hard to spell;
> Only one hundred nights ago
>   I learned it very well.
>
> I mean her *actions* were
>   So great she got a name,
> And thousands spoke with praise
>   That should have spoke of shame.
> While here she had so many callers
>   And toated [sic] off six thousand dollars.
>
> Tell me, dear father, why great acting did she do
> That people would borrow three dolors [sic] to go and
> See her? Tell me all about her, for I don't know,
> And I saw hundreds that did go, and they—

> My son, you are 15 minutes late for school, and
> Go at once, my child, and don't ask me any
> More foolish questions about nothing.
> [*News* 28 Feb. 1881: 4].

For others in Indianapolis, however, Bernhardt was "something," rather than "nothing." Welcomed on February 26 with a combination of excitement and concern, she again became the subject of pulpit morality and journalistic bombast. While churchmen and poetasters raged against her, the *Indianapolis Journal* published a flowery welcome in French, proclaiming her name to be the "Open Sesame" for both hearts and purses. She was assured that although America's streets were unlike those of the Champs Elysées, Americans both appreciated and adored art; she was asked to remember, at the end of her very long and fatiguing days, that many were torn between the joy of seeing her and the sorrow of bidding her farewell (26 Feb. 1884: 4). Others besides those in the French community felt the same way. Ignoring, or perhaps responding to comments like those of the Presbyterian minister who claimed that "the nudity of the drama [was] veiled in the French language," visitors flocked from the surrounding cities and towns of Vincennes, Terre Haute, Lafayette, and Richmond to welcome her at Union depot and to see her perform.

The 1200 fans who hoped to catch a glimpse of the diva were disappointed when her car was switched off at the west end and she was hurried into a carriage for her matinée performance of *Froufrou* at the Park Theatre. The confusion was exacerbated at the theatre by a printing error that produced tickets for both matinée and evening performances on the same color stock (*News* 25 Feb. 1881: 4). Because of the overflow audience, the orchestra was displaced to make room for additional seating, and as at other venues, speculators who had purchased the three back rows for the evening, hoping to sell each seat for $10, found themselves the victims of public distaste for profiteering and earned little more than fifty cents per seat (*Journal* 26 Feb. 1881: 8). Despite naysayers like McKenzie and his ilk, ticket sales were reputed to be over $5,000 even before she arrived. Thrifty souls who believed the rumor that she cleared $6,000 in Indianapolis alone and expected to return to France with $35,000 were only marginally appeased by a public relations announcement that although she was extended the courtesy of Bates House, where she dined and occupied three parlors, "she insisted on paying for everything, as is her rule" (*Journal* 27 Feb. 1881: 5).

Her Indianapolis performances received three kinds of reviews: economic, theological, and literary. She was called "the most stupendous sell ever perpetuated upon a willing but too easily victimized city," and she was denounced as a pariah from the pulpit. Apparently her earlier threat, impractical at best, to record offensive comments and sue the clergy, was dropped. According to Rev. Dr. Bartlett of the second Presbyterian Church, the worst plays posed a danger: "Their impure plots and indecent exposures, and profanity, utterly worthless frivolity emasculate the minds of youth, inflame passions, give false notions of life, and ruin them for all serious and noble living." Since he immediately gave a synopsis of the plots of *Froufrou* and *Camille*, his target was unmistakable. As his source for censuring "this frivolous French woman [who] will starve the intellect and destroy the soul," he cited Canon Wilberforce's Westminster Abbey attack on Bernhardt, in which she was accused of bringing illegitimate offspring to England and "flaunting her skirts in the very face of royalty." Wilberforce's heartfelt cry seemed to suggest that Prince Albert was the only bulwark against immorality in both England and America: "O how deeply virtuous England regrets the premature death of the good Prince Consort! Had he been living to-day this could never have happened" (*News* 28 Feb. 1881: 4).

While legitimate reviews of her performances gave a nod to the proprieties, they were, in miniature, a reprise of the many-faceted attitude evidenced earlier in Louisville. The *Journal* reviewer discussed her appearance and her private car, and observed philosophically that the play's "immorality and unchastity ... makes it popular"; that having been said, he went on to praise her "thorough naturalness," her "intelligence and forcefulness," and the "horrible realism" of the death scene. She was better than Modjeska, the writer concluded, and in *Camille* had reached the apex of her art. Moved to adopt a melodramatic tone, he provided a critique stylistically reminiscent of Olive Logan. Bernhardt was

> [a]ble to lead us out of ourselves and that which surrounds us into the clearer, higher region of the universal humanity, away from the petty littlenesses of that which is, to our common partnership in the great heart of humanity with its infinite burden of affection and suffering, life and death [27 Feb. 1881: 5].

The underlying sincerity of this extravagant tribute, as well as the recognition that Indianapolis's relationship with Bernhardt was a mixture of adulation and fear of the unknown, was reflected in a farewell verse published in the Indianapolis *Journal*. Bernhardt did command a goodly amount of money, the versifier conceded, but her audiences, most of whom understood little or no French, were nonetheless enthralled by her, worshipping her photograph and flocking to her performances:

> O Sarah-Sara-Sairie—thou divine,
>   First favorite of all the sister arts!
>   Though breaker of our pocket-books and hearts!
> Thou naughty sorceress we all malign,
> Yet worshipfully bow us at thy shrine,
>   And praise thee as thou stalkest through thy parts—
>   Forget our wives, and o'er Sarony's cartes,[1]
> When thou are gone, muse on that form of thine.
> O Sarah, we be men of little wit,
> And hence we marvel much what charm compels
>   Us to pay three dollars just to sit
> As many hours and stare at nothing else—
>   Since all thy French availeth not a whit—
>   Unless, indeed, we know its v(o)ice, if not the words of it.
>   [27 Feb. 1881: 5].

Bernhardt went on to evoke a similarly mixed response in the North Central towns she visited. After Indianapolis, she traveled along the Vandalia line via St. Louis to St. Joseph, Missouri, and then spent one night in Leavenworth, turning east for her engagements in Quincy and Springfield, where she performed *Camille*. An argument over dividing the gross receipts in Kansas City ended in cancellation; in any case, the anti–Semitism displayed by the *Kansas City Times* reporter who commented snidely on Marcus Mayer, her business manager, hardly promised Bernhardt an unbiased welcome.[2] By the time she reached Milwaukee on March 5, she had already begun to loop back to the Northeast and the end of her tour.

Her unusual two-night stay in St. Joseph on February 28 and March 1 was restorative in more ways than one. The relatively empty platform that greeted her at the Eighth Street Depot at 1:30 A.M. may have been a welcome sight. The *St. Joseph Daily Gazette* joked that "the well known piety of the people of St. Joseph prevented a large assembly," but she and her sister, exhausted from their travels, retired immediately to their eight-room suite and slept almost around the clock, rising for an afternoon rehearsal and then sightseeing. Refreshed by the hiatus, she was energized by a rousing welcome from a city that that traced its roots to a French founder and that served as a cultural hub for surrounding communities. Like the French reporter in Indianapolis, the *Daily Herald* reviewer greeted her with a nostalgic paean, asking that economic considerations give way to aesthetic appreciation: "[H]ow many amongst us can see even in a vision the flowing drapery of the fugitive past?" This "child of artistic traditions" will make the "dead fair ones of Arsene Houssaye's[3] magic pages live again and Paris,

6. "We be men of little wit": Audiences in the Midwest 139

the beautiful city, the heart of Bohemia, is ours again and Saxon morality ... and ugliness will fade away.... Let us have for a while again the tempest of the heart instead of the woes of the pocket and the griefs of the head...." Not only was she welcomed in extravagant terms, but, more practically, special efforts were made to attract an audience from other towns in Missouri, Kansas, and Nebraska. Many railroad lines, including the Hannibal, St. Joseph & Western, Kansas City, Narrow Gauge, Missouri and Pacific, and the Nebraska B. & M., ran excursion fares; the governors of the three states received special invitations; two hundred unreserved (and reportedly well-upholstered) chairs were added to the gallery; and a spate of gossipy stories appeared. These efforts at times overstepped the bounds of theatrical courtesy, much to the disgust of the business agent Marcus Mayer; what seemed to be a hospitable offer from St. Joseph to run special trains and make tickets available to area residents, including those in Kansas, on further analysis proved to be a device for insuring a full house at the expense of the house in Leavenworth (*Leavenworth Standard* 1 March 1881: 4).

Because St. Joseph was small, all news was at a premium, and so rumor and fact were equal grist for the reporters' mills. One sympathetic article retold a story first aired in Paris, about Bernhardt's supposed "father" M. Bernhardt, a French provincial actor maniacally obsessed with the idea that he was a talented baritone (*Daily Herald* 22 Feb. 1881). More to the point, her entire contract was printed in the *Daily Gazette*, providing interested readers with a host of details about police coverage and other demands, including six musicians and a five thousand dollar fee (21 Feb. 1881). The amount was large enough to evoke a sweetly malicious comment from the French songstress Marie Roze, the wife of impresario Col. Mapleson; in her interview, printed in the *Evening News*, she suggested that Bernhardt chose to perform in St. Joseph because the Parisians paid even better actresses less and because her physique was "too weak ... for emotional parts" on her native ground (8 Feb. 1881). On a pleasanter note, the *Herald* offered theatre owner Milton Tootle a warm vote of thanks for his citizenship and foresight in making the city world-class, the actual quotation belying such status: "And they say Sally is writing a book, a book of travels. Just think of it. Within a few months all Paris will be talking about Song Yose!"—a somewhat inflated hope, given the cursory mention of countless one-night stands in Bernhardt's memoirs.

The schedule was taxing, and like her sister Jeanne, who complained about exhaustion to the *Dayton Daily Journal*, Bernhardt confided in a French-speaking *Gazette* reporter who sneaked into the theatre for an interview. No matter how warm the welcome, she was dismayed by the way her trunks had been handled and unhappy about the lack of dressing-room space. Anxious about her own success, she deplored the "very, very unenthusiastic" New Orleans audiences and admitted to struggling with English, "such a hard, uncouth language." Finally, she was as "tired to death with people trying to talk boarding school French" as she was of "the rattling of the Libretto pages" (1 March 1881).

Despite this farrago of woes, her presence in the small, Midwestern town was a boon to the critics, less so to the non–French speaking public. The *Herald* gave high praise to Bernhardt's greatness in conveying "art which conceals art" and to her "extraordinary magnetism and power to elicit sympathy" in *Froufrou*, although the librettist was taken to task as a "diabolical fool who turns good French text into English insanity." Meanwhile, a typical theatergoer, described as a "gentleman from the wilds of Nebraska," expressed frustration typical of the theatrically naïve: "Well, sir, that was about the darndest thing last night I ever saw. Why I sat there all evening within twenty feet of the stage, and drat my pictur if I could understand a single word that was said" (1 March 1881). The Francophone *Gazette* paid considerable attention to the audience, suggesting once again that in many small towns, the real actors were seated in the theatre. The crowd, which displayed itself as "a brilliant levee," was "expectant" and understood the plot "with great intelligence," despite the language disparity. Torn between writing a critical review and a human-interest story, the reporter applauded the "rich toilets" and elegance of the ladies and then explained tactfully that many were "so strikingly attractive as to deserve individual mention did not their number preclude any attempt to do equal justice." He gave a glimpse, moreover, of local practice, when he commended the audience for refraining from "that rat-a-tat-tat chorus of impatient feet which ordinarily precedes the rising of the curtain" (qtd. in *Quincy Daily Herald* 3 March 1881: 1–2). Her appearance was successful, judging by the $3700 in receipts for *Froufrou*, noted the *Leavenworth Times*.

After leaving St. Joseph, the farthest point west on her hegira, Bernhardt stayed one night in Leavenworth, where the journalistic preparation for her visit mirrored the prepublicity in larger cities. In late February prospective viewers were advised that the architectural advantages of the new, small Opera House guaranteed everyone an excellent seat, unlike the case "in many of the long halls in Western cities," and they were told about Bernhardt's newly constructed dressing room, "an elegant budoir" suitable for preparing her "magnificent toilets" (*Leavenworth Standard* 27 Feb. 1881: 4; 1 March 1881: 4). Her enthusiastic welcome was coupled with repeated expressions of local pride in Leavenworth's dramatic *savoir-faire* and the assurance that she would be warmly welcomed. Perhaps to assuage the lingering moral issue, the *Times* resorted to publishing its own "Bernhardt

6. *"We be men of little wit"*: Audiences in the Midwest   141

Sermon," grandiloquently urging its readers to ignore rumor and engage in Christian charity:

> If the way chance to have been rugged and thorny and trodden with bruised and weary feet; if, in passing through the wilderness, the wayfarer may have fallen, and gathering up her strength with what courage she might still struggled on past the pitfalls set ever to trap the unweary [sic], one might suppose a Christian charity, if not a manly courtesy, should seal the lips of judgment, and lead us to emulate the example of Him who, stooping, wrote the record of woman's weakness upon the sand, that with the shifting of its ever-restless particles it might soon be effaced [2 March 1881: 4].

This call for compassion was marred only by one incident, and that caused by Bernhardt's own company. Reported by the *Leavenworth Times* as a scheme calculated to increase publicity, the story was both confused and confusing: according to one version, after the *Camille* performance, business manager Marcus Mayer had gotten into an altercation with the company's treasurer, and both drew pistols. Bernhardt, already in her nightgown, became the "divine peacemaker in a drama not on the bills": "It was real Bernhardt entertainment, strikingly novel, in one act and with nary an *encore*" (4 March 1881: 4). A week later the *Standard* reported the incident at second hand, reprinting a *Chicago Times* article about "a drunken brawl" between town and theatre people broken up by Bernhardt's sudden appearance in her nightgown. The writer speculates, then dismisses the idea that the "loud, boisterous and bloody" fight was an advertising ploy: "A woman who will equip herself with a skeleton by way of seeming fat in comparison, and will make her bed in a coffin by way of nothing but caprice, is capable of advertising herself so as by her night-clothes" (9 March 1881: 1).

Other disputes were the kind of verbal competitions engaged in by journalists everywhere. Several made an effort to meet her well before her arrival in Leavenworth. The *Standard* reporter missed his headline because he decided not to wait for Bernhardt's train, late as usual, at the northern depot; his story was scooped by a *Kansas City Times* reporter, who, he reports with some pique, "had the bad taste to publish [his interview] in French," but who was laudatory and ebullient, especially about the expression in her eyes: "They reflect, oh, so truly! The calms and tempests of a soul which, fired by genius, has ne'ertheless been taught that genius does not bring happiness and peace." He provided, as well, a corrective to the "hubbub ... raised about her emaciation." To his eyes, she weighs close to one hundred and thirty pounds, her hair is "a lovely brown," and her nose is "well defined" (*Standard* 1 March 1881: 4). By March 3, when Bernhardt had left Leavenworth, the *Standard* reporter had readied his response. "A Charming Interview with Bernhardt" is a burlesque of his fellow reporters' tactics, with special reference to Kansas City journalists (3 March 1881:1). "Dominus Vobiscum," says the *Kansas City Times* correspondent, consulting the wrong phrase book; "dulce et decorum as pro patria mori," he continues, as the *Press* journalist comes aboard, accompanied by his "yaller" dog Kate. Asked about her reported "ecstacy" over Kansas City scenery, Bernhardt soon puts him right:

> I well remember the occasion. I glanced up as we entered Kansas City, and saw a goat chewing a clothes line and three children tied to a fence to keep from falling over a precipice which the mother was washing near by. I was affected to tears and wished myself back in France.

A first-hand human interest story, however, reported that Bernhardt appeared beautiful but care-worn, her face showing evidence of pastimes that tended to "unwoman her constitution," presumably like the reportedly "pleasant French game of cards" she played between St. Joseph and Leavenworth. The *Times* reporter garnered an interview with one of the four Pinkerton detectives traveling with her, who claimed that they were there as much to protect her from the "gags" of the onlookers as from jewelry theft, although she had been concerned at seeing a familiar but unidentifiable individual shadowing her. These tidbits were presumably as welcome to the *Times* readers as the hodgepodge of other information: she was a hearty diner; she wrote on notepaper edged with slate; someone in the audience at *Camille* tried to play "Yankee Doodle." Many undoubtedly looked for and found their names listed individually in the column, along with descriptions of their clothing and their comments about how well they enjoyed the performance (3 March 1881: 4).

Once the serious reviewer assessed her performance, however, the focus was on her fine acting and on the well-bred nature of the crowd that had come to meet her at the depot late in the afternoon before the performance. The article is as laudatory of the actress as it is of its local readers, whom it calls both "conservative and well-balanced." In one of the most lucid expressions of pride in this "new world, vigorous, ambitious and thoroughly appreciative of the best talent," the reporter frames a periphrastic sentence that lays the intensity of her performance to her desire to invigorate "an embryo world of art":

> She seemed to understand that she, who for a time by the grace of genius wears the laurels of the stage, had come from her far-off city on the Seine which for centuries has been the home of art, to touch the heart of this new world and help to give the higher drama an impetus that will make it coequal with the marvelous material development of the West.

Bombast aside, the reviewer points out that as *Camille* progressed, the "intellectual and thoughtful" audience moved from focusing on the "gorgeousness of bonnets and the intricacies of dress" to the "idea and pathos" of the drama itself, as librettos were ignored for the experience itself.

Despite their journalistic and theatrical competitiveness, St. Joseph and Leavenworth were sister cities in their appreciation of Bernhardt's talent, and the actress, sensitive to her audience's mood, seemed to respond in kind. She was received warmly in Quincy, Illinois. Traveling on the Hannibal and St. Joseph rail line, she arrived on March 3 at 5:30 P.M., but not without adventure. Her risky approach to New Orleans repeated itself less spectacularly: to reach Quincy, she had to cross an unstable bridge, this one temporarily constructed over a flooded Brush Creek under the supervision of the city's general superintendent. An enthusiastic crowd, which had second-guessed the time of her arrival, welcomed her warmly, giving a hint of the glowing press reviews to come. When she did perform in *Camille*, the *Quincy Daily Herald* reporter was unabashedly excited, praising the "acting in her eyes [that] speak to you in a language that you understand" and extolling the naturalness of her death scene, "the finest acting probably ever witnessed in our Opera House" (4 March 1881: 1).

Unlike critics in small Midwestern towns, who were openly grateful for her presence even when they did not understand her spoken language, reporters in larger cities like Cincinnati and Springfield disguised ignorance with flippancy and brashness. When Bernhardt offered *Camille* at the Springfield Opera House on March 4, the major papers largely ignored serious reviewing for a wealth of human-interest commentary. The *Illinois State Journal* was among the few that sedately mentioned Bernhardt's cordial reception and encores, "a rare thing" in Springfield. The *Illinois State Register*, on the other hand, adopted a cheeky, provincial tone, conveying an attitude that would have been familiar to Bernhardt as she traveled through what was for a cultured French woman alien territory. Typical of this kind of humor was a squib that incorporated rumors about her eating habits and her clear complexion, beautiful smile, and slender stature:

> Sarah Bernhardt is said to travel on her muscle, and as she is about to visit us we take back anything we might have thought of her, and

say right here that she never paints, drinks with the boys, don't wear false teeth, and that she can make a shadow on a clear day, and we take our solemn oath that she don't look an inch over 16, and is just too awfully sweet for anything [*Illinois State Register*, 26 Feb. 1881: 4].

Such buffoonery, which glosses French manners with American slang, is a type of reverse snobbery that tries to deflate elitism by democratizing it. Seeking to recreate and domesticate her as an American artifact, it creates a fiction that manifests the writer's own lack of understanding. Unlike the French-speaking Dayton journalist, whose polite visit resulted in a revealing personal interview, the *Illinois State Register*'s attempt to see her was derailed. When the reporter tried to enter the special car, he saw only the business agent J. H. Haynie and the Pinkerton guard Captain Cleary, who "were holding sweet communion together over a bottle of wine." They allowed him to peek into Bernhardt's train compartment, but she had already gone to the Leland Hotel for a much-needed rest. He then tracked the company down to a Monroe Street restaurant, where the translator M. F. Brisse confided unhelpfully that at Quincy, "The opera house was too dingy and smelled bad." At a loss for news, he draws an unattractive picture of the company: "The party was having a jolly time, and as they are gone the reporter will say that an uglier lot of ladies and freer with their tongues he has never seen. Card playing and cooking was going on, and the fumes of garlic drove the reporter out ..." (5 March 1881: 4).

Unable to see Bernhardt at her hotel, he followed the *Chic* tradition of creating a satirical diversion, but without the delicacy and whimsy of the New York humorist. Since he cannot reproduce the French mispronunciations, he slips into Germanic transliteration. Indeed, the beginning of the "interview" sounds believable—Bernhardt commenting on the hugeness of the prairies and on Lincoln's tomb and the State House—but as the column progresses, she waxes rhapsodic about a host of local characters:

> [Bob Hazlett] just too sweet for anyzing. And dose nice young man, Pratt. I see him. He much fall in love mit me, but I much scorn him. And den dat Mierolowski. Oh, just old sweetness. I kiss him much (in mine mind).... He buy me one leetle herring and I eat him not, I save him to remind me of him I loves so much.... Monsieur Vinceet ... He von leetle darling. I luff him ever so much and I peg von leetle lock of his whiskers, which I will take mit me to Paree...."

The reporter, too, claims that he receives a salutation: bidding him "a diew," Bernhardt says, "I gif you von little kees, it is von new vune an haf nevare been used" (6 March 1881: 4).

That kind of breezy attitude was also evident in some of the Springfield reviews of *Camille*, although others confounded or sidestepped the ethical issues. One preview of the play, for instance, naively identified Bernhardt the artistic performer with the fictional heroine. Reader and audience "must confound the two," the reporter maintained: they are the same in physical description, in "moral character," and in "nervous constitution which made one the wanton and the other the great actress." In tone the article was sympathetic to Armand's "tender, thoughtful love," but it ended with equivocation—"Whether rightly or wrongly, let him who is pure enough to judge alone say"—rather than with condemnation, as was the case in Chicago. Yet, once she left ("She Has Visited Us, And Like The Arab, Has Folded Her Tent—And Gone To Milwaukee," one headline read), the reviewer seemed himself as baffled by a performance in French as he claimed the audience was. While acknowledging the warm applause at her appearance, he was reduced to facetiousness: "[w]e thought we detected something that sounded like 'Oh cheese it' from Sarah, when her lover tried to steal a back-handed kiss and mussed her back hair" (*Illinois State Register* 4 March 1881: 4; 5 March 1881: 4).

Such waggishness had small effect on her popularity in Milwaukee, where tickets went on sale at the Academy of Music on March 1 at 3 P.M., with an anticipated three-hour wait. Orchestra seats were added in anticipation of the crowd, "luxurious seats improvised and the greatest elegance established," as the *Evening Chronicle* assured its readers in an unintentional oxymoron. One reporter enlivened the scene with a running narrative about "Anna Maria," who braved the lengthy ticket line herself. Raising her hands "in holy horror as she saw a surging line of men and women," she tried to cajole a policeman, who told her, "Jine the crowd, ma'am, and git into the line an' you'll git the tickets in yer turn." Squeezing to the front, she was pummeled front and back, right and left, and engaged in conversation by an Irish maidservant: "That's a foine hat ye have. Air ye goin' to see Sarie Barnyhard in that hat? My missus as sint me down for the sates has a brand new one wid white feathers ..." Heckled for her effrontery in jumping line, she was escorted to the end, where she waited for three hours to buy dress-circle tickets. Finally returning home "[w]ith hair disheveled, dress torn and soiled, hair like a bird's nest, and face streaked with perspiration and dirt," she calculated that the six-dollar tickets cost, in addition, another forty-eight dollars in damaged clothing plus the price of a new theatre outfit (2 March 1881: 4).

That account notwithstanding, Milwaukee's welcome to Bernhardt on March 5 was comparatively more sophisticated than Springfield's, with two exceptions. Again, her arrival was not without incident. Leaving Springfield after the *Camille* performance, the train encountered a twelve-foot high snowdrift outside of Bloomington; there, the male members of the troupe tackled the obstacle with shovels. They had to repeat their efforts outside Chicago, when the engine balked at another drift four feet high and 250 feet long. After struggling to arrive in Milwaukee, Bernhardt was greeted with news that her old acquaintance, the whale, had arrived at the La Crosse Depot on February 1. No wonder, then, that she refused to speak to anyone—"some of the young reporters were frantic in their grief," reports the *Daily Sentinel* (7 March 1881: 8).

By the time she arrived, comparisons had already been drawn between Bernhardt and the whale. The *Evening Chronicle* praised Fred Englehardt's entrepreneurial spirit: "[T]his is a pretty good example of a Yankee showman's enterprise, and Engelhardt says he would not trade his whale for Sara Bernhardt, especially as an object of curiosity for the west." "Jewhilican what a fish!" exclaimed the amazed reporter, who waxed eloquent over the monster's sixty-foot length and punned on Bernhardt's Boston adventure: "If you want a private apartment for a party at cards, fetch on the furniture and walk into his mouth.... Then look at the bones! And to think that Bernhardt took only one! Herein Shahara failed to get her de-serts" (*Evening Chronicle* 1 Feb. 1881: 4; 3 Feb. 1881: 4).

The whale was not her only welcomer in the city. As the *Daily Sentinel* explained, she narrowly escaped being greeted as well by a "Milwaukee lady" who, unable to wait for her local appearance on March 5, had traveled to Chicago in January to see *Froufrou*. The would-be Olive Logan allowed extracts from her letters to be published; in one, she admitted lying in wait at Palmer House for "the slightest encouragement" from Bernhardt "to go up and salute her in the French style on both cheeks." The writer, who preferred Clara Morris to Bernhardt, reflected the view current in Chicago that the actress "has all the *body* of art, but *not the soul.*" Her critical commentary, however, was directed at Bernhardt's costumes and physical appearance, rather than at the performances. She daydreamed about refurbishing her own wardrobe to mimic the fabric "poems" she saw on stage; and she found fault with Bernhardt's ears, which were "enormous. She drags a wisp of crimpled hair over each ear to hide their ugliness." Finally, seizing on current artistic gossip, she declared that Bernhardt's artworks were "flattering likenesses of herself" and that "probably someone else made them [the sculptures] for her" (1 March 1881: 8). The pre-publicity that ushered in Bernhardt's Saturday arrival was plentiful, but local reviews were sparse, because Sunday was a day of restricted publication. Such a backdrop for the matinée of *Camille* and evening performance of *Froufrou* would hardly seem to have guaranteed—as it seemed to do—the "most appreciative audiences and the impression in her favor" that the Monday *Chronicle* reports (7 March 1881: 4).

At her next two Midwestern stops—Detroit and Toledo—she faced cities that responded like Tweedledee and Tweedledum. After some hesitation, Detroit was enthusiastic, trying to overcome its lack of theatrical expertise and its penchant for judging entertainers on the principle of "utility": as one reporter commented earnestly, "It is a serious doubt with many if after all there is any pleasure of a transitory character worth as much money as ... Bernhardt" (*Detroit Post and Tribune*, 13 March 1881: 4). The Toledo papers expressed more serious reservations, although they commented positively on the lack of "gush" in her welcome (*Toledo Blade* 14 March 1881: 3) and published lame jokes about being on the "tip-toe of expectation" since "she is rather slender, but she usually draws pretty stout houses" (*Blade* 10 March 1881: 3). The "stout" houses, however, were composed of unsympathetic audiences, their attitude colored by anti–Semitism and characterized by rustic humor. Whether the reception in Toledo was a reflection of Bernhardt's own exhaustion from a fatiguing schedule is difficult to say. Throughout her travels, a friendly reception in one city was no guarantee for the next; rather, the opposite often held, possibly a function of raised expectations.

In Detroit the drama reviewers, taking the high critical ground, won a minor skirmish over the importance of legitimate editorial commentary. To be sure, they lost the first volley: the March 3 ticket sale for Bernhardt's performances at Whitney's Grand Opera House was heralded not by analysis but by an article on the sartorial elegance of gloves, including a medley of verses about gloves and lost loves, a glossary of glove gestures, and a lament about the buttonless "Sarah Bernhardt" glove, which reached to the elbow and "wrinkled like an old stocking." This "slovenly" style emphasizes the "look of emaciation," the writer complained (*Free Press* 6 March 1881: 9). The reviewers, on the other hand, explicitly declined to judge Bernhardt on any other score but acting and invoked the aid of a "literary lady" of the city to write "a woman's opinion" of Bernhardt's earlier performance in New York at Booth's theatre. What the audiences had to look forward to, she claimed, was "marvelous grace," an extraordinary voice, and eloquence of gesture that overcame the language barrier. As was the case elsewhere, however, the writer maintained that Bernhardt had no intrinsic genius—that her artificiality allowed the audience to admire, not to feel—yet she was a success, despite "her narrow mental and moral vision, and her poverty of soul" (6 March 1881: 7). This kind of double focus—on

Bernhardt-related trivia and on mildly deprecatory criticism—placed Detroit in the middle position of enjoying small-town gossip but aspiring to large-town theatrical sophistication.

Despite that somewhat ambiguous introduction, Detroit audiences warmed up to Bernhardt. If they were slow to do so, they had a surfeit of riches: Fanny Davenport was on the boards at the same time, with a mirror repertory. The "empty benches" that consequently greeted Bernhardt in *Froufrou* the first evening must have been unsettling, but the *Post and Tribune* reviewer blamed the city's "conservative and critical class" rather than competition. The *Free Press* reviewer was honest about the language barrier, maintaining that the best effects occurred in scenes that were supposed to be mute, where Bernhardt's "inspired" performance revealed "the tragic force within the great actress." He also avoided effusiveness about her appearance, laying to her credit "a talent for looking beautiful" while not being so (9 March 1881: 1). All seemed to dislike the stage setting, complaining that Abbey refused Manager Whitney's "liberal provision" of "$2000 worth of elegance" in favor of "meager mountings," a criticism that seems to echo the ongoing clash of cultural expectations about spectacle and subtlety (*Evening Wisconsin* 4 March 1881: 4; *Free Press* 10 March 1881: 1). Her art, her years of hard study, her devotion to the theatre: these qualities were generally what the reviewers stressed.

Perhaps the informal interview in the March 7 *Detroit Post and Tribune* guaranteed that Whitney's would be jammed with 1800 theatergoers eager to see *Camille* the next night. The reporter was enthralled by her charm and grace: slipping into her dressing room between acts, he watches her costumier at work and sees her transformed into a peasant girl—"no corset, no *jupon*," she says, smiling at him, a comment that evoked his heartfelt comment about her costume being "a more complete reform habit for her sex than any yet offered." Yet while such Continental freedom of speech and gesture was charming in person, on stage it was held to be more dangerous: the same newspaper protested the "false and mawkish sentiment" of *Camille* and, although rejoicing that the presentation in French obscured the moral message, disliked the realism that "goes too far when it exalts and apotheosizes a wanton" (10 March 1881: 4).

Ultimately, the twin performances of Davenport and Bernhardt may have increased the popularity of both. One versifier alliteratively expressed his suspicions of their managers' collusion:

> Sara, Slim, sinuous, soulful;
> Fanny, fastuous, fresh, florid, full:
> Tremendous team.

> Curiously co operative commigration;
> Marvelous managerial maneuvering;
> Shekels superabundant.
> [*Plain Dealer* 16 March 1881: 4].

Such cooperation may have been at work at the serenade that followed the performance of *Camille*, no matter how spontaneous it seemed. That night Spell's Band turned up at Russell House, where the actresses were lodged, to serenade Davenport with "Secret Love," the "Star Spangled Banner," and "Yankee Doodle." Afterward, the American actress "waved an elegant floral banner" and thanked the musicians; then she leaned out of the window and graciously asked them "not to forget our neighbor—a stranger; give her 'The Marsellaise [sic]'" (*Plain Dealer* 15 March 1881: 4). Davenport was cheered and called "noble-hearted" for what can only be described as generous one-upmanship—or good managerial planning.

Despite the competition from Davenport, Detroit was sincere in its praise for Bernhardt, as the effusive paean from George Parsons Lathrop[4] testified:

> Not for to-night, not for to-night alone
>   The death we saw; our tears
> Springing to mingle with your passion's moan.
>   No: Through the unvoiced years
> Such death shall outlive life; your art's pure tone
>   The waiting future hears.
>   [rpt. *Post and Tribune* 9 March 1881: 4].

Toledo, Bernhardt's next stop, put aside turgid sentimentality for the type of raw humor that Springfield's wits indulged in. Angry at what they felt was an "exorbitant" ticket price of $3 (the going rate), theatergoers complained vigorously about the cuts in *Camille* as well as about the lengthy speeches delivered in an unfamiliar language. The "not so cordial" but "large and fashionable" audience expressed a stated preference for Modjeska and Morris, for whose performances they did not need librettos. Many in the audience were said to have attended out of curiosity rather than aesthetic enjoyment, and an editorial about "the talented Jewess" revealed underlying anti–Semitism (*Blade* 11 March 1881: 2, 3). The dislike seemed to be mutual: in an interview, Abbey "sneer[ed]" at the city as being unable to support an artist of Bernhardt's caliber, and the *Blade* sneered back, offended that she had shortened *Camille* "in the most inartistic manner" and performed as if "under pressure." Yet the demands Toledoans made upon her private time were incessant. A young man who wanted

Bernhardt's autograph for his photo album paid a District Telegraph Office message boy to present his album to Bernhardt. Abbey was furious at the intrusion: "She never writes her autograph for the amusement of snobs," he grumbled. "You may tell the fellow who sent you here that Miss Bernhardt's manager invites him very politely to go to the devil" (14 March 1881: 3).

Audience naïveté was perhaps the fundamental reason for the dissatisfaction, as an interview with a Toledo street urchin suggests. After earning a free pass to *Camille* by helping a scalper hand out advertisements, the boy tells the interviewer about Bernhardt's appearance, using colorful language reminiscent of O. Henry. She is "a heap thinner" than the papers report, he says: "Talk about water-pipes, billiard-cues, an' gun-bor's—why they ain't a circumstance to Sary. She's like a streak o' gas-light fallin' on a wall through a crack in a door"; her mouth is "like a cistern"; and her gloves "sot on her arms like a pair of rubber boots would fit a pair o' stilts." He goes on to provide verbal snapshots of the audience, all of which suggest why Bernhardt was less than successful in Toledo. One viewer, convinced that the play is in Italian, explained the confrontation between Armand and his father over Marguerite's letter of farewell in this way:

> The fellar wot pretended to understand Italian said that was a partiklar nice passage.... *Armong* had just got a tailor's bill handed to him, an' as soon as he saw the old man come in he wanted him to pay it. He said "*Mong pair,*" was the Italian fur "Money, parent."

Another tells his date that while "it was the correct thing to say that they enjoyed Sary's actin' tremenjus, ... for his part he would ruther see a Humpty Dumpty show or Buffalo Bill." A third, railing at his wife after the play, adds up the amount of provisions he could have bought for the price of the tickets and complains about the waste of money (12 March 1881: 5).

Some of Toledo's unhappiness followed Bernhardt to Cleveland— "Bernhardt Be Blanked!" announced a headline in the Cleveland *Penny Press*, which engaged in belittling the actress and her accoutrements. When she arrived via the Lake Shore railroad on March 11, she was greeted by "plenty of policemen, but no crowd"—except for two hundred onlookers who had waited in the freezing cold for the train, which arrived an hour late. The troupe looked "hardly as well" as their American counterparts, and the "City of Worcester" was said to be "inferior." Bernhardt, tired of

6. *"We be men of little wit"*: Audiences in the Midwest   151

her fans' insistent gawking, had let it be known through Jarrett that she "hated to be stared at and thinks the American people very impudent, ... their habit of staring at her an insult worthy of a slap in the face" (*Penny Press* 12 March 1881: 2). Nonetheless, the crowd pressed close when she disembarked, and the *Penny Press* reported on their disappointment—"a laugh almost derisive went up"—when she appeared muffled to the eyes and dressed plainly in dark traveling clothing. Clearly, her fans expected spectacle as a reward for their perseverance; just as clearly, Bernhardt had decided not to oblige. Followed closely by a Pinkerton detective holding her leather case of jewelry, she was taken to Kennard House, where she had scarcely time to rest before she left at 6 P.M. for the theatre (11 March 1881: 3).

Although the unfriendly tone of the report indicated that Bernhardt was unapproachable, the Cleveland *Plain Dealer* journalist found an immediate welcome, despite her punishing schedule. Perhaps his bilingualism helped: he sent up his card and was received by the actress, who after months of traveling commanded "tolerably good English," despite the reporter's willingness to conduct the interview in French. He was won over by her expressive eyes and her charm. Nearing the end of her tour, she said that America was beautiful but "*so cold*" and that she was "tired out" and longed to return home. When the reporter left, he called at Jarrett's room, only to be told brusquely that Bernhardt was unavailable; learning that the reporter had simply knocked at her door, Jarrett "became decidedly chagrined and said something about a want of courtesy" (12 March 1881: 1). While Bernhardt herself could be tart on occasion, Jarrett's own lack of temper and efforts to protect his charge may have occasioned some of the ill feelings in the smaller venues.

The disparity between the *Penny Press*'s antagonism and the *Plain Dealer*'s relative civility suggests that they represented opposite sides of the readership. The *Penny Press* estimated that only 25 percent of the *Froufrou* audience at the Euclid Avenue Opera House were serious, the others "curiosity seekers" there to evaluate her dressmakers' skill. The reported consensus was that her costumes failed to live up to those of other performers—her "cheap-looking riding habit, in which she looks like a telegraph pole in boots" was particularly unbecoming. While she is praised for her true-to-life presentation and technical facility, she is taken to task for lack of "sympathy" (12 March 1881: 2). On the other hand, although the *Plain Dealer* made sport of her stature—"It would seem at times as though she gathered her skirts tightly about the limbs and posed for the sole benefit of those horrid male skeptics who will never believe such things can be until they have seen them"—it was enthusiastic about her talent, insisting that a "serious review ... is not necessary" because she was "a really great actress," as her *Froufrou* performance attested. The reporter applauded the audience for their "conscientious minds interested far more than the usual degree in the stage and its advancement" (12 Mar. 1881: 4). In the final analysis, the Cleveland reviewers seemed to have found what they looked for and presented the picture most appealing to their readership. Thirty-six years later, after countless American tours, she might have laughed at their final assessment:

> ... it is not likely she will ever visit "the dear Americans" a second time and it is a matter for serious speculation whether the Americans care to have the very dear Bernhardt come over on a second financial crusade [*Plain Dealer* 15 March 1881: 4].

After her equivocal welcome in Cleveland, Bernhardt began the trek back to the more theatrically sophisticated Northeast, through the gateway city of Pittsburgh. There, however, her arrival was preempted by Fred Engelhardt's exhibit. Housed in the Pennsylvania Railroad metal yard in a specially constructed building, "Monsieur, the Whale" drew immense crowds, despite some evidence of decay. "The general impression is that the mammal's characteristics have been misrepresented," comments the *Pittsburgh Telegraph*, unconsciously echoing some of the criticism that followed Bernhardt. The *Pittsburgh Daily Post* reporter is one of the few to have made an explicit connection between the actress and her Nemesis: "It is rather a queer coincidence that the arrival of Mlle. Bernhardt and that of the whale should be syncronious," he comments; "She saw him when he was taken from the water at Boston and formally christened him the 'Prince of Whales'" (16 March 1881:4).

While the curious flocked to see the whale and theatergoers avidly bought tickets for "one of the best weeks of the season," Bernhardt and her troupe took a Sunday's worth of rest, retiring to Monongahela House and then scheduling a night rehearsal at the Pittsburgh Opera House. Her indefatigable drive was rewarded during the week by a series of serious reviews, which, while tinged with Puritanism, helped to counteract the antagonism displayed in Toledo and in Cleveland. Even the vein of resentment at Bernhardt's profits—"La Bernhardt ... says she will come back and rake in the pretty American gold when she learns to play in English" (*Daily Post* 14 March 1881: 4)—is well balanced by the focus on theatrical matters. The *Post* reviewer, although reminding his readers that *Camille* is both "dangerous" and "harmful" and ought to be "banished," offers high praise of the actress's interpretation of Gilberte. "[T]his little outgrowth of the social hot-house" is a universal type, he maintains; because of Bernhardt's "exquisite diction, her deliciously measured voice and her marvelous comprehension of the effect of the slightest tone," the audience sat entranced, forgetful of their librettos. In the midst of his encomium, the reviewer pauses to lambaste both the speculators, who had held many of the empty best seats for a high price, and the local officers: "There were several ill mannered, uncouth politicians in the house, and they stood near the railing and disturbed the people by profanity and loud talk" (*Daily Post* 15 March 1881: 4).

The foreignness of her acting—in other words, French realism—was well received by audiences in this industrial city. Reviewers took a high tone, although the *Pittsburgh Commercial Gazette* complained about "unnatural selection" in her omitting classical French drama from her repertory: in *Camille*, for instance, which the *Pittsburgh Telegraph* insisted "has no moral expressed or implied," Bernhardt is commended for her refusal to pander to "American sentimental tastes" (16 March 1881: 4). The *Gazette* agreed, praising her for not playing to the audience, even though many were clearly lost in trying to understand her rapid French. The *Post* took up the issue, defending her from the prevailing charge of lacking the "strong emotional capacity" that Clara Morris displayed. Her conception of the character as being consumed by a "smothered fire," the realism of the dining and death scenes—"it was as though one had peeped through the window of a *café* or into a gay Parisian house"—had, the reviewer said, "never been equaled in this city. Those who say that Mlle. Bernhardt is overrated may have had cause for it, but we cannot understand wherein her defects lie" (16 March 1881: 3). Her Sunday rest and rehearsal had borne fruit.

At this point Bernhardt looked forward to the end of her exhausting tour, with only Titusville, Bradford, Erie, Buffalo, and Niagara Falls on the books before she said farewell in New York. Perhaps the enthusiasm of her welcome in these smaller venues militated against her tiredness. If Indianapolis, insecure about being out-bargained, and Cleveland, proud of its "plain dealing," were suspicious of succumbing to an aesthetic experience, the *Petroleum World* and Titusville *Herald* were beside themselves with anticipation. Bernhardt with her "wonderful natural gifts" was seen as a modern-day Horatio Alger, a talented painter, sculptor, and actress surpassing even Rachel; she has succeeded "solely by her own exertion and inspiration" (*Petroleum World*; qtd. in *Erie Morning Dispatch* 17 March 1881: 1). Her "brilliant" performance of *Camille* at the Titusville Opera House was honored by "a magnificent critique" in the *Herald* on March 17, which billed itself as the only review in French that had appeared during her tour. Apparently, the evening was marred by only one flaw. In the past Bernhardt's performances had been interrupted by snow, by falling scenery, and by a fire; this time Marie Colombier was again to blame. While the *Herald* claims that Colombier fainted because of "*Gustave* flattening out a weak-kneed chair in a most ludic[r]ous manner" (qtd. in *Erie Morning Dispatch* 17 March 1881: 1), she was more likely dissolved in laughter, but the incident did little to damp Titusville's enthusiasm.

The troupe continued on to Bradford, and then, as word of her success spread, the Erie Park Opera House manager prepared for an estimated 1500 enthusiasts on March 18 for *Camille*. So warm a welcome helped make up for her often unpredictable reception in the Midwest, yet like those in Toledo, Erie journalists engaged in a fair share of flippancy, a reminder that she had moved into the Northeast. While the *Erie Morning Dispatch* prepared a lengthy and sympathetic synopsis "for the Benefit of Those Who No 'Parlee voo Francis,'" the *Morning News* ironically noted that the crowd of fifty at the depot stood "for two hours waiting to fall down and worship the idol that Abbey has set up." Bernhardt's best defense against such derision was her own naturalness: surprising her critics by stepping out of the train and kissing a child on the platform, she also, contrary to custom for a one-night stand, proceeded to a hotel. There, at Reed House, as the newspaper reported, "not at all hoggish with her thinness," she ran gossiping from room to room and then took a walk outside with Jeanne. As usual, she was afforded little privacy. Crowds gathered outside her door while she ate, and the ever-present reporter admitted that leisurely Continental dining put "American voracity" to shame. He joked that "So many trays went in that the anxious watchers became alarmed about her, and fears were entertained that her slenderness would be destroyed.... It was a mystery how she disposed of that dinner without adding to her circumference" (19 March 1881: 4).

On the subject of her talent, however, the joking stopped: the *Morning News* review of *Camille* was a laudatory essay on "one of the grandest exhibitions of dramatic art ever witnessed." It was a "dramatic revolution" characterized by perfection; Bernhardt's "ease and naturalness" overcame the language barrier. Again, the death scene brought down the house. For the reviewer, Bernhardt's expression of "utter hopelessness, that finds voice in a plaintive wail [is] more eloquent and soul-touching than any language that ever flowed from mortal pen" (19 March 1881: 4).

Perhaps because the Erie audience was different from Toledo's, the *Morning News* was unable to produce a street urchin to comment on the performance; but it did invent its own rustic humorist to provide a tongue-in-cheek interview. Aristotle, the office boy purportedly sent to see Bernhardt behind the scenes, had difficulty gaining access—he was thrown into a painted bed of roses replete with nails—but threatening to "give the whole party such a racket in the next issue that 'ud bust up the entire company," he was allowed to see the *artiste*. In her dressing room, he hung his hat on a spitoon and watched her unobserved as she rehearsed an attack on the *Observer*, a competing newspaper. "*Bete! Scelerat! Monstre!*" she shouted. At that, he interrupted her to carry on a conversation in fractured French:

> "I have come to intervoo you," said I, "are you in *conditione* [presentable, in good condition]?" I wanted to let her see I knew French also.
> "A *peu pres* [Almost]", said she, and that settled it....
> "A *posteriori*, how have you made out since you arrived in America?" I thought I'd fire off some Latin for effect.
> "A *tout hazard* [On the off chance], my engagemong have been a *toute entrance* [at every entrance] ever wher I go."
> "That's bully" said I.
> "What baggage have you?" I next asked.
> "You are an '*ame de boue* [soul of mud, the lowest of the low],'" said she, and then she called a fellow named Garcon, and he came in and fired me out of the apartemong [*Erie Morning News* 19 March 1881: 4].

In reality, Bernhardt may have wished to deal with many an intrusive, inquisitive reporter in that way; but as the record shows, she was remarkably accessible to those who were courteous. She also knew when to withdraw and how to create the spectacle her public hoped for. Indeed, although her personal life was flamboyant, her public behavior in America was modest and her notoriety was often a fabrication of the press or creative staging by Jarrett. Aside from costumes created for carefully orchestrated presentations, receptions, or theatrical performances, her daily traveling attire was unpretentious and her manner unassuming. Repeatedly, reporters comment that she is like a schoolgirl in her enjoyment of gossip, of new acquaintances, or of adventures. What hid these qualities from midwestern reporters was their own sense of inferiority and difference, and their own way of dealing with foreignness through belittlement and sarcasm. At its best, this typical brand of American humor sought to domesticate Bernhardt; at its worst, it confirmed a native bias against aesthetic experimentation. In her travels through the Midwest, she was often exposed to American brashness, independence, and a determination not to be hoodwinked, so her success or lack of it at one venue was no guarantee of her reception at another. Yet her many curtain calls at the gateway to the East were auspicious, allowing her to bid farewell to "men of little wit" and move to the Northeast to complete her tour.

7

Home, Sweet Home

"Oh, it is magnificent; it is so large and so beautiful. There are some funny people here, but, of course you find them everywhere..." [*New York Times* 5 May 1881: 8].

Her lengthy tour of the "magnificent" United States ending, Bernhardt could look back on a series of victories. Most gratifying must have been her personal triumph during a tour conceived, in part, to pay her debt to the Comédie Française: that august company was not the premier French acting troupe in America—hers was, and in America she need answer to no one but herself. She was director and actor, tragedienne and comedienne, both on stage and off. In England, she had met with royalty; in America, she *was* royalty, despite all the efforts to democratize her by introducing her to literary lions and shysters, artists and critics, university professors and ragamuffins. Her realistic acting and spare stage sets called into question American theatrical conventions, and her presence provoked moral and ethical sparring matches. She was a disruptive factor, bringing elements of cultural heterogeneity to the more conservative elements of the towns she visited, but she was also a created spectacle. As a foreigner, she was expected to be alien, exotic, and strange, as much a member of Abbey's and Jarrett's menagerie as the wild animals she kept in her own. Yet she learned from the Americans, adapting their language and some of their business savvy to her own operations. They learned from her, too. By the time she returned to the Eastern seaboard, she found that her "foreignness" had to some degree become a part of the texture of American theatrical culture.

After leaving Erie, Pennsylvania, Bernhardt traveled once again to Canada, where she performed *Camille* and *Froufrou* in Toronto on March 19. Her reception was uneventful, marked, in fact, by only minor protests in the newspapers. Matinée attendance was more affected by those with "scruples," as the *Toronto Mail* reported; the Grand Opera House was less than half full. The audience's coolness about *Camille* was, however, more than compensated for by the warmth of the review and the crowd in the evening—"one of the best audiences, socially speaking, Toronto has ever turned out." The *Camille* reviewer, who was ecstatic about her "simply perfect" death scene and the naturalness that pervaded her entire performance, was equally happy with her evening performance of *Froufrou*, in which her "magnificent picture of approaching death" redeemed the conventional melodrama of the last two acts. And, judging from the remarks about "Burny," purportedly from a "gallery boy" who was sneaked into see *Camille* as a reward for helping to post bills, others were just as admiring: the actress was "jist a daisy," he reported to his friends (*Mail* 21 March 1881: 8).

The quiet tone of the visit was set by the editorial in the *Toronto Daily Mail* that took a ranting letter-writer to task. "The whole world is fully acquainted with [Bernhardt's] lax code," the editor observed, "and no good purpose is to be gained at this late day by drawing further attention to it." More remarkable, perhaps, is his movement from moral condemnation to public defense of art: as he points out, "on the stage [people] do not see the woman's morals, but only her clever portrayal of character" (17 Mar. 1881: 4). For his part, the letter-writer, a clergyman, acknowledges Bernhardt's talent—in fact he bewails it; her acting makes "the path of virtue more difficult" as her devotees "turn aside to worship a genius that persistently, defiantly, notoriously, disobeys the law He made beautiful." The letter clearly outraged several readers, who responded two days later with a variety of well-written defenses. One pointed out that the first chapter of Romans classes "malignity and backbiting" with murder; another, referring to adultery proceedings against Talmage, asks why the clergyman "did not warn his flock not to go to the Grand Opera when a certain Brooklyn minister lectured there."

Despite her more friendly welcome, Bernhardt was eager to return to the United States and especially excited about visiting Niagara Falls, which she had glimpsed before 7:30 A.M. as she traveled north on the Great Western railway. Given her earlier reception in Canada, where she evoked anathemas from the religious establishment and a riotous welcome in the streets, her comment on the renaming of the Canadian city from Clifton to "Niagara Falls" was deceptively mild: "*Mais comme ces Canadiens sont gourmand* [How greedy these Canadians are]!" (*Niagara Falls Gazette* 23 March 1881: 3).

The local newspapers were more interested in Bernhardt's impression of the American side of the Falls, and the *Toledo Blade*, *Gazette*, and *Buffalo Courier* published lengthy accounts of her excursion. The *Courier* reporter, however, whom Jarrett invited to accompany the party, had a coveted first-hand view for his March 21 report. The day at the Falls began at 8 A.M., when two carriages set out, one carrying Bernhardt, her sister, Marie Colombier, and Angelo; and the other, Abbey, agent Mayer, *Gaulois* reporter Haynie, and the *Courier* journalist. The rest of the troupe broke into smaller groups, and all met at Prospect Park, where, after riding on the inclined railway, Bernhardt impulsively led her party up an ice mountain. It was far different from her ascent of the whale in Boston: reaching the icy summit with the aid of "steel pointed creepers," she stood "radiant from her violent exercise and joyous and exultant." As the group debated how to get down, she laughingly gathered her skirts, waved good-by, and descended in the time-honored way, "at a rate of speed greater than any toboggan ever went down a snow-slide."

After this exercise, the party repaired to Prospect House for a breakfast arranged by proprietor David Isaacs. Bernhardt's response to children was always warm: she hugged and kissed Isaacs's young son and wrote in English (either in the hotel journal or the mother's journal, depending on the account): "How good God is to have created such beautiful things. With enthusiasm, Sarah Bernhardt, 1881" (*Toledo Blade* 23 March 1881: 1). Fortified by breakfast and protected by oilskins, the group set out and walked in back of the Falls. There, Bernhardt declared herself "not a bit fatigued" and much to the astonishment of "the bewildered looking guide" whimsically decided to perform "a most careful and interesting rehearsal" of the final act of Dumas's *La Princesse Georges*, a new addition to her farewell repertory. Finally, talking volubly all the time, they ate lunch. Like others before him who had spoken personally to the actress, the *Courier* reporter was captivated by her charm: she had a "sweet and interesting" manner; "her rosy cheeks glowed with health"; and her very movements "bespeak the refined French woman that she is." She was complimentary in return, praising the Falls above all other natural wonders she had seen— "all paled into utter insignificance, when compared with the glories of the grand old cataract." After the long day, they withdrew to their special cars at 5 P.M. at the New York Depot and were whisked away "from the gaze of a large crowd" to the next venue.

Her energy and playfulness suggest that this brief interlude was very welcome before she again faced the prospect of reportorial cacophony and social squabbling that often accompanied her appearances. As before, tandem performances initially called forth opposite reactions. In Buffalo, where she performed *Camille* on Monday, March 21, she was celebrated as "the greatest society actress that ever visited the Queen City of the Lakes" (*Gazette* 23 March 1881: 3); a day later in Rochester, she was grudgingly welcomed by the *Daily Union and Advertiser* in an editorial on "The Coming Sarah Bernhardt Imposition." Indeed, she would have been welcome to stay longer in Buffalo, where Academy of Music representatives John and Henry Meech tried unsuccessfully to negotiate with Abbey for a two-night stand. Expecting an overflow crowd, they decided on an effective move, albeit unpopular with scalpers—limiting the number of tickets to ten per person. Three days before the performance, only fifty front-row seats remained to be sold (*Courier* 10 March 1881: 2; 18 March 1881: 2). Their managerial counterparts in Rochester, however, suffered from a storm of complaints about Bernhardt's projected appearance. Smarting from an earlier cancellation by Mlle. Roze,[1] scheduled to perform in *Carmen*, one vocal reporter lambasted the brokers for substituting Bernhardt's mediocre talent and then gloating over their profits. He fulminated about the "next promised instance of managerial greed" with the "exhibition" of Bernhardt, a "commodity of commerce," and he reproached the managers, who "seem to have taken a fiendish delight in catering to the most depraved instincts and most morbid curiosity" in order to attract the curious to her performances. He goes on to warn readers against spending three dollars (the equal of "nine months' interest on a $100 bond") to see someone who has "worn herself out" and whose language they will not understand (*Daily Union and Advertiser* 16 March 1881: 2).

In light of these hostile comments, the enthusiastic reviews of her preceding day's performance of *Camille* in the Buffalo papers provided a nice salve, both economic and emotional. The Buffalo *Courier* reviewer, who refused to discuss "her eccentricities" or to deal with "what some people have regarded as her advertising feats," maintained that "she advertises no more than she can make good"—and that is "depth and delicacy of feeling" with no meretriciousness. Her "dramatic genius [is] of the very highest order," he concluded (22 March 1881: 2). The Rochester reporters never capitulated completely, but after her performance admitted to being impressed by the talent and charm that had overcome critical dyspepsia elsewhere. The Rochester *Daily Union and Advertiser*, convinced that the "craze" was over (16 March 1881: 2), nonetheless conceded that although Bernhardt lacked "vivacity," she exhibited grace, self-control, and "magnetism," characteristics rarely seen in American actresses; and it went on to congratulate her on achieving such "perfect sympathy" with her audience that she overcame the language barrier (23 March 1881: 2).

In Albany and Troy, her next stops after performing at the Syracuse

Opera House on March 23 and 24, she was greeted with unfriendly curiosity and a singular lack of understanding. Business owners, however, immediately co-opted her for advertising purposes, as they had in Atlanta, Indianapolis, and other cities: the enterprising Church & Phalen Co., for instance, featured a "Sarah Bernhardt Pin for the Hair" (*Troy Daily Times* 26 March 1881: 3). In Albany the almost all-female crowd that engulfed her at the railroad station was aggressive and unhappy that she had arrived almost one and one-half hours late. Dismayed at such a welcome, the troupe received little sympathy from the reporters, who professed to be puzzled when "a tall, black moustached French gentleman" who paced back and forth on the jammed platform was heard to mutter, "It ees a shame to ze American people." Bernhardt, casting a startled look at the surging crowd, muttered "Mon Dieu!" and took refuge in her Delavan House suite before performing the same evening, the 25th. The audience's coldness during the first half of *Froufrou* was fair recompense, one reviewer ungenerously suggested, for her failure to live up to the accounts published about her. "She was not surprisingly thin, or beautiful, or gorgeously attired. Her action, manners, movements and speech were simple, unaffected, natural, devoid of ordinary stage tricks...."—in short, the real-life spectacle fell short of the spectacle created for her by the press. By the third act, however, her talent broke through the audience's reserve, and they gave her "deafening applause" and encore after encore. Still, whether the audience "had seen the greatest living actress" or someone on a level with Morris and Modjeska was debatable, after-show comments implied; many would have preferred her to speak in English for the sake of "popular approval." She left for Boston with an economic loss. The Albany performances earned under $2500: Leland Opera House was at least twenty percent empty on the 25th, and even more so for the next day's matinée of *Camille*.

After six months of touring, Bernhardt was no longer a public relations phenomenon. In November, her created spectacle often worked in her favor to attract audiences; in March, that image sometimes worked against her, especially in small Midwestern and Northeastern towns. In larger venues, moreover, she was recognized as an accomplished actress whose talent carried the day and who no longer needed extensive public relations support. Because she had returned as a known quantity, then, she was less likely to be reviewed extensively. Such was the case in Boston, where her reception was polite, but cooler than her first visit, "the furor ... having been spent and the high prices ... debarring the masses," as the *Clipper* said with some tartness (9 April 1881: 46). Her grotesque companion, the whale, had vanished, but even so, her memories of their initial encounter were vivid:

> I think I was oftenest struck by the flaming posters that met my gaze at every turn. On nearly every bill-board Bernhardt, McCullough and the Boston Whale were to be found in close proximity. One would almost have thought, so inseparable were we, that we were travelling in conjunction for the same manager.... I believe it was generally conceded that the Whale was not the least interesting of the three [qtd. in *Boston Commonwealth* 9 April 1881: 3].

The satirists, too, had found other victims or had become devoted admirers. With her approval Thatcher and Ryman brought *Sarah Heartburn* to Boston; her enthusiastic account of the absurdities of the January 7 performance had gained the company a Paris invitation, and they were ready to sail for France.

Serious reviewers, however, were hesitant about her new offerings. The *Clipper*, for instance, found *L'Étrangère* to be wearying and disappointing because it began late, finished just before midnight, and did not offer enough stage presence for the star; moreover, Bernhardt's failure to appear in the finale was "a dire disappointment." Other performances were subject to unpopular changes, too. The debut of *La Princesse Georges*, initially scheduled for March 31, was put off, and *Hernani* offered in its place. The new play was finally given as an invited full-dress rehearsal on April 1 and as a public performance for the first time in America on April 2. The *Clipper* was unusually terse, commenting that it was "modern in tone, but of questionable purity," yet still "of great interest." An incident in which the drop curtain was unexpectedly raised, giving a view of the female troupe members in various stages of undress, might have evoked a comic verse or sketch during the first visit; now it is accorded only a brief mention (9 April 1881: 46).

At this point, Bernhardt was eagerly looking forward to occupying her berth on *L'Amérique*, yet she had five scheduled performances (four, once her April 5 performance at Fall River, Massachusetts, had been cancelled) before her New York farewell. The first—Worcester—rekindled the freshness of her early 1880 appearances. The audience greeted her enthusiastically, although her stay was short: in an attempt to avoid both crowds and an overnight stint in her parlor car, she arrived from Boston at 4:15 P.M. on April 4 and left immediately after her performance at 11:30 P.M. The *Daily Spy* and *Evening Gazette* recorded the special efforts undertaken to prepare the Worcester Music Hall, now the Worcester Theatre, including new carpets and paper for the "star" dressing room, which was also "otherwise made attractive and suitable for the owner of such a costly wardrobe." Local heroes included those who had set up the special effects scenery:

John D. Chollar was responsible for the new furniture and Mr. Merrifield for the upright pianoforte, said to be necessary because the French are "much more particular" than others. Again the American desire for a furnished stage ran counter to French realism, which was interpreted as thrift. The Music Hall directors were concerned that "Mlle Bernhardt would not act on a bare stage, even if the management desired to economize" (*Worcester Evening Gazette* 8 July 1965).

The anticipation in Worcester ran high, in both serious and absurd ways. Not only were audiences told that they might expect "dramatic art in perfection," but they were given an introduction to the evening's performance of *Camille* "condensed for busy folks":

Act I—Paris

He—You are sick. I love you.
She—Don't. You can't afford it.

Act II—Paris

She—I think I love you. But good-bye; the Count is coming.
He—That man? Then I see you no more. But no! An idea! Let us fly to the country.

Act III—The Country

His Father—You ruin my son! Leave him.
She—He loves me.
His Father—You are a good woman. I respect you. Leave him.
She—I go.

Act IV—Paris

She—You again? I never loved you.
He—Fly with me, or I die.
She—I love you; but good-bye now.

Act V—Paris

She—(Very sick.) Is it you? Is God so good?
He—Pardon me. My father sent me.
She—I pardon you. I love you. I die. [*Dies. Tears. Sensation. Curtain.*]
[*Evening Gazette* 4 April 1881].

The *Evening Gazette*'s serious review of the performance was enthusiastic, reiterating what was by this time a common assessment: that she won over the audience by her polished performance, melodious voice, and mobile, expressive face. Sounding a rare note, however, the reviewer also praised her "versatile, ever changing spirit of intelligence." Although he had not seen her entire repertory, he was certain that classical tragedy was not her forte and that compared to *Froufrou, Camille* was her most successful impersonation: "Camille is a real woman struggling against pestilent surroundings and a hard fate, while *Froufrou* is only a spoiled child, with herself to blame...." It was Bernhardt's air of "quiet refinement" that made the play "tolerable," even attractive. Some of the success of the Worcester performance, which garnered $1200 in receipts—a large amount, considering the size of the music hall—he attributed to the location, which, although smaller than Booth's or the Globe, had better acoustics and sight lines.

Bernhardt's willingness to appear in a small town like Worcester had an element of *noblesse oblige* that the local audience responded to warmly, but that was not the case in Fall River, where the performance was cancelled because of lack of interest (*Providence Evening Bulletin* 4 April 1881: 6). As at other times in her tour, a lack of success in one town was hardly a good prognosticator of her next performance. The reviewers and audience in Providence were laudatory about her *Camille*: "[T]he charm of her voice, the grace of her movement, and the pathos and power of her acting, made conquests last evening of those who understood no word of French, and who were inclined to be prejudiced against her" (*Providence Evening Bulletin* 7 April 1881). A different kind of conquest, reminiscent of the Rice burlesque in Philadelphia, was attempted by Chace, Griffin, and Mason in *Sarah Burnheart* at the Providence Theatre Comique; the piece was one of several, including Professor H. M. Parker and his Wonderful Mastodon Dog Circus. In Newark, her next stop, she faced a double disadvantage. The mothers who had in 1880 worried about their sons being led astray were still a very real anti-theatrical presence, and the city's proximity to New York meant that audiences had an alternative theatrical venue. In an attempt to overcome both problems, pre-publicity was unusually bombastic. The performance, a "phenomenal event," was billed as the "crown of theatrical sensations"; and the special scenery was said to be "on a scale commensurate with its importance." The Park Theatre managers, wanting to assure a profit, held a pre-ticket sales subscription poll from March 28 to April 1. As the *Newark Daily Advertiser* reported, women and resident foreigners preferred *Froufrou*; others voted overwhelmingly for *Camille*, presumably because the plot was better known.

These tactics, calculated to create an audience, were coupled with safeguards against an overflow crowd, and the latter perhaps worked too well. Since the boxes were auctioned by mail, box office sales were quiet, and only a handful of speculators appeared on line at 6 A.M. on April 2; consequently, the theater was only half-full. The *Advertiser*, which speculated that "many prominent patrons of the drama" had already seen Bernhardt in New York, balanced between Puritanical guilt and aesthetic pleasure:

That she completely triumphs in spite of the well understood prejudices against her personal character, and the repugnant standard of foreign manners she represents, was a testimony of her supreme command of her art, and its close enough resemblance to nature to "make the whole world kin" [8 April 1881].

More explicit in its disappointment at the small house, the *Newark Daily Journal* lamented the "blow to enterprise in bringing to Newark first-class talent." The blame was laid not only upon the high ticket prices but upon the Lenten season. Since the city is "a churchly place," the reporter believed that churchgoers stayed away for fear of being thought morally indifferent to Bernhardt's character.

In order to make New York her farewell city, Bernhardt traveled south to Washington and Baltimore and then circled back to Philadelphia and New York. She claimed to the *Evening Star* reporter that her Washington audience was "the most appreciative" she had played to and that she especially appreciated that their proficiency in French made librettos unnecessary, an ironic comment in light of the reporter's confessed ineptness in the language. The genial tone of the interview was maintained by Bernhardt herself. When the reporter commented that "the newspapers have had a good deal fun" about her, she claimed not to be offended: "I don't understand half of it. What I do understand I laugh at," she said, perhaps forgetting her angry response eight months earlier to the "skeleton" caricature (9 April 1881: 1). The Washington theatrical reviews mirrored the audiences' appreciation, temporizing about the moral issues raised by the "anti-eleventh commandment romance" otherwise known as *Froufrou* but waxing eloquent about the way in which Bernhardt's performance in *Camille* illustrated "a grand moral through the use of corrupt elements." The *Post* was outspoken, calling the language "tawdry," "the women disgusting," and the tone one of "morbid and slimy sentimentality." Through it all, however, the reviewer is ecstatic about the way in which Bernhardt portrays the "goodness of a heart, polluted but not destroyed, ris[ing] to the act of supreme self-abnegation" (*Washington Post* 9 April 1881: 2; 10 April 1881: 4).

Her brief stop in Baltimore was a reflection of her Washington performances. There, she was greeted by another minstrel show, this time by Carncross's Minstrels at Albaugh's Holliday Street Theatre. There, she was burlesqued as "Sara Barnyard" in "Calmeel; or the Fate of a Croquette," reportedly an "indescribably ludicrous burlesque ... given with remarkable spirit" (*Baltimore American* 7 April 1881: 1, 2). More seriously, the *Baltimore American*'s drama reviewer provided an intelligent analysis, one that granted her to be "better than the best of other actresses, "but also one that sensed the loss of immediacy that exhaustion in a part can produce. His suggestion—that she remove herself from the star system and return for a time to the Comèdie Française, where the entire company is the star—was well thought out, and although it mentioned her acting as a money-making business, he tried to make the point that Bernhardt needed this at this stage in her career of "drama as an art" (10 April 1881: 3).

The warm welcome in the Washington area at an end, Bernhardt had still to weather a Philadelphia audience afflicted by a combination of *déjà vu* and the same Lenten conscience that had hampered playgoers in Newark. In January her Philadelphia visit had been ushered in by a full-scale pulpit attack on theatrical immorality; in April, her detractors were different. *Philadelphia Evening Bulletin* readers were taken to task not by ministers but by editors for being "gay fasters" who divested themselves of jewelry and fancy clothes but who nonetheless went to the theatre. Once there, as the warning went, they were likely to see characters that were less than virtuous and plays that were unsuitable, like *L'Étrangère*, which was scheduled for Good Friday. Lest that caution prove ineffective, the *Bulletin*, which predicted lower than expected receipts, recommended that managers refrain from scheduling performances so as not to tempt the churchgoers (11 April 1881: 4). The Philadelphia correspondent to the *New York Mirror* thought it enough to declare "The Bernhardt craze is over" (16 April 1881: 10).

Given that kind of pressure, Philadelphians were reluctant to come to her opening performance of *Adrienne Lecouvreur*. On April 11, the Chestnut Street Theatre was only twenty-five percent full, a situation that taxed Bernhardt's self-confidence despite her proven success elsewhere (Jarrett, it was said, like the proverbial man in search of wedding guests, would go out into the streets in such a case to drum up an audience). Theatergoers may have remembered that in January, *Adrienne Lecouvreur* was substituted for *Phèdre* because of Marie Colombier's lateness in reaching the theatre. The play, moreover, had a long history of problems in other engagements. Used as a debut, as it was in New York and later in Baltimore, Chicago, and Cincinnati, its subtleties were often wasted on first-night audiences who expected more flash and glamour from a woman whose way had been paved with scandal.

Once on the boards, however, Bernhardt treated the "small, select, critical" audience to a noteworthy performance, even though the *Philadelphia Inquirer* reviewer grumbled that she received too much publicity. As a backhanded compliment, the reviewer called the death scene disappointing, pale in comparison to her "wonderfully mobile face" and to her second act triumph, "one of the most marvelous and delicate interpretations of the actor's art" (12 April 1881: 8). The *Evening Bulletin* agreed that although the play lacked novelty, her performance ranked "with the best as a refined, artistic, elegant, and occasionally impassioned" interpretation. That review focused primarily on the modulations of her voice and her artistic "trick of changing her tone suddenly and completely." The death struggle, however, was "unnecessarily horrible": Bernhardt lacked sympathy for her character, being careful to place herself near a chair before she fell and kicking away the train of her dress—"a woman who is being devoured by poison probably does not hunt for a chair when the paroxysms are fiercest, and it is unlikely that she will give much attention to her petticoats," the reviewer argued (12 April 1881: 5).

Although finding fault wherever possible, the *Inquirer* reviewer was quick to use Bernhardt's visit as a lever in his attack on the Chestnut Street Theatre management on behalf of Philadelphians embarrassed at the "slovenly state" of the theatre. Unlike Worcester, Philadelphia had not spruced up the theatre for the French visitors, who, the reviewer says, must feel as though they have "fallen into absolute barbarism ... everything is either old, shabby, dirty, tawdry, cheap and out of place; ... poverty shows itself in every chair and carpet and scene, and ... bad management advertises itself...." The setting for *Camille* was especially disappointing: "The furniture looked as if it had been hired for the occasion from a South street auction store; the scenery was faded and dirty, the properties of a former generation, and all signs of bad management, with poverty or sloth, being painfully apparent" (*Inquirer* 12 April 1881: 8; 13 April 1881: 8). These complaints, a repetition of those published in January, suggest that the management was determined to remain oblivious to the state of the theatre as long as profits continued.

Despite the uncomfortable venue and low attendance, the reviews for *Camille*, the second offering, were enthusiastic. The *Inquirer* made fun of the "strutters, posers and snivelers" who had previously undertaken to portray Marguerite as a passionate, fleshly woman, unchanged at the end by her love or by the prospect of death. What made Bernhardt popular was her transformation into "redeemed, ennobled, purified womanhood." Indeed, the description given of her interpretation as "the highest expression of humanity rescued from spiritual death through the death of the body" would seem to make an improper Lenten play into one appropriate to the season. The "small and exceedingly irresponsive audience" became carried away by a performance in the "most perfect mould" and "surrendered absolutely to her grace, tenderness, passion, sweetness, gentleness and charming expression of ennobled, beautified womanhood" (13 April 1881: 8).

Despite the positive reviews, the size of the audience seemed to galvanize both Bernhardt and Abbey. Unhappy about performing to empty seats, she may have fallen psychosomatically ill. In any case, Abbey, facing declining profits, decided to mend matters by granting a special interview on April 13 to the *Evening Bulletin*. On the heels of his announcement that Bernhardt had never been ill in the United States, only "tired and fatigued" (3), she abruptly walked off stage during that night's performance of *La Princesse Georges*. The doctor in the house, duly summoned, diagnosed a "congestive chill" and "inflammation of the lungs." On this occasion, the audience, having made the effort to attend the theatre, proved difficult to disperse. Even after everyone had been reimbursed, the manager had to eject a number of front-row occupants who stubbornly maintained that they could not leave until the end of the play, because the ladies' wraps had been checked. The next evening, April 14, Bernhardt appeared in front of a "cordial" audience displaying no hint of illness to mar her performance as Froufrou. Whatever turned the tide—Abbey's interview, rave reviews, or spectator curiosity—the audience was the largest and most fashionable of the week. Most of the newspapers, having commented on her performance in January, deliberately avoided full reviews. Even so, the *Inquirer* again took aim at the managers, pointing out that Bernhardt's "fire of genius and ... grace and finish of the highest art" was displayed against a backdrop of "sordid meanness of management which made a single rickety and faded suit of furniture do duty for the apartments in Paris and for those in Venice as well" (15 April 1881: 7). Of her final performances, *L'Étrangère* was least well received, not because of her acting but rather because "it was poor stuff in a dramatic sense" (16 April 1881: 3).

Although her stay in Philadelphia was again not the happiest, Abbey's interview with the *Bulletin* provided a thoughtful coda. He was described as "businesslike," and the readers were warned that they would get not sentiment but "facts" about the woman preparing to leave "bearing in her bosom golden sheaves worth not less than $200,000." Abbey described Bernhardt as never "out of temper once" and admirable in sticking to her contract; "cupidity is not her weakness"—her liking for spacious quarters had more to do with seeking inspiration, he said, than love of ostentation and profit. He spent some time attempting to clarify the record about their business agreement. Contrary to the common assumption that he paid all her expenses, he insisted that because her company was so large, he had contracted to provide only a specified portion each week. About her notorious spendthrift habits, he is critical. She is "too liberal," he said; "she will have what she fancies and wants other people to do the same."

One of Abbey's goals seemed to be to temper the reporter's assumptions about the trip's lucrative nature. Profit was not his main interest, he maintained, but rather doing "what was promised"—in the face of dire predictions that Bernhardt was too fragile to perform nightly, she was "as keen as a briar," despite months on the road. He provided details for the curious: the company traveled early in the morning, slept until eleven, ate breakfast, and then prepared to face that day's performance. Bernhardt had no "hangers-on," Abbey declared irritably, and denied both a "pet dog" and a "pet son": "By the way, what an outrage that story is! She has no son with her, and has had none with her, and she has too much sense to carry a poodle with her." In the end, the ever-practical Abbey portrayed her "a business woman, on a business trip.... She has a fund of common sense which would be a fortune to some of our advertising people. She came with an end in view—artistic repute and money" (*Bulletin* 13 April 1881:3).

It was, indeed, as a successful businessman that he spoke. A detailed account of his financial deal with Bernhardt was published in the *New York Sun* on 25 November 1880 (3). Abbey, bidding against Theodore Moss of Wallack's Theatre and T. Henry French, as well as theatre manager Stetson and others, agreed to guarantee Bernhardt's American success by depositing a trust fund of $50,000 in Paris, five times her average yearly earnings. With considerably less in hand, he persuaded out-of-town managers to put their share in a similar New York fund and thus achieved liquidity. Other deals attributed to him included a $10,000 cash advance from Weber and Rullman for exclusive rights to theatre librettos, with one-third going to Bernhardt; and at least $1500 from Sarony, who by November had more than recouped what he had paid for rights to Bernhardt's photographs. Some claimed that Abbey took a cut from the speculators: choice orchestra seats were available only at selected hotel stands—the Fifth Avenue Hotel, for instance, where the broker Tyson cleared $1500 the first week. Most of the objections, however, seemed to come from those who were unable to share in the earnings generated by the popular actress.

The complaint about her personally profiting at the expense of her audiences, heard loudly in New York when Bernhardt debuted in November, was muted in April, when her reputation as a successful businesswoman was accepted as a matter of course. Also as a matter of course, however, New Yorkers had followed particulars of her receipts in the major cities, and they read about her graciousness and charm. Perhaps reports like those from Niagara, where she was pictured as an appreciative spectator and pleasant guest—"She is thankful for any attention shown her, and expresses herself, although in poor English, in a most agreeable manner" (*New York Times* 21 March 1881: 5)—contributed to her diva's welcome in

New York. Despite local performances by other popular groups on April 18, the house at Booth's was said to be "immense" by the *New York Times*.

Reviewers, inclined on her second visit to deal with matters other than scandal and profit, published farewell assessments as well as serious commentaries on her new offering, Dumas's *La Princesse Georges*. New Yorkers spoke more strongly than their Philadelphia counterparts about this work which, "richly spiced with immorality," came from an author so entranced by his theories that his "wit ... carried him into paradox and artificiality," as both the *Mirror* and *Times* complained (23 April 1881: 2; 19 April 1881: 4). The *Sun* likewise objected to Dumas's "hazardous freedom of idea and expression," shocking even those "hardened to ... robust indecency." The playwright was applauded by the *Times*, however, for his compassionate viewpoint toward women, despite the immorality of the plot. The *Graphic* went a step further and combined the arguments, insisting more philosophically that the important point "is not a law of sexes, but of absolute right. Evil is individual, not masculine, feminine or neuter ..." (18 April 1881: 364).

Despite these caveats, The *Times* uniformly praised Bernhardt's "flexible, polished, and womanly talent" and agreed with the Worcester reviewer about her acting in *Camille*: unlike others—Clara Morris, for instance—Bernhardt was a realist who succeeded in "elevat[ing] the character to her own taste" (19 April 1881: 4). Similarly, the *Graphic* appreciated Bernhardt's delicacy of interpretation, arguing against those who called for a more passionate approach: "true acting is a rounded whole and not a series of loud weepings and wailings and gnashing of teeth" (18 April 1881: 364). One sour note was sounded by the *New York Mirror*, whose reviewer called her performance a "colorless, even display of mediocre acting that was tedious." Her travels had weakened her emotionally and physically: "an interminable bore," she was "thoroughly fagged out ... and thinner" (23 April 1881: 2). Apparently, Marie Colombier suffered from the opposite complaint. The *Graphic* reporter found her "alarmingly generous in anatomical display. Gentlemen smiled disguisedly at this prominent feature of the performance, while the ladies wondered where it all came from" (18 April 1881: 364).

To be sure, other problems and peevish comments bubbled up through the serene and successful surface of her final New York appearances. Jeanne Bernhardt also came in for her share of unwelcome notoriety when a hypnotic session went awry. The effort—perhaps an attempt to control her addiction to morphine—failed: Bernhardt herself, reputedly "so magnetic that it is impossible to mesmerize her," failed to show up to observe the session at the Clarendon Hotel. Jeanne succumbed, but to hysterics rather than to mesmerism, and Professor E. B. Jennings abandoned the attempt

(*Philadelphia Evening Bulletin* 23 April 1881: 3). Furthermore, Bernhardt and Abbey were jointly vilified, one as the "great French Humbug" who had tricked audiences into "fall[ing] prey to an actress's unsubstantial newspaper notoriety," the other as a poor manager who had made Booth's unpopular and uncomfortable for the audiences. The speculators, too, were outraged, as their business suddenly turned unprofitable; the *Mirror* complained that most took a two-thirds cut on tickets to *Adrienne Lecouvreur* in order to salvage their investment (7 May 1881: 7).

These remarks were, however, muted compared with the cacophony that had occurred during her November debut. Her remaining performances were accorded notices or brief reviews, and the audiences were uniformly large and warm. The final assessment was that her acting was polished and realistic, and she was praised for spiritualizing the heroines, irrespective of their moral or social stature. By this time, too, audiences had become tutored in understanding the delicate nuances of her acting, so that they no longer demanded that she "rant and rave and 'slop over,'" as the *Daily Graphic* put it (22 April 1881: 389). New Yorkers joined with audiences in Chicago, New Orleans, and Boston, in disliking *L'Étrangère*: it was "tedious" and "worthless," the *Times* complained, and the main character, Mrs. Clarkson, was "like one of Dryden's bombastic heroines—big with purpose and small with meaning" (28 April 1881: 5). The *Sun* went further, echoing some of the naïve comments from midwestern critics: the play, offensive to "wholesome-minded people," is tolerable only because the French tongue provides the "thin ice ... that conceals the slough of offence beneath" (28 April 1881: 3).

Bernhardt's fellow actors had no such complaints about the special matinée of *La Princesse Georges* that she gave to honor them on Thursday, April 21, before her evening performance of *Froufrou*. The afternoon was a resounding success, although such performances had developed a questionable reputation: when receipts were low, "professional matinées" of Rice and Neunnemacher's *Pirates of Penzance* and Steele Mackaye's *Hazel Kirke*, for instance, had been opened to customers who flocked to see the well-known actors in the audience. In Bernhardt's case, however, no seats were sold—all were given to members of the profession or friends, who were seated on a first-come, first-served basis and who "rapturously greeted ... and frequently applauded" Bernhardt in her role as Severine (*Clipper* 30 April 1881: 4, 6). *Puck*, whose squibs and cartoons Bernhardt detested, congratulated Abbey (as did the ordinarily acidic *Mirror*) for handling the performance in a professional manner, instead of as a ploy to attract customers. *Puck*'s approval was short-lived, however: a week later, it complained about Abbey, noting that given the amount of Bernhardt's earnings, she was "admirably managed," and the public should be thanked as well (27 April 1881: 131; 4 May 1881).

After her hegira through the Midwest and return appearances on the East Coast, Bernhardt was visibly happy to have completed her tour and ready to return home. She gratefully and publicly thanked her professional supporters: her note to Marcus Mayer, Abbey's agent, was reprinted in the *New York Mirror*. As the author of "The Usher," the dramatic column, whimsically claimed, "the epistle bears Sara's arms—a rampant pair of hairpins":

> Mon Cher Monsieur Marcus Mayer :
> Avant de partir de la belle Amerique je viex vous remercier du devrousment [dévouement] que vois avez deploye dans notre long voyage. Grace a votre zele je ne me suis pas aperçu de la riguer de l'hiver ni de la longuer du voyage.
> Merci donc et au revoir.

With grace, then, Bernhardt bid farewell to those who had arranged her trip, expressing appreciation for their devotion and energy in so smoothing the way on her journey that she felt neither the severity of the winter nor the length of the voyage.

The large crowd that gathered early at Morton Street to see her aboard *L'Amérique* was kept waiting until the last moments; Jeanne arrived shortly after nine, and Bernhardt a quarter of an hour later. The *Times* published the fullest account, and other newspapers, like the *Graphic*, filled in details. "[A]s she did not have the physical strength of a President of the United States," the *Times* wryly commented, she shook only a few hands and hurried on board, directly to the saloon, which was festooned with flowers. There, she spoke to the Transatlantic Lines agent Louis de Bebian and accepted a number of impressive floral tributes: "Two representing full rigged ships, composed of the rarest and most fragrant flowers, were each three feet in length by four in height," and another, in the shape of a sunshade, was fashioned from leaves, roses, and mignonettes (*Graphic* 4 May 1881: 482; *Sun* 5 May 1881: 3). When she saw the crowd around her reaching for papers and card cases, she avoided signing autographs by retreating to her dressing room. She was followed by the *Times* reporter, whose greeting in French evoked a flood of native Parisian. She intended, she told him, to play in English and to see San Francisco on her next tour, and she murmured gently about her fans' demands:

> I hid myself on purpose; they have come out of curiosity, and to get me to write my autograph in their albums and pocket-books. Wherever I go every other person asks me for my autograph, and

it is quite a bother to keep writing my name over and over again, much as I like to please them.

According to the *Sun*, although she did not like the fatigue of traveling, she thought the Americans were "generous and open-hearted. They have treated me splendidly. How can I help liking them?" (5 May 1881: 3).

After the warning bell, she joined her sister on the hurricane deck, a fashionable figure in mauve plaid dress, cream coat, silver belt, and gold Gainsborough hat trimmed in purple and yellow (according to the less fashion-savvy *Sun* reporter, she was wearing a straw "poke bonnet"). There she waved her handkerchief at the crowds, unaware of the comments the *Times* reporter purportedly overheard: "'Aint she horrid looking,' remarked one [lady] to her companions. 'She's a perfect fright,' added another. 'And how she is painted up,' broke in a third, on whose own fair face the bloom of art was radiant" (5 May 1881: 3, 8). After *L'Amérique* weighed anchor at 10:12 A.M., it was followed for some distance by a tugboat, whose passengers were members of the New York acting profession escorting their French sister out of the harbor.

As she grew closer to home and to her son, she forgot that she was an actress. At Le Havre, she saw a tugboat coming to meet her, with sixteen-year-old Maurice on board:

> She trembled ... turned paler than ever, cried, waived [sic] her arms, ran from one part of the vessel to another, shouted out his name time and again, and would, in all probability, have sprung into the sea, had not the ever-faithful Claude been by to prevent her. Finally the two boats were lashed together, and the son was soon enfolded in his mother's arms. It was a touching sight. No acting now [*Times* 31 May 1881: 5].

Bernhardt, nearly bankrupt when she left France in October 1880, had returned with considerably more earnings and stature than either she or her managers had expected. As Abbey had said, she was interested in "artistic repute," and that is precisely what she gained. No longer the ugly child in the ill-fitting, poorly dyed silk; no longer the uncertain actress, whose stage-fright left her weeping with frustration in her dressing room; no longer the grisette, making a name for herself in the theatrical demimonde—rather, a vivacious actress, a talented artist, and a shrewd businesswoman,

Opposite: Self-portrait in marble. Photograph of sculpture by Sarah Bernhardt. Harry Ransom Humanities Research Center, the University of Texas at Austin.

confronting and overcoming the New World's skepticism and chauvinism. One might argue that her success was a permutation of the world's oldest profession, in which she was trained by her mother; to succeed, Bernhardt, with the help of her agents, had to sell herself, her costumes, her jewelry, her mannerisms—her lifestyle, in short. Yet while doing so, she was also learning to act in the hardest school of all. Performing in a language foreign to her audience, she nonetheless learned to convey the emotions, the plot, the very rationale of her plays, and all that to an audience accustomed to sensational effects rather than realistic acting. She also faced the clamor of a public unused to Continental standards, so although they expected immorality, they were vocal about not countenancing it. What surprised them was the sharp wit, business shrewdness, and imagination of a sophisticated Frenchwoman determined to be a success, *quand même*. Before the stuffy social set in New York, the theatrically naïve of the small towns, and the bigoted moralists in the pulpit, Bernhardt brought her paintings and sculpture, her acting and directing. Ultimately she was judged by theatrical standards, and despite the reviewers' self-conscious attempts to create a critical climate so as not to be swept away by either her charm or elitist appeal, they could not help, even in their criticism, to pay homage to *la Liberté*.

Appendix I.
Plays Performed in
the United States, 1880–1881

Adrienne Lecouvreur (1849)—Augustin Eugène Scribe and Ernest Legouvé
La Dame aux Camélias [Camille] (1852)—Alexandre Dumas fils
L'Étrangère Alexandre (1876)—Alexandre Dumas fils
Froufrou (1869)—Henri Meilhac and Ludovic Halévy
Hernani (1830)—Victor Hugo
Le Passant (1869)—François Coppée
Phèdre (1677)—Jean Baptiste Racine
La Princesse Georges (1871)—Alexandre Dumas fils
Le Sphinx (1874)—Octave Feuillet

Appendix II. Bernhardt's Traveling Art Show

The following list is taken from the *Sarah Bernhardt Souvenir, Including the Authorized Catalogue of Her Paintings and Sculpture* (Harvard Theatre Collection, Houghton Library).

Paintings

"Retour à la Maison" (*Returning Home*)
"Parisienne" (*Parisian*)
"Incroyable" (*Dandy*)
"Petite Bretonne Assise" (*Little Breton Girl Seated*)
"Petite Bretonne Debout" (*Little Breton Girl Standing*)
"Jeune Fille et la Mort" (*Young Girl and Death*)
"Femme au Bord de la Mer" (*Woman on the Sea-shore*)
"Au Theatre" (*At the Theatre*)
"Espagnole au Repos" (*Spanish Girl Reposing*)
"Le Modele" (*The Model*)
"Perroquets" (*Parrots*)
"Jeune Fille et Garçon" (*Young Girl and Boy*)
"Vase de Fleurs" (*Vase of Flowers*)
"Marine" (*Sea View*)
"Jeune Fille" (*Young Girl*)

Sculpture

Buste de M. de Girardin (Bronze)
"Primavera" (Marble)
"Encrier Fantastique" (Bronze)
Statuette de Sarah Bernhardt (Marble)
Buste de Regina Bernhardt (Marble)
"Ophelie" (Marble)

Appendix III.
Performance Chronology

Date	Place	Venue	Performance
8 November (Monday)	New York	Booth's Theatre	*Adrienne Lecouvreur*
9 November (Tuesday)	New York	Booth's	*Adrienne Lecouvreur*
10 November (Wednesday)	New York	Booth's	*Froufrou*
11 November (Thursday)	New York	Booth's	*Froufrou*
12 November (Friday)	New York	Booth's	*Froufrou*
13 November (Saturday)	New York	Booth's	*Adrienne Lecouvreur*
14 November (Sunday)			
15 November (Monday)	New York	Booth's	*Camille*
16 November (Tuesday)	New York	Booth's	*Camille*
17 November (Wednesday)	New York	Booth's	*Camille*
18 November (Thursday)	New York	Booth's	*Hernani*
19 November (Friday)	New York	Booth's	*Hernani*
20 November (Saturday)	New York	Booth's	*Froufrou*
21 November (Sunday)			
22 November (Monday)	New York	Booth's	*Froufrou*
23 November (Tuesday)	New York	Booth's	*Phèdre*
24 November (Wednesday)	New York	Booth's	*Camille*
25 November (Thursday)	New York	Booth's	*Le Sphinx*

Appendix III. Performance Chronology 179

Date	Place	Venue	Performance
26 November (Friday)	New York	Booth's	Le Sphinx
27 November (Saturday)	New York	Booth's	Camille
28 November (Sunday)			
29 November (Monday)	New York	Booth's	Hernani
30 November (Tuesday)	New York	Booth's	Froufrou
1 December (Wednesday)	New York	Booth's	Camille
2 December (Thursday)	New York	Booth's	Phèdre
3 December (Friday)	New York	Booth's	Le Sphinx
4 December (Saturday)	New York	Booth's	Hernani (two performances)
5 December (Sunday)			
6 December (Monday)	Boston	Globe Theatre	Hernani
7 December (Tuesday)	Boston	Globe	Froufrou
8 December (Wednesday)	Boston	Globe	Adrienne Lecouvreur
9 December (Thursday)	Boston	Globe	Le Sphinx
10 December (Friday)	Boston	Globe	Phèdre
11 December (Saturday)	Boston	Globe	Froufrou
12 December (Sunday)			
13 December (Monday)	Boston	Globe	Camille
14 December (Tuesday)	Boston	Globe	Froufrou
15 December (Wednesday)	Boston	Globe	Camille
16 December (Thursday)	Boston	Globe	Adrienne Lecouvreur
17 December (Friday)	Boston	Globe	Camille
18 December (Saturday)	Boston	Globe	Camille; Froufrou and Adrienne Lecouvreur (selections), and Le Passant
19 December (Sunday)			
20 December (Monday)	New Haven	Carll's Opera House	Camille
21 December (Tuesday)	Hartford	Roberts's Opera House	Froufrou
22 December (Wednesday)	Burlington		(cancelled)

Appendix III. Performance Chronology

Date	Place	Venue	Performance
23 December (Thursday)	Montreal	Academy of Music	*Adrienne Lecouvreur*
24 December (Friday)	Montreal	Academy of Music	*Froufrou*
25 December (Saturday)	Montreal	Academy of Music	*La Dame aux Camélias* (matinée); *Hernani*
	Springfield(?)		
26 December (Sunday)	Springfield(?)		
27 December (Monday)	New York (visit)		
28 December (Tuesday)	Wilmington	Grand Opera House, Masonic Temple	*Camille* (cancelled)
29 December (Wednesday)	Baltimore	Academy of Music	*Adrienne Lecouvreur*
30 December (Thursday)	Baltimore	Academy of Music	*Froufrou*
31 December (Friday)	Baltimore	Academy of Music	*Camille*
1 January (Saturday)	Baltimore	Academy of Music	*Camille* (matinée)
2 January (Sunday)			
3 January (Monday)	Philadelphia	Chestnut Street Theatre	*Phèdre* (replacement for *Adrienne Lecouvreur*)
4 January (Tuesday)	Philadelphia	Chestnut Street	*Froufrou*
5 January (Wednesday)	Philadelphia	Chestnut Street	*Camille*
6 January (Thursday)	Philadelphia	Chestnut Street	*Hernani*
7 January (Friday)	Philadelphia	Chestnut Street	*Le Sphinx*
8 January (Saturday)	Philadelphia	Chestnut Street	*Camille* (matinée); *Froufrou*
9 January (Sunday)			
10 January (Monday)	Chicago	McVicker's Theatre	*Adrienne Lecouvreur*
11 January (Tuesday)	Chicago	McVicker's	*Froufrou*
12 January (Wednesday)	Chicago	McVicker's	*Le Sphinx*; *Le Passant*
13 January (Thursday)	Chicago	McVicker's	*Camille*

Appendix III. Performance Chronology

Date	Place	Venue	Performance
14 January (Friday)	Chicago	McVicker's	*Phèdre*
15 January (Saturday)	Chicago	McVicker's	*Froufrou*; Benefit for George Carpenter
16 January (Sunday)	Chicago	McVicker's	
17 January (Monday)	Chicago	McVicker's	*Camille*
18 January (Tuesday)	Chicago	McVicker's	*L'Étrangère*
19 January (Wednesday)	Chicago	McVicker's	*Froufrou*
20 January (Thursday)	Chicago	McVicker's	*Hernani*
21 January (Friday)	Chicago	McVicker's	*Froufrou*
22 January (Saturday)	Chicago	McVicker's	*Camille*
23 January (Sunday)			
24 January (Monday)	St. Louis	Grand Opera House	*Froufrou*
25 January (Tuesday)	St. Louis	Grand	*Le Sphinx* (matinée); *Le Passant*
26 January (Wednesday)	St. Louis	Grand	*Camille*
27 January (Thursday)	St. Louis	Grand	*Adrienne Lecouvreur*
28 January (Friday)	St. Louis	Grand	*Hernani*
29 January (Saturday)	St. Louis	Grand	*Camille* (matinée); *Froufrou*
30 January (Sunday)			
31 January (Monday)	Cincinnati	Pike's Opera House	*Adrienne Lecouvreur*
1 February (Tuesday)	Cincinnati	Pike's	*Camille*
2 February (Wednesday)	Cincinnati	Pike's	*Froufrou*
3 February (Thursday)	Cincinnati	Pike's	*Camille* (matinée); *Hernani*
4 February (Friday)			
5 February (Saturday)			
6 February (Sunday)	New Orleans	Grand Opera House	*Froufrou*
7 February (Monday)	New Orleans	Grand	*Phèdre*
8 February (Tuesday)	New Orleans	Grand	*Camille*
9 February (Wednesday)	New Orleans	Grand	*Hernani*

Appendix III. Performance Chronology

Date	Place	Venue	Performance
10 February (Thursday)	New Orleans	Grand	*Le Sphinx* (matinée); *Le Passant*
11 February (Friday)	New Orleans	Grand	*L'Étrangère* (cancelled)
12 February (Saturday)	New Orleans	Grand	*Camille* (matinée); *Froufrou*
13 February (Sunday)	New Orleans	Grand	*Adrienne Lecouvreur*
14 February (Monday)	Mobile	(cancelled—late arrival)	
15 February (Tuesday)	Mobile		*Camille* (cancelled)
16 February (Wednesday)	Atlanta	DeGive's Opera House	*Camille*
17 February (Thursday)	Nashville	Masonic Theater	*Camille*
18 February (Friday)	Memphis	Leubrie's Theatre	*Froufrou*
19 February (Saturday)	Memphis	Leubrie's	*Camille* (matinée); *Adrienne Lecouvreur*
20 February (Sunday)			
21 February (Monday)	Louisville	Macauley's Theatre	*Froufrou*
22 February (Tuesday)	Louisville	Macauley's	*Camille*
23 February (Wednesday)	Cincinnati		
24 February (Thursday)	Columbus	Comstock's Opera House	*Camille*
25 February (Friday)	Dayton	Music Hall	*Froufrou*
26 February (Saturday)	Indianapolis	Park Theatre	*Froufrou* (matinée); *Camille*
27 February (Sunday)			
28 February (Monday)	St. Joseph	Tootle's Opera House	*Froufrou*
1 March (Tuesday)	St. Joseph	Tootle's	*Camille*
2 March (Wednesday)	Leavenworth	Opera House	*Camille*
3 March (Thursday)	Quincy	Opera House	*Camille*
4 March (Friday)	Springfield	Opera House	*Camille*
5 March (Saturday)	Milwaukee	Academy of Music	*Camille* (matinée); *Froufrou*

Appendix III. Performance Chronology

Date	Place	Venue	Performance
6 March (Sunday)			
7 March (Monday)			
8 March (Tuesday)	Detroit	Whitney's Grand Opera House	*Froufrou*
9 March (Wednesday)	Detroit	Whitney's	*Camille*
10 March (Thursday)	Toledo	Wheeler's	*Camille*
11 March (Friday)	Cleveland	Euclid Avenue Opera House	*Froufrou*
12 March (Saturday)	Cleveland	Euclid Avenue	*Camille* (matinée); *Adrienne Lecouvreur*
13 March (Sunday)			
14 March (Monday)	Pittsburgh	Opera House	*Froufrou*
15 March (Tuesday)	Pittsburgh	Opera House	*Camille*
16 March (Wednesday)	Titusville	Opera House	*Camille*
17 March (Thursday)	Bradford	Opera House	*Camille* (?)
18 March (Friday)	Erie	Park Opera House	*Camille*
19 March (Saturday)	Toronto	Grand Opera House	*Camille* (matinée); *Froufrou*
20 March (Sunday)	Niagara Falls		
21 March (Monday)	Buffalo	Academy of Music	*Camille*
22 March (Tuesday)	Rochester	Grand Opera House	*Camille*
23 March (Wednesday)	Syracuse		*Camille* (?)
24 March (Thursday)	Syracuse		?
25 March (Friday)	Albany	Leland Opera House	*Froufrou*
26 March (Saturday)	Albany	Leland	*Camille* (matinée)
	Troy	Rand's Hall	?
27 March (Sunday)			
28 March (Monday)	Boston	Boston Theatre	*Camille*
29 March (Tuesday)	Boston	Boston	*L'Étrangère*
30 March (Wednesday)	Boston	Boston	*Froufrou*

184   Appendix III. Performance Chronology

Date	Place	Venue	Performance
31 March (Thursday)	Boston	Boston	Hernani (replacement for La Princesse Georges)
1 April (Friday)	Boston	Boston	Adrienne Lecouvreur
2 April (Saturday)	Boston	Boston	Camille (matinée); Adrienne Lecouvreur
3 April (Sunday)			
4 April (Monday)	Worcester	?	Camille
5 April (Tuesday)	Fall River		(cancelled)
6 April (Wednesday)	Providence	Low's Opera House	Camille
7 April (Thursday)	Newark	Park Theatre	Camille
8 April (Friday)	Washington	National Theatre	Froufrou
9 April (Saturday)	Washington Baltimore	National Academy of Music	Camille (matinée) Camille
10 April (Sunday)			
11 April (Monday)	Philadelphia	Chestnut Street Theatre	Adrienne Lecouvreur
12 April (Tuesday)	Philadelphia	Chestnut Street	Camille
13 April (Wednesday)	Philadelphia	Chestnut Street	La Princesse Georges (cancelled)
14 April (Thursday)	Philadelphia	Chestnut Street	Froufrou
15 April (Friday)	Philadelphia	Chestnut Street	L'Étrangère
16 April (Saturday)	Philadelphia	Chestnut Street	Camille; Froufrou
17 April (Sunday)			
18 April (Monday)	New York	Booth's Theatre	La Princesse Georges
19 April (Tuesday)	New York	Booth's	Camille
20 April (Wednesday)	New York	Booth's	Hernani
21 April (Thursday)	New York	Booth's	La Princesse Georges (benefit); Froufrou
22 April (Friday)	New York	Booth's	Adrienne Lecouvreur
23 April (Saturday)	New York	Booth's	Camille
24 April (Sunday)	New York		
25 April (Monday)	New York	Booth's	La Princesse Georges

Appendix III. Performance Chronology

Date	Place	Venue	Performance
26 April (Tuesday)	New York	Booth's	Camille
27 April (Wednesday)	New York	Booth's	L'Étrangère
28 April (Thursday)	New York	Booth's	Froufrou
29 April (Friday)	New York	Booth's	Camille
30 April (Saturday)	New York	Booth's	Froufrou
	Brooklyn	Academy of Music	Froufrou
1 May (Sunday)			
2 May (Monday)	New York	Booth's Theatre	Benefit

Notes

Introduction

1. Bernhardt's father has not been identified. Two possibilities are commonly reported: either "a highborn naval officer named Morel or a brilliant young law student named [Edouard] Bernhardt," who posed as her uncle (Gold and Fizdale 11; Skinner 2). According to Basil Woon, Bernhardt's family name was Paul de Thérard; as Woon says, the young man's penchant for "*l'adventure amoureuse*" made him "one of the wildest youngsters in the Latin Quarter" (42–43).

2. These and other well-known details from Bernhardt's life may be found in both Cornelia Otis Skinner's *Madame Sarah* and Arthur Gold and Robert Fizdale's *The Divine Sarah*.

3. Bakhtin, whose model of carnivalization is helpful in understanding Bernhardt's cultural impact and American responses to her, suggests that pageantry and ritual are earmarks of a transformative change. In his model, social laws are suspended to allow "free and familiar contact among people"; "profanation," parodies, "blasphemies," or "debasings" abound; and, finally, the result is "universal" and "joyous laughter" that speaks of new beginnings" (*Problems* 122-3).

4. For Bakhtin, "heteroglossia" is a specialized term, referring in part to the multi-voiced nature of a work that presents both "the direct intention of the character who is speaking, and the refracted intention of the author," and also the "oppositions ... [that] are submerged in social heteroglossia, ... surface upheavals of the untamed elements ... that play *on* such individual oppositions" ("Forms of Time" 324-6). In other words, in a fictional situation, many levels of discourse occur at once, their conflicting messages representing not simply a logical or linguistic opposition but rather a conflict of forces. The displacement of a customary, single mode of discourse for a new, multiple one disrupts ordinary modes of thought and behavior and forces reassessment of assumptions. Just as French words and new tonal values invaded linguistic understanding, so Bernhardt invaded the American consciousness.

5. Given her lifestyle and achievements, Bernhardt would likely have agreed with

Julia Kristeva that women are allied with the "explosion of social codes" and with revolution (qtd. in Jones 363).

6. These ideals are discussed by Barbara Welter in *Dimity Convictions*.

Chapter 1

1. Henry Eugene Abbey's sponsorship of Bernhardt gained him the sobriquet "Napoleon of managers." He managed a number of theaters, including the Park (in New York, Boston, and Philadelphia), Booth's, Wallack's, the Grand Opera House, and the Metropolitan Opera House, where he introduced such operatic notables as Lilli Lehmann, the famous German Wagnerian soprano; Emma Eames, the American lyric soprano, known for the "singularly pure and beautiful quality" of her voice; and Emma Calvé, the French soprano, whose rendering of Carmen made her famous ("Lehmann"; "Eames"; "Calvé"). Despite the financial risks, Abbey brought well-known operatic and theatrical performers to smaller towns across the United States, expanding their performance venues outside of major cities. A full discussion of his life and theatrical management are available in an unpublished dissertation by Richard Hossalla. The agent Henry C. Jarrett is sometimes confused with the theatrical manager of the same name; Jarrett the manager, who died on 15 October 1903, initiated the "system of traveling combinations" and produced the spectacle *The Black Crook*, thereby beginning the modern musical ("Jarrett"; *New York Times* 16 Oct. 1903: 7; *London Times* 19 Oct. 1903: 9). Bernhardt's business agent, referred to as "Edward Jarrett" in Skinner and in Gold and Fizdale, accompanied Bernhardt on her 1886 South American tour; ill with a throat disease, he died in Buenos Aires on 2 August 1886 (*New York Times* 12 Aug. 1886: 8).

2. The Swedish operatic star Christine Nilsson made her debut in October 1864 in Paris and appeared as Elsa in *Lohengrin* in 1873–74 in the United States; she sang the title roles in a number of first performances, including *Mignon* at Drury Lane and *Mignon* and *Mephistofele* at the Metropolitan Opera House. Her last professional appearance in America was the 1882–1883 season. Marie Van Zandt, the daughter of the operatic singer Mme. Zanzini, was an American soprano, who, tutored in Europe, debuted in Mozart's *Don Giovanni* in Turin; in 1880 she signed a five-year contract with the Opéra-Comique, where she created the title role in Delibes's *Lakme* (1883). She debuted at the Metropolitan Opera House in 1891. Pauline Lucca, an Austrian *mezzo soprano*, was contracted to the Berlin Opera House before she came to New York, where she received high praise for her 1872 debut at the Academy of Music ("Nilsson"; "Van Zandt"; "Lucca").

3. Cornelia Otis Skinner's *Madame Sarah* and Arthur Gold and Robert Fizdale's *The Divine Sarah* give an account of this time period without providing background for the anti–Semitism that surfaced. Gold and Fizdale quote without a source a letter that warns her to keep her "horrible Jewish nose" away from the Molière celebration lest she be pelted with potatoes (155). See my Chapter Two for an examination of the way in which anti–Semitic attitudes shaped the American response to Bernhardt. A 1971 unpublished dissertation by Richard Gordon Smith on the factors in Bernhardt's success in America gives a host of details about the 1880–1881 New York critical response, but omits her experiences in other cities; he also provides popular assessments of her hair, figure, and voice, but does not explore the anti–Semitic innuendoes in the press.

4. These actresses were all successful Englishwomen, who, nominally under the management of impresarios, had a substantial say in arranging their performances and

handling their finances during their American tours. Ellen Terry was one of these: resoundingly popular in Shakespearean and classical drama, she publicly declared her enjoyment of Shaw and dislike for Ibsen ("Ellen Terry"). Geneviève Ward was another: she began her career under her own name—Ginevra Guerrabella—as an opera singer and then achieved an international reputation in Herman Merivale and F. C. Grove's *Forget-Me-Not* ("Geneviève Ward"). The others faced public outcries because, like Bernhardt, they performed "fallen women." The *New York Dramatic Mirror* called the much-loved Madge Kendall "crude, noisy, and vulgar" when she appeared in Arthur Wing Pinero's *The Second Mrs. Tanqueray*, and Lillie Langtry was taken to task for playing a "fast" society woman in *The Degenerates* ("Madge Kendall"; "Lillie Langtry"). Nethersole was made party to a lawsuit against Clyde Fitch's *Sapho*, which opened 5 Feb. 1900. She eventually published "Sex Dramas To Day and Yesterday" in *Green Book* magazine, a manifesto in favor of openness on the stage:

> We are learning through [the "white-slave-plays"] and the frank language employed in them, that sex questions are not immoral, that the stage is the place to speak the truth, show the truth, and rid ourselves of the hypocritical opinion of the past that there are certain things better left unsaid, that there are certain cess-pools which it would be better to leave covered, and that women, particularly, should not enter into a discussion of these things ["Olga Nethersole"].

5. As Bernhardt's stature as actress increased and she moved more confidently from the easygoing courtesan culture of her mother's house into the demimonde of the professional actress, Marie Colombier moved from intimate confidante to scandal-monger. Her burlesque *Les Mémoires de Sarah Barnum* (1883) infuriated Bernhardt, as did her earlier *Les Voyages de Sarah Bernhardt en Amérique*, which appeared before Bernhardt could capitalize on her own memoirs. Angelo, as supporting actor, received uniformly tepid reviews in the United States; Jeanne, who joined the company in New York, was praised by the press for her beauty.

6. In Lysiane's account of the incident, Bernhardt prevented the mother-to-be from leaping overboard and lectured her about the rewards of parenthood: "I, too, was afraid for [Maurice] and afraid that I should not be able to look after him. Then I decided to live for him, and my whole existence became beautiful and purposeful...." During the birth, Bernhardt was sickened by the noxious odors in the steerage. As the story goes, she cowed one of the passengers, "sniggering and imitating her, sniffing at a filthy piece of rag and screwing up his nose in disgust," into washing out a basket for the new baby. Lysiane ends with a touching scenario in which a woman appears as she is leaving and says, "'Ah! Madame Sarah Bernhardt! How they are going to love you in America....' And Sarah, utterly worn out with weariness and emotion, fell into the arms of an old lady who had helped to deliver the baby. It was Mrs. Abraham Lincoln" (Bernhardt, Lysiane 117–8).

7. *Chic*, an ephemeral comic paper that appeared in 1880, flourished for only a year. Its origins are obscure, but its brand of humor, plentiful line cuts, elaborate weekly lithograph, drama reviews, campaigns against political corruption, and topical commentary make it a fit predecessor of *Life* magazine, the much-admired "gentle satirist" that gave name, if not contents, to the modern periodical of the same title (Mott 3.267; and see, for instance, my "'Sal' Bernhardt and the Men About Town: Theatre Resources in *Chic*."). The longer-lived *Puck* began as a comic weekly published in German by Joseph Keppler, first in St. Louis and then in New York; the actor Sydney Rosenfeld became the first editor of the English version, which began publication in 14 March

1877. By 1880, Henry Cuyler Bunner was the editor, a post he held until 1896. The artist Joseph Keppler, who drew cartoons that were the equivalent of graphical fisticuffs in the campaign against political corruption, was joined by J. A. Wales and Frederick Opper. The very brashness and vigor of *Puck*'s crusades, both political and cultural, gave it a distinctively American cast (Mott 3.520–32).

8. In many American newspaper reports, French words and phrases are misspelled or otherwise incorrect. I have quoted these solecisms without correction; in some cases (not here) they are part of the satiric intent of the author. As early as August 7, the *New York Mirror* foresaw the language problem and claimed that "metropolitan critics go around with little yellow-covered 'French in Twenty-Minutes' books, and mutter such mysterious remarks as 'Nous avons de tres bon café et d'excellent the,' or 'L'enfant de la boulangerie est petit.' Alas, poor critics!" (7).

9. A fine description of spectacle and the issues connected with it—limelight vs. electric illumination, color massing, the relation between historical and scene painting, the role of the director and the critic in evaluating setting—occurs in Michael Booth's *Victorian Spectacular Theatre 1850-1910*.

10. What added to her distress was that the silk had been provided by Mr. Berentz, one of Bernhardt's early suitors. He and his father, both tanners, had supplied the family with oilcloth printed with "medallions representing the French kings"; there, Bernhardt writes, "I learned my history best" (*Memories* 67). Details about the son differ somewhat depending on the source. He was so in love that he was willing to forgo a dowry, offering to settle 500,000 francs on her if she agreed to marry him (Skinner 26); he was shy but ambitious, beginning to make his fortune by selling Passover cakes that he brought to Bernhardt at the convent (*Memories* 66); he had big ears and bad teeth (Woon 78); he had "black hairs sprout[ing] from his cheeks and chin, his nose and ears, and he had "hands ... like furry paws" (Gold and Fizdale 33). What is clear is that he was as desperately in love with Bernhardt as she was in love with acting.

11. Male members of the company mentioned in the article include M. Defossez, the stage manager and former manager of the Theatre Royal at The Hague; M. Gally, leading young man; M. Dorsey, the second leading gentleman; M. Chamounin, first comedian; M. Joliet, second comedian; M. Bouillot, first old man; M. Thefer, young walking gentleman; M. Gangloff, character man; M. Deletraz, young utility man; and M. Biron, general utility man. The female members were Mme. Deletraz, second leading lady; Mlle. Mea, first old lady; her daughter Mlle. Carpentier, soubrette; Mlle. Sidney (or Sydney), second leading lady; Mlle. Blanche Martel, general utility; Mlle. Lafleur, soubrette; Mlle. Joliet, prompter; and Jeanne Bageard, children's roles. Marie Colombier and Edouard Angelo, who followed with Bernhardt on the *L'Amérique*, were also listed.

12. Hossalla quotes the invitation as it was published in *The New York Dramatic Mirror*. He also recounts an anecdote about Abbey's lateness, which delayed the welcoming party by forty-five minutes (412–13).

13. The emphasis on her nose and hair suggest a concern about her Semitic background; see Chapter 2 for a fuller analysis. A measure of the disagreement about her attributes may be gleaned from the lengthy list of descriptions compiled from a host of newspapers and sent to the *Daily Graphic* by a contributor (3 Nov. 1880: 19). Part of the list is quoted here:

>Nose aquiline and prominent.—*Sun*
>The nose was strong yet delicate...—*Graphic*
>Teeth good but not regular.—*Sun*

Teeth two rows of pearls.—*Graphic*
The hair was a tawny gold, clustering caressingly over a bold and intellectual brow.—*Graphic*
This aerial hair stuck out at least a foot from under the back of a Gainsborough hat.—*Sun*
Petite actress.—*Graphic*
Somewhat above the average height.—*Post*
It (face) is very lovely, and more than lovely.—*Graphic*
Mille. Bernhardt is not a handsome woman, nor even a pretty woman.—*Poet*

14. One of the *Daily Graphic* reporters, who spoke French, records no mention in his extended conversation with Bernhardt of her experience of delivering a baby in steerage; indeed, as she says in his report, she scarcely left her room, and then only to be seasick in the English Channel. Discrepancies abound in these interviews, but they all testify to a variety of experiences influenced by whether the reporters spoke directly to Bernhardt or to Jarrett and the degree to which they believed her, their own preconceptions, or Jarrett's version of events, delivered with an eye to advertisement.

15. What Bernhardt complained about—the focus on externals like her accent, her costumes, and her thinness—was a way for the artists and journalists to understand her foreignness. In 1880 Bernhardt was already a practiced poseur, creating theater wherever she went, and the reporters, looking for "story," were an eager audience. In 1917, when she was seventy-three years old, the effect was different; the American public looked past the living caricature, a "ruined old woman, crippled, grown fat," and saw the legendary Bernhardt, who brought down the house playing the nineteen-year-old Joan of Arc (Kobler 65).

16. The presidential campaign was in full swing, with Republicans James A. Garfield and Chester A. Arthur running against Democrats Winfield Hancock and William H. English.

Chapter 2

1. Published details about the contract differ according to the source (see also Chapter 7). Hossalla agrees with Louis Verneuil that each performance yielded $1000, but says that her weekly expense account amounted to $200 and that she received fifty percent of the receipts over $4000 (410). The sporting magazine *Spirit of the Times* (Mott 2.203) offered inside knowledge about the offers in a tongue-in-cheek paragraph that parodied the characteristic tone of the managers: "Jim Meade tempted her with fifty per cent, and a half clear benefit, with a church choir concern on the off-nights. Stetson telegraphed that he would rent her the Globe Theatre, Boston, adding the attractive line, 'Come, here is another world for you to conquer, and I do all the posters at my own job office'" (qtd. in Hossalla 408). John Stetson, a blustery, aggressive impresario known for his malapropisms, managed theaters in Boston, including Howard Athenaeum, the Olympic, the Globe, and the Park; and in New York, including Booth's, Fifth Avenue, the Standard, and the Star. ("Stetson").

2. The *Spirit of the Times* gave a lively picture of the first-nighters that packed Booth's Theatre, over 3,000 strong:

> By 8 o'clock Twenty-third Street was so jammed with ticket-holders that the police were obliged to prevent the carriages from depositing any more people.

Ladies in elegant costumes were crushed in the crowd, and gentlemen in opera-hats counseled patience and called "Order!" Speculators in tickets, librettos, Lives of Bernhardt, were packed in with our best society. It was nearly nine o'clock before the front of the theatre was cleared of ticket-holders, and an outside throng of curious spectators remained there until after the performance... [qtd. in Hossalla 252].

3. Skinner (195), followed by Gold and Fizdale (188), incorrectly gives the caption as "The Jewish Danae" and a publication date in April 1881, during Bernhardt's farewell visit to New York.

4. The Union League Club was formed in 1863 to foster the Union Cause and to house a library, a display of trophies, and a gallery. In New York, it maintained two club houses, one at 26 East 17th Street and one at Madison Avenue and 26th Street; members engaged in a variety of causes, including sponsoring a Black regiment and contributing to the Sanitary Fair and to the Metropolitan Museum (Mooney).

5. Gustave Doré, who died two years after Bernhardt's first American tour, was both painter and sculptor; but it was as illustrator that he achieved fame, completing drawings for a long list of such diverse masterpieces as the Bible and *Don Quixote*. His collaboration with the British journalist Blanchard Jerrold produced *London: A Pilgrimage*, which vividly brought to life the disparities occasioned by rank and wealth (Chazal).

6. Louise Abbéma's first publicly acclaimed portrait was of Bernhardt in 1876; from there she went on to a career as a successful portraitist, attracting well-known theatrical and artistic personalities and private citizens as her subjects. She was strongly influenced by Japanese painting in the 1880s and was in much demand for her decorative work (Lobstein).

7. Georges Clairin, whose later Orientalist paintings were influenced by his association with the theatrical world, also gained fame for his large, decorative murals in public buildings such as the Paris Opéra (Rosenthal). Gold and Fizdale, who reproduce one of Clairin's sumptuous portraits of Bernhardt on the cover of their biography, comment that "no lady of the faubourg would have allowed herself to be pictured in such intimate attire or in so inviting a position" (135).

8. In an impartial way, Opper lampooned other stage figures in the drawing. Fanny Davenport lounges as a plump odalisque, Clara Morris walks a tightrope, and Rose Eytinge balances on an obelisk. These figures would have been well known to readers. Davenport debuted at Niblo's Garden in 1862 and joined Augustin Daly's Fifth Avenue Theatre Company five years later; eventually, she formed her own company and gave English-language premieres in America of Bernhardt's plays, including *Fédora* (1883), *La Tosca* (1888), *Cleopatra* (1890), and *Gismonda* (1894) ("Davenport"). Morris specialized in high emotions—she was called the "queen of spasms and the mistress of the tricks of the acting trade." She joined Daly's company in 1870, went on the road (performing *Camille* and other plays), and ended her career in vaudeville ("Morris"). Eytinge's 1852 debut was in Dion Boucicault's *Old Guard*; known as a temperamental actress in high comedy and tragedy, she worked with Lester Wallack's, Daly's, and A. M. Palmer's acting companies ("Eytinge").

9. Hector Rosenfeld, a contributor to *Puck*, produced the following:

> "Great heavens, what is this I see!"
> With terror-stricken voice he gasped,
> And sinking weeping on his knee,
> Her rigid hand in his he clasped.

> "O, dearest, thour't not dead, oh, say
>   Thou still dost live, my darling wife!"
> But stiff and motionless she lay
>   And gave no outward signs of life.
>
> He placed his hand upon her heart
>   And waited, breathless, for its beat;
> And see! What was it made him start,
>   In joyous rapture, to his feet?
>
> "Run for a doctor, quickly, fly
>   While yet a spark of life remains."
> But look, the figure winks its eye,
>   And with a laugh its feet regains.
>
> "O stop your shouting and your crying
>   You silly boy," exclaims the minx,
> "Why, can't you see that I was trying
>   To show you Sarah in 'The Sphynx?'"
>   [8 Dec. 1880: 224].

10. For everyone, translation posed difficulties. Bernhardt eventually became more adept in understanding and responding in English, but at the beginning of her tour, miscommunication was the rule. A *Clipper* reporter packages the rumors, the plays she performed in, and the impossibility of clear communication in one verse called "Gallic Echoes":

> I interviewed Sal at rehearsal
>   To query a number of things;
> I hoped she would pardon intrusion,
>   As actors, like riches, take wings;
> And, knowing I'd find her at three in—
>   She whispered politely: "Adrienne!"
>
> I told her I was a Bohemian,
>   Who "wrote up" the stage for his board,
> And came to report for The Clipper,
>   That made it a point to record
> Whatever to nature was drew true—
>   She dreamingly murmured: "Oui, Frou-Frou!"
>
> I asked if they kept her together
>   While posing in different parts,
> Because her slight frame like her acting,
>   Was made up of natural arts;
> And when on the stage she became ill—
>   She smilingly echoed: "Oui, Camille!"
>
> I then sought to know if she scuptured
>   And painted, or was it a dodge
> To hoodwink the newspaper critics,
>   Who said her work was but bodge,
> Exhibited merely to fete her—
>   Indignant, she answered: "Oui, Phedre!"
>
> I asked if she slept in a coffin,
>   Or rattled her bones in a bed;
> And whether she ever was married,
>   Or never had chosen to wed;

> And should she have time to learn Annie—
> She cut me off short with: "Hernani!"
>
> I wished her opinion of Gotham,
>   Our ladies, and babies, and men,
> The public, their money, and Abbey,
>   And how he should manage it when
> Her dresses caught in the west wings—
> She winked as she answered: "Oui, Le Spinx!"
>   [11 Dec. 1880: 302].

11. Rachel, the stage name of Élisa Félix, was a classical French tragedienne who debuted in Corneille's *Horace* with the Comédie Française in 1838. Like Bernhardt, she had a reputation for capriciousness; after years of disagreement with the Comédie Française over her freedom to accept personal contracts, in 1849 she moved to annul her contract as *sociétaire* and then had herself rehired as *pensionnaire*, a position that gave her a salary and 6 months' leave yearly in which to pursue other contracts. Her emotional presence and nuanced vocal expression made her internationally famous: she was called "an inspired natural performer, with an ability to give to the text a strong human quality and to make it sound as if it were being heard for the first time. She also had very clear diction, a sense of musical rhythms and an economy of gesture ..." ("Rachel").

12. J. Hudson Kirby, born in London, made his 1837 debut at Philadelphia's Walnut Street Theatre. He specialized in "blood and thunder" melodramas; it is said that "Kirby's scene-chewing technique gave rise to the expression 'wake me up when Kirby dies.'" The Bowry Theatre, whose pit persisted well into the 1860s, was known for its rowdy audiences. It opened in 1826 and burned for the final time in 1929. By the time Bernhardt arrived, it had been renamed the Thalia; located in a predominantly immigrant neighborhood, it staged plays in German and Yiddish ("Kirby").

13. Frederic Jaher discusses the anti–Semitism of the Populists in detail in "Were the Populists Anti–Semitic?" As he points out, the Populists saw the Jew as alien: "He lived in the city, usually did not perform ennobling manual labor, spoke a strange tongue, and dressed exotically" (80). These reservations might equally well be applied to Bernhardt.

14. Anthony Comstock began his career as moral guardian by shooting a rabid dog and then crusading against its owner, who traded in whisky, by breaking into his shop and smashing his stock of liquor bottles. Comstock, who joined the YMCA campaign against vice, was also influential in formulating 1873 legislation against mailing obscene materials. As one commentator said, "It is clear that he did not know how to distinguish between good art and bad, or indeed between art and morals." He pursued quacks and liberal thinkers like Victoria Woodhull with equal furor; he attacked the Art Students' League; and he began proceedings against George Bernard Shaw ("Comstock").

15. Roscoe Conkling, known as the great Republican "spread eagle" orator, had a long political career as a congressman, beginning in 1858. Known for his support of political patronage, he ran the New York Custom House along with Chester Arthur and Alonzo Cornell and insisted on his right to oversee federal administration in New York. Stymied by James Garfield over patronage, he resigned his congressional seat in May 1881 ("Conkling"). Henry Ward Beecher, whose career as a pulpit orator began in 1847 at the Brooklyn Heights Plymouth Congregational Church, was sued for adultery with the wife of Theodore Tilton, who followed him as editor of the *Independent* (Findlay).

Not all stories about cats had such overtones. Bernhardt was fond of animals, and so the anecdote about her "passionate affection for a cat of extremely ugly physique" which she had smuggled into the Albemarle may contain some truth. Frustrated at the hotel's refusal to deliver food for residents' pets, as the story goes, Bernhardt wrapped herself and the cat in a shawl and flew out the door to a butcher shop, where, because she could not make the owner understand French, she seized a knife and sawed away at a piece of meat. The *New York Sun* reporter, trying to track the story down, reports that the Albemarle desk clerk said, "'I give it up. She may have an orang-outang and a baby elephant, for all we care. She's the nicest guest that ever lived" (5 Dec. 1880: 5).

Chapter 3

1. The term "melting pot," anathema to some in the twentieth-century culture wars, was taken from Isreal Zangwill's play of the same name, in which a character named David Quixano exclaims, "America is God's Crucible, the great Melting-Pot where all the races of Europe are melting and re-forming!" (33). More recently, in a speech in Pittsburgh on 27 October 1976, President Jimmy Carter redefined the idea as "a beautiful mosaic. Different people, different beliefs, different yearnings, different hopes, different dreams."

2. *Chic*'s readers would be familiar with the references. Boston Common, originally a public pasturage, was, and is, an urban park. Faneuil Hall, a city landmark, became a public gathering place in 1842; here Bostonians planned the Revolutionary War. Plymouth Rock is assumed to be where the Pilgrims disembarked from the *Mayflower* in 1620 to establish the first permanent settlement.

3. According to the web site "Boston Online" (June 14, 2000. http://www.bostononline.com /faq.html#beantown),

> In colonial days, a favorite Boston food was beans baked in molasses for several hours. Back then, Boston was sort of awash in molasses—it was part of the "triangular trade" in which slaves in the Caribbean grew sugar cane to be shipped to Boston to be made into rum to be sent to West Africa to buy more slaves to send to the West Indies. Even after the end of this practice, Boston continued as big rum producing city—the Great Molasses Flood of 1919 (which killed 21), ocurred [sic] when a tank holding molasses for rum production exploded.
> Today, Boston baked beans are something of a rarity—there are no companies in the city making it and only a few restaurants serve it.

4. The "Autocrat" is an allusion to Oliver Wendell Holmes, whose essays, first published in *The Atlantic Monthly*, were collected as *The Autocrat of the Breakfast Table*. In the poem Bernhardt begs Abbey to cancel her tour in Boston, the cultural "Hub," even though she will be scolded by the popular Holmes, who is one of the Boston Brahmins.

5. As Francis Jehl reminisces, Bernhardt finds parallels between Edison and Napoleon: "I am sure that one compartment of their brains would be found to be identical. I do not compare their genius. One was destructive, and the other creative" (232).

6. According to Skinner, Bernhardt had scrawled the phrase "*Quand même*," which means "all the same" or "for all that," defiantly across her dressing room mirror during her disastrous *Comédie Française* debut in Jean Racine's *Iphigénie* (36–7). It became her motto, an expression of courage and determination to succeed in the face of great odds.

7. This obscure artist is described in Max Beerbohm's "Dandies and Dandies" in this way:

> How very delightful Grego's drawings are! For all their mad perspective and crude colour, they have indeed the sentiment of style, and they reveal, with surer delicacy than does any other record, the spirit of Mr. Brummell's day. Grego guides me, as Virgil Dante, through all the mysteries of that other world. He shows me those stiff-necked, over-hatted, wasp-waisted gentlemen, drinking Burgundy in the Café des Milles Colonnes or riding through the village of Newmarket upon their fat cobs or gambling at Crockford's. ... The formal way in which Mdlle. Mercandotti is standing upon one leg for the pleasure of Lord Fife and Mr. Ball Hughes; the grave regard directed by Lord Petersham towards that pretty little maid-a-mischief who is risking her rouge beneath the chandelier; the unbridled decorum of Mdlle. Hullin and the decorous debauchery of Prince Esterhazy in the distance, make altogether a quite enchanting picture [1].

8. Depending on the account, details differ. Skinner says, for instance, that Bernhardt asked Jarrett to set up the whale-walk and that he had arranged with a Mr. Gordon, a respectable Bostonian, to escort her on the adventure. Bernhardt, on the other hand, writes that Gordon had met them serendipitously at the hotel with his little daughter, who was eager to see the whale, and that he had asked her to drive the coach, thinking that doing so would distract her from her uncomfortable encounter with the whale (*Memoirs* 174–75).

9. An excerpt from Mrs. Moulton's account is reprinted in Gold and Fizdale (177–78), but the date is given incorrectly as January 1881; at that time Bernhardt would have been performing in Philadelphia, Chicago, and St. Louis. Skinner also retells the tale (173).

10. Bernhardt refers to Chang, "The Celebrated Chinese Giant." Eight feet in height, he was known as a kindly and generous man. After marrying Catherine Santley from Liverpool, he settled his family at Bournemouth, where he ran a bazaar and tea room; his home is now the site of the Ashleigh Hotel. He died in November 1893, four months after his wife ("The Gentle Giant"). The *Toronto Daily Mail* published a column about the prodigious appetite he displayed on tour in Brooklyn (21 March 1881: 6).

11. The hidden joke in the comment involves a pun about acting in Longfellow's "The Psalm of Life," which begins with the familiar lines "Tell me not in mournful numbers, / Life is but an empty dream!—." The poet goes on to exhort the reader to remember—

> Not enjoyment, and not sorrow,
> Is our destined end or way;
> But to act, that each to-morrow
> Find us farther than to-day.
>
> Art is long, and Time is fleeting,
> And our hearts, though stout and brave,
> Still, like muffled drums, are beating
> Funeral marches to the grave.
>
> ... Trust no Future, howe'er pleasant!
> Let the dead Past bury its dead!
> Act,—act in the living Present!
> Heart within, and God o'erhead!

12. Frederic Crowinshield was a Boston artist who had studied in London, Rome, and Paris. His studio was housed in the Boston Museum of Fine Arts, where he was a lecturer on anatomy and an instructor in painting and drawing. In 1886 he moved to New York; he became well known for his murals and stained glass which were installed in a number of locations, including the Waldorf and Manhattan hotels, and Harvard Memorial Hall ("Crowinshield").

13. The nervousness with which some of her visitors approached her at the art reception is illustrated by a tale about fractured French in *The Boston Journal*. A young man drilled himself in saying "Mademoiselle, j'ai l'honneur de vous salue." He assiduously studied the words, written on a little slip of paper; he practiced until he was letter perfect, addressing the statue of Benjamin Franklin, the state house, and his own astonished relatives. Despite his preparation he became speechless upon being presented to Bernhardt, and walking home crestfallen, he paused to speak to a statue of Washington: "'George, I have made an ass of myself.' In the dim moonlight of a leaden sky he thought he saw the horse whisk its tail, and from the brazen lips of the great captain came forth in thunder tones: 'J'ai l'gonneur de vous salue'" (rpt. in *The Chicago Times* 26 Dec. 1880: 2).

14. Adelaide Ristori, a prominent Italian tragedienne known for her grand style and impulsive outbreaks of emotion, rose to fame during Rachel's waning popularity. She appeared in the United States for the first time in 1866 and the last in 1884 and achieved renown for her performance in *Phèdre*. Fanny [Francesca] Janauschek, a Czechoslovakian tragedienne, debuted in New York in 1867, when she was already a well-known actress in Prague and Frankfurt; she was said to have a "statuesque figure, emotional power and vibrant but controlled voice." The Polish-born Mme. Modjeska emigrated to the United States in 1876, already a star; she debuted the next year in *Adrienne Lecouvreur* and became famous for her performance as Camille ("Ristori"; "Janauschek"; "Modjeska"). For Rachel, see Ch. 2, endnote 10.

15. La Fontaine's *Les Deux Pigeons* is a cautionary fable about a pigeon who, desiring new sights, travels away from its nest and falls into a series of adventures from which it barely emerges with its life. Lovers, in short, should remain contentedly together and not seek greener pastures.

16. Sophie Croizette was Bernhardt's childhood friend and stage rival at the Comédie Française. Croizette, who was tall, blonde, and well-endowed—the opposite in appearance from Bernhardt—became the mistress of Emile Perrin, the company's director. When the two played in *Le Sphinx*, their rivalry and their unparalleled acting created the "Croizettistes" and the "Bernhardtistes." Bernhardt played her role of the betrayed wife with quiet intensity; Croizette, in her suicide scene, "turned a sinister green, terrorizing the audience with what looked like a severe case of lockjaw and delirium tremens combined" (Gold and Fizdale 120 and *passim*).

17. The actor-manager Tommaso Salvini was a well-known Shakespearean actor, much praised for his empathetic projection: "Endowed with rich physical attributes—a powerful, sonorous voice, striking and muscular figure, stage presence, and perfect command of gesture and movement—he brought intelligence and imaginative perception to his preparation and execution of roles ..." ("Salvini"). He began his 1880–81 American tour in November in Philadelphia. David Fennema's unpublished dissertation "Tommaso Salvini in America: 1873–1893" is a rich source of details about his life and theatrical tours (140).

Chapter 4

1. Fanny Davenport, who was managed by Augustin Daly, was said to add "dazzling beauty, splendid presence, and blooming health" to his ensemble. She performed in *La Dame aux Camélias* in 1853 and relied heavily on Bernhardt as a precedent in producing her roles, especially those in *Fedora*, *Tosca*, and *Gismonda*. Matilda Heron performed in an English version of *La Dame* in 1857; she was noted for her "intelligent reading and fine acting," although it was said that "she was not an especially attractive woman. Even by the standards of the time her figure was 'ample'...." The London-born Laura Keene, the stage name of Mary Moss, was one of the first female theater producers. She was an actress until 1855, when she opened her own playhouse, a rival to Wallack's. Because of economic difficulties related to the Civil War, she returned to acting and was performing at Booth's when Lincoln was assassinated. ("Heron"; "Keene"). For Davenport and Morris, see Ch. 2, endnote 8; for Mme. Modjeska, see Ch. 3, endnote 14.

2. Salvini had four children with Clementina Cazzoli, an actress with whom he regularly performed in the late 1850s. Italian divorce laws were complicated, and while Cazzoli obtained a legal separation from her husband Giacomo Brizzi, also an actor, she never married Salvini. (Fennema 14).

3. The full text of Louis Frechette's poem is reprinted in Appendix Two of Hathorn's *Our Lady of the Snows* (276–78).

4. Such a "caprice" seems innocent in light of the kinds of "theatrical nuisances" the *Baltimore American* editor complains about the previous week. Using Zanesville, Ohio, as the scapegoat, he quotes the rules printed in the playbill and comments, "Unexceptional as these rules appear, they seem to ... show the dark interior of provincial theatre manners.... [W]hat must be the natural condition of the theatre where the yelling, whistling, nut-devouring, smoking and hat-wearing impulses of the audience riot in unpruned and unchastened luxuriance!"

5. The St. Louis *Spectator*'s pejorative comments about Schwab reflect the anti–Semitic innuendoes common on the East Coast. His "simian countenance indicates that he got a very late start in the majestic system of evolution"; he is "a supercilious, offensive, insufferable cad" whose profits from Bernhardt's visit are supposedly enormous, since he holds the rights to her photograph and libretto translations, which are "wretchedly executed." The *Connecticut Courant* joined in vilifying Schwab by repeating a piece of gossip: "It is understood that at the close of the season he will sell at auction the second-hand dresses and the *lingerie* of Miss Bernhardt ..." (29 Jan. 1881: 224).

6. According to Edward Le Roy Rice's memoirs, Add [John Addison] Ryman, who created the company on December 20, 1880, was "one of the greatest burlesque actors that minstrelsy ever knew." In his company was the blackface performer George Thatcher, famous for the burlesque monologue, which he claimed to have invented in an attempt to outdo his rival Billy Emerson (Rice 122, 190).

7. The Shakespearean Sarah Siddons, best known for her role as Lady Macbeth, performed in Garrick's company at Drury Lane and eventually moved to Covent Garden in 1871. The comedian best known for his role in Boucicault's *Rip Van Winkle*, Joseph Jefferson was both actor and stage manager; his fortunes turned in 1857 when he was hired by Laura Keene. Sir Henry Irving, who achieved fame for his chilling performance in *The Bells*, managed the Lyceum brilliantly for twenty years; he hired well-known actors and actresses and attracted such figures as Sir Arthur Sullivan to write incidental music and Burne-Jones to design stage sets ("Siddons"; "Jefferson"; "Irving").

8. The amount of luggage was notorious enough to justify the a piece of advice to youngsters printed in the *N.Y. Commercial Advertiser*: "Study, little girl, persevere, be eccentric, sleep in a coffin, sculp skulls, and you may yet own as many trunks as Sarah Bernhardt" (qtd. in *Puck* 24 Nov. 1880: 198).

9. The complete poem, published in the *Spectator* on January 29, is as follows:

I

I do not know what leaf you love;
What flow'r brings gladness to your eyes;
If plant beneath, or star above,
Smile-lights your ever-changing skies.

II

But this I know: If chance e'er came
To place an offering on your shrine,
I'd light the fields with memory's flame,
And seek for token that's divine.

III

I know where such a token's found;—
Where whitened clover sweetly breathes,
Whose leaves speak, all the wide world 'round,
More meaning than your laurel leaves.

IV

I'd place a shamrock at your feet,—
The triple-leaf, the sainted one
Held high, that Tara's hosts might greet
The union of three gods in one.

V

This trinity of leaves I'd deign
To offer you, its counterpart,
Who—painter, sculptress, actress—reign
A living trinity of art.

Chapter 5

1. Mme. Guérard became a second mother to Bernhardt; a widow, she lived above Youle's apartment. Her early devotion to the little girl lasted throughout her life (Gold and Fizdale 26).

2. In her later career, Logan (a pen name for Mrs. Wirt Sikes) argued for both equal labor rights and education under the rubric of "True Womanhood," which recognized women's domestic nature and domestic importance. By the time she was interviewing Bernhardt in St. Louis, she had been married twice and her public popularity was on the wane. The most detailed accounts of Logan may be found in dissertations by Mardia J. Bishop and J. Robert Wills, Jr., and the American *Punchinello* published a satirical biography of her as a "speakeristess" on 17 Sept. 1870.

3. Adelina Patti, noted for bel canto and coloratura, was gifted with a pure, sweet voice. She had international debuts, including the Academy of Music and Covent Garden, where she was London's first Aida in 1876. Three years later she toured the United States with the impresario Col. Mapleson. Giulia Grisi, a scintillating operatic

performer, debuted at La Scala, but left in 1832; after 1834, she alternated performing in London and Paris. (Forbes, "Patti" and "Grisi").

4. Kate Claxton, who debuted in Chicago in 1869 and in New York under Augustin Daly in 1870, had small success as a manager. When she returned to acting, she was seen as a theatrical jinx—she was performing during a number of theater fires, including the devastating one that destroyed the Brooklyn Theatre in 1876 ("Claxton").

Chapter 6

1. Napoleon Sarony, who photographed over 30,000 actors or actresses, was the co-founder of a lithographic firm that popularized the modern theatrical poster. After his wife died, he studied art in Europe, but his interest was captured by the new art of photography; he returned to America in 1865, after beginning his photographic career in London with Ada Isaacs Menken in *Mazeppa* as his subject ("Sarony").

2. According to an interview with Mayer, who was in charge during Abbey's absence, the *Kansas City Times* had published a spurious interview with Bernhardt in deplorable French. The tone of Mayer's report indicates the liveliness of the rivalry and double-crossings characteristic of the journalism of the day:

> A very elegantly dressed young man came on board the cars and represented himself to me as a St. Joseph reporter. Knowing that St. Joseph reporters always dress elegantly, I believed him ... what I regret most is that he drank about a quart of my best brandy... . that interview was pretty well cooked up, however, but the French was horrible. Nobody could read it or understand it. It was worse than Choctaw. But, then, that's all one could expect from the mouth of the Kan [*St. Joseph Daily* 1 March 1881].

3. Arsène Houssaye, who published six volumes of confessions and innumerable novels, served as the director of the *Comédie Française* ("Houssaye").

4. The novelist and editor George Parsons Lathrop, married to Nathaniel Hawthorne's daughter Rose, had an influential journalistic life. In 1883 he founded the American Copyright League, which finally secured the international copyright law, and helped found the Catholic Summer School of America. He published verse, critical works, novels, travel essays, and histories, and edited the standard edition of Hawthorne's works ("Lathrop").

Chapter 7

1. Marie Roze, a French soprano, debuted in Paris in 1865 and in London's Drury Lane in 1872. She was a member of Col. Mapleson's company until 1881 (Forbes, "Roze").

Bibliography

"Abbey, Henry [Edwin]." *Oxford Companion to American Theatre*. Bordman.
Appel, John. "Jews in American Caricature: 1820–1914." *Journal of American History* (Sept. 1981): 103–133. Rpt. in Gurock 47–77.
Appel, John, and Selma Appel. "Anti-Semitism in American Caricature." *Society* 14 (1986): 79–84. Rpt. in *American Immigration & Ethnicity*. Vol. 15. *Nativism, Discrimination, and Images of Immigrants*. Ed. George E. Pozzetta. New York and London: Garland, 1991.
Auerbach, Nina. *Woman and the Demon: The Life of a Victorian Myth*. Harvard UP: Cambridge, MA, and London, 1982.
Bakhtin, M. M. "Forms of Time and the Chronotype in the Novel." *The Dialogic Imagination*. Ed. Michael Holquist; trans. Caryl Emerson and Michael Holquist. U of Texas P Slavic Series, No. 1. Austin: U of Texas P, 1981.
____. *Problems of Dostoevsky's Poetics*. Ed. and trans. Caryl Emerson. Intro. Wayne C. Booth. Theory and History of Literature, Vol. 8. Minneapolis and London: U of Minnesota P, 1984.
Banham, Martin, ed. *The Cambridge Guide to Theatre*. Rev. ed. Cambridge, New York, and Melbourne: Cambridge UP, 1995.
Beerbohm, Max. "Dandies and Dandies." *The Works of Max Beerbohm*. New York: Scribner's, 1896.
Bernhardt, Lysiane. *Sarah Bernhardt, My Grandmother*. Trans. Vyvyan Holland. London: Hurst & Blackett, n.d.
Bernhardt, Sarah. *The Art of the Theatre*. Trans. H. J. Stenning. Pref. James Agate. 1924. Freeport: Books for Libraries Press, 1969.
____. *The Memoirs of Sarah Bernhardt: Early Childhood Through the First American Tour and her Novella* In the Clouds. Ed. and intro. Sandy Lesberg. New York and London: Peebles Press, 1997.

———. *Memories of My Life*. 1908. New York and London: Benjamin Blom, 1968.
———. *My Double Life: The Memoirs of Sarah Bernhardt*. Trans. Victoria Tietze Larson. Albany: State U of New York P, 1999.
———. *Sarah Bernhardt Souvenir, Including the Authorized Catalogue of Her Paintings and Sculpture*. New York: 1880 [?].
Bishop, Mardia J. "From 'Wax-Doll Prettiness' to a 'Lifeless Dough Doll': The Actress in Relation to the Images of 'Woman' in Mid-Nineteenth-Century America." Diss. Columbus: Ohio State, 1993.
Booth, Michael. *Victorian Spectacular Theatre 1850–1910*. Boston, London, and Henley: Routledge & Kegan Paul, 1981.
Bordman, Gerald, ed. *The Oxford Companion to American Theatre*. New York and Oxford: Oxford UP, 1984.
"Boston Online." 14 June 2000, http://www.boston-online.com/faq.html#beantown.
"Bowry Theatre." *Oxford Companion to American Theatre*. Bordman.
"Calvé, Emma." *The New Grove Dictionary of Opera*. Sadie.
Chazal, Gilles. "Doré, Gustav." *Dictionary of Art*. Ed. Jane Turner. New York: Grove, 1996. 34 vols.
"Claxton, Kate." *Oxford Companion to American Theatre*. Bordman.
Cogan, Frances B. *All-American Girl: The Ideal of Real Womanhood in Mid-Nineteenth-Century America*. Athens and London: U of Georgia P, 1989.
Cohen, Naomi W. "Antisemitism in the Gilded Age: The Jewish View." *Jewish Social Studies* (Summer/Fall 1979): 187–210. Rpt. in Gurock 263–86.
Colombier, Marie. *Les Mémoires de Sarah Barnum*. Ed. and Pref. Paul Bonnetain. New York: S. W. Green, 1884.
———. *Les Voyages de Sarah Bernhardt en Amerique*. Paris: C. Marpon, 18??.
"Comstock, Anthony." *Dictionary of American Biography*. Vol. 4. Johnson and Malone.
"Conkling, Roscoe." *Dictionary of American Biography*. Vol. 4. Johnson and Malone.
Conot, Robert. *A Streak of Luck*. New York: Seaview, 1979.
"Crowinshield, Frederic." *Dictionary of American Biography*. Vol. 4. Johnson and Malone.
———. *Who was Who in American Art*. Ed. Peter Hastings Falk. Madison, CT: Sound View Press, 1985.
"Davenport, Fanny." *Oxford Companion to American Theatre*. Bordman.
"Eames, Emma." *The New Grove Dictionary of Opera*. Sadie.
"Ellen Terry." *Famous Actors and Actresses on the American Stage*. Young. Item 189.
"Eytinge, Rose." *Cambridge Guide to the Theatre*. Banham.
Fennema, David Harold. "Tommaso Salvini in America: 1873–1893." Diss. Indiana U, 1979.
Findlay, Jeff. "Beecher, Henry Ward." *The Encyclopedia of New York City*. Ed. Kenneth T. Jackson. New Haven and London: Yale UP, 1995.

Forbes, Elizabeth. "Grisi, Guilia." *The New Grove Dictionary of Opera*. Sadie.
_____. "Patti, Adelina." *The New Grove Dictionary of Opera*. Sadie.
_____. "Roze, Marie." *The New Grove Dictionary of Opera*. Sadie.
Foushee, Eric Fontaine. "Through the Eyes of Sarah Bernhardt: A Study of Ophelia, Artistic Tradition, and Feminism." Diss. Southern Methodist U, 1994.
"The Gentle Giant." 3 September 2001, http://www.ashleighhotel.co.uk/chang.html.
Gilbert, Pamela. *Disease, Desire, and the Body*. Cambridge Studies in Nineteenth Century Literature and Culture. Ed. Gillian Beer and Catherine Gallagher. Cambridge: Cambridge UP, 1997.
Gold, Arthur, and Robert Fizdale. *The Divine Sarah: A Life of Sarah Bernhardt*. New York: Knopf, 1991.
Gurock, Jeffrey S. *Anti-Semitism in America*. New York and London: Routledge, 1998. Vol. 6 of *American Jewish History*. 8 vols. 1998.
Handlin, Oscar. "American Views of the Jew at the Opening of the Twentieth Century." *Publications of the American Jewish Historical Society* (June 1951): 323–44. Rpt. in Gurock 187–208.
Hathorn, Ramon. *Our Lady of the Snows: Sarah Bernhardt in Canada*. Currents in Comparative Romance Languages and Literatures, Vol. 38. New York: Peter Lang, 1996.
_____. "Sarah Bernhardt's Canadian Visits." Canada House Lecture Series No. 52. London: Canadian High Commission, 1992.
"Heron, Matilda." *Oxford Companion to American Theatre*. Bordman.
Higham, John. "Anti-Semitism in the Gilded Age: A Reinterpretation." *Mississippi Valley Historical Review* (March 1957): 209–28. Rpt. in Gurock 559–77.
_____. "Social Discrimination Against Jews in America 1830–1930." *Publications of the American Jewish Historical Society* (Sept. 1957): 1–33. Rpt. in Gurock 229–61.
Hossalla, Richard J. "Henry E. Abbey, Commercial-Manager: A Study of Producing Management in the Theatre of the Late Nineteenth Century (1870–1900)." Diss. Kent State U, 1972. Ann Arbor: UMI, 1985.
"Houssaye, Arsène." *Oxford Companion to French Literature*. Comp. and ed. Sir Paul Harvey and J. E. Haseltine. Oxford: Clarendon Press, 1959.
"Irving, Henry." *Cambridge Guide to the Theatre*. Banham.
Jaher, Frederic Cople. "Were the Populists Anti-Semitic?" *Doubters and Dissenters*. By Jaher. New York: Macmillan, 1964. Rpt. in *Antisemitism in the United States*. Ed. Leonard Dinnerstein. New York: Holt, 1971. 78–86.
"Janauschek, Fanny [Francesca]." *Cambridge Guide to Theatre*. Banham.
"Jarrett, Henry C." *History of the American Stage*. By T. Allston Brown. 1870. New York and London: Benjamin Blom, 1869.
"Jefferson, Joseph." *Oxford Companion to American Theatre*. Bordman.

Jehl, Francis. *Menlo Park Reminiscences*. Dearborn: Edison Institute, 1937.
Johnson, Allen, and Dumas Malone, eds. *Dictionary of American Biography*. 20 vols. New York: Scribner's, 1928–1958.
Jones, Ann Rosalind. "Writing the Body: Toward an Understanding of l'Écriture féminine." *The New Feminist Criticism: Essays on Women, Literature, Theory*. Ed. Elaine Showalter. NY: Pantheon, 1985.
"Keene, Laura." *Oxford Companion to American Theatre*. Bordman.
Kendall, John Smith. "Sarah Bernhardt in New Orleans." *Louisiana Historical Quarterly* 26.3.
Kent, Christopher. "Image and Reality: The Actress and Society." *A Widening Sphere: Changing Roles of Victorian Women*. Ed. Martha Vicinus. Bloomington and London: Indiana UP, 1977.
"Kirby, J. Hudson." *Oxford Companion to American Theatre*. Bordman.
Kobler, John. "Bernhardt in America." *American Heritage* July/August 1989: 52–65.
La Fontaine, Jean de. *Oeuvres completes*. Pref. Pierre Clarac and ed. Jean Marmier. Paris: Éditions du Beuil, 1965.
"Lathrop, George Parsons." *Dictionary of American Biography*. Vol. 11. Johnson and Malone.
"Lehmann, Lilli." *The New Grove Dictionary of Opera*. Sadie.
"Lillie Langtry." *Famous Actors and Actresses on the American Stage*. Young Item 119.
Lobstein, Dominique. "Louise Abbéma." *Dictionary of Women Artists*. Ed. Delia Gaze. London and Chicago: Fitzroy Dearborn, 1997. 2 vols.
Longfellow, Henry Wadsworth. *The Letters of Henry Wadsworth Longfellow*. Cambridge: Belknap Press of Harvard UP, 1966.
"Lucca, Pauline." *The New Grove Dictionary of Opera*. Sadie.
"Madge Kendall." *Famous Actors and Actresses on the American Stage*. Young Item 116.
Maiden, Lewis S. "Three Theatrical Stars in Nashville, 1876–1906." *Southern Speech Journal* 31 (1965): 338–47.
Marks, Patricia. "'Sal' Bernhardt and the Men about Town: Theatre Resources in Chic." *American Periodicals* 1.1 (1991): 86–101.
Michie, Helena. *The Flesh Made Word: Female Figures and Women's Bodies*. New York and Oxford: Oxford UP, 1987.
"Modjeska, Helena." *Cambridge Guide to the Theatre*. Banham.
Mooney, James E. "Union League Club." *The Encyclopedia of New York City*. Ed. Kenneth T. Jackson. New Haven and London: Yale UP, 1995.
"Morris, Clara." *Oxford Companion to American Theatre*. Bordman.
Mott, Frank Luther. *A History of American Magazines 1865–1885*. Vol. 3. Cambridge: Harvard UP, 1966.
"Nilsson, Christine." *The New Grove Dictionary of Opera*. Sadie.
"Olga Nethersole." *Famous Actors and Actresses on the American Stage*. Young Item 156.

Patmore, Coventry. *The Angel in the House*, Book 2: Canto XII, Husband and Wife. June 7, 200. Galileo English Poetry: 600–1900 (Chadwyck-Healey). http://www.galileo.peachnet.edu.
"Rachel [Élisa Félix]." *Cambridge Guide to Theatre*. Banham.
Reed, Isaac G. As *"Too Thin;" Skeleton Sara. Her "Realistic" Life and Adventures in America*. NY: Evans & Kelly, 1880.
Rice, Edward Le Roy. *Monarchs of Minstrelsy, from "Daddy" Rice to Date*. New York: Kenny, 1911.
Richardson, Joanna. *Sarah Bernhardt and Her World*. NY: Putnam, 1977.
"Ristori, Adelaide." *Cambridge Guide to Theatre*. Banham.
Rosenthal, Donald A. "Clarin, (Jules-)Georges(-Victor)." *Dictionary of Art*. Ed. Jane Turner. New York: Grove, 1996. 34 vols.
Sadie, Stanley, ed. *The New Grove Dictionary of Opera*. London: Macmillan; New York: Grove's Dictionaries of Music, 1992. 4 vols.
"Salvini, Tommaso." *Cambridge Guide to Theatre*. Banham.
"Sarony, Napoleon." *Oxford Companion to American Theatre*. Bordman.
"Siddons, Sarah." *Cambridge Guide to Theatre*. Banham.
[Sims, Frank H.]. *The Amours of Sara Bernhardt. The Secrets of Her Life Revealed*. New York: John W. Morrison, 1880.
Singerman, Robert. "The Jew as Racial Alien: The Genetic Component of American Anti-Semitism." *Anti-Semitism in American History*. Ed. David A. Gerber. 103–128. Rpt. in Gurock 343–68.
Skinner, Cornelia Otis. *Madame Sarah*. Boston: Houghton, 1967.
Steele, Valerie. *Fashion And Eroticism: Ideals Of Feminine Beauty From The Victorian Era to the Jazz Age*. Oxford: Oxford UP, 1985.
Talmage, Thomas De Witt. *The Life of T. DeWitt Talmage, Together with Thirty-One Sermons, Also a History of the Brooklyn Tabernacle*. New York: John Alden, 1890.
Taranow, Gerda. *Sarah Bernhardt: The Art Within the Legend*. Princeton: Princeton UP, 1972.
"Van Zandt, Marie." *The New Grove Dictionary of Opera*. Sadie.
Verneuil, Louis. *The Fabulous Life of Sarah Bernhardt*. Trans. Ernest Boyd. New York and London: Harper, 1942.
"Ward, Geneviève." *Cambridge Guide to Theatre*. Banham.
Welter, Barbara. *Dimity Convictions: The American Woman in the Nineteenth Century*. Athens: Ohio UP, 1976.
Wills, Jr., J. Robert. "The Riddle of Olive Logan: A Biographical Profile." Diss. Case Western Reserve U, 1971.
Woon, Basil. *The Real Sarah Bernhardt: Whom Her Audiences Never Knew. Told to Her Friend Mme. Berton ...* New York: Boni and Liveright, 1924.
Young, William, ed. *Famous Actors and Actresses on the American Stage*. 2 vols. New York and London: Bowker, 1975.
Zangwill, Isreal. *The Melting-Pot*. New York: Macmillan, 1926.

Serials

Atlanta Constitution
Atlantic
Baltimore American
Boston Commonwealth
Boston Evening Transcript
Boston Globe
Boston Globe Supplement
Boston Herald
Boston Journal
Boston Post
Buffalo Courier
Chic (New York)
Chicago Inter-Ocean
Chicago Play
Chicago Times
Chicago Tribune
Cincinnati Daily Enquirer
Cincinnati Saturday Night
Cincinnati Star
Cleveland Penny Press
Cleveland Plain Dealer
Columbus Dispatch
Columbus Evening Dispatch
Connecticut Courant
Dayton Daily Journal
Detroit Free Press
Detroit Plain Dealer
Detroit Post and Tribune
Erie Morning Dispatch
Erie Morning News
Evening Wisconsin
Harper's
Hartford Daily Times
Hartford Times Supplement
Illinois State Journal
Illinois State Register
Indianapolis Journal
Indianapolis News
Kansas City Times
Leavenworth Standard
Louisville Courier
Memphis Daily Appeal
Memphis Herald
Milwaukee Daily Sentinel
Milwaukee Evening Chronicle
Nashville Daily American
New Haven Palladium
New Haven Register
New Orleans Daily Picayune
New York Clipper
New York Commercial Advertiser
New York Daily Graphic
New York Express
New York Herald
New York Mirror
New York Sun
New York Times
New York World
Newark Advertiser
Newark Daily Journal
Niagara Falls Gazette
Norristown Herald
Ohio State Journal
Oil City Derrick
Petroleum World
Philadelphia Bulletin
Philadelphia Evening Bulletin
Philadelphia Inquirer
Philadelphia Press
Pittsburgh Commercial Gazette
Pittsburgh Daily Post
Pittsburgh Telegraph
Providence Evening Bulletin
Puck
Punchinello
Quincy Daily Herald
Rochester Daily Union and Advertiser
St. Joseph Daily Gazette
St. Joseph Daily Herald
St. Joseph Evening News
St. Louis Daily Globe-Democrat
St. Louis Post-Dispatch
St. Louis Republican
St. Louis Spectator
Springfield Republican
Titusville Herald
Toledo Blade
Toronto Daily Mail
Troy Daily Times
Washington Post
Worcester Daily Spy
Worcester Evening Gazette

Index

Abbéma, Louise, 39, 192
Abbey, Henry E. 10–12, 17, 24, 34, 47–48, 59, 65, 67–68, 87–88, 90, 96, 105, 111, 117, 126, 132, 137, 148–149, 154, 156, 158–159, 167–168, 170–172, 188, 190, 194–195, 200
Academy of Music (Baltimore, MD) 88
Academy of Music (Buffalo, NY) 159
acting: Bernhardt as a new Rachel 3, 49, 74, 76, 87, 106, 108, 119, 128, 133, 153, 194, 197; death throes 46, 99, 106; stamina 5, 6, 11, 16, 22, 50–51, 102, 133, 152; tragedy 5, 49, 73, 76, 88, 119, 128, 131, 148, 156, 194, 197
Adrienne Lecouvreur (Legouvé and Scribe) 19, 45–46, 48–49, 70, 74, 86–88, 91, 98, 105, 107, 113–114, 119, 165, 170, 193, 197
advertisement 17, 28, 32, 37, 46, 58, 67, 69, 70, 79, 81, 84, 86, 88, 90, 96, 101, 108, 118, 120, 121–123, 132, 134, 141, 150, 159, 160, 168, 191; *see also* spectacle
Albany, NY 159; arrival 160
Albemarle Hotel 25, 26–27, 195
L'Amérique: birth of baby 13, 61, 189; championship of emigrants 9, 14, 189, 191; *mal de mer* 13, 15, 191; Mrs. Lincoln 13, 25–26, 144, 189, 198
Anderson, Mary 114

Angelo, Eduoard 13, 49, 111, 116, 133, 158, 189, 190
Anti-Semitism 1, 4, 11–12, 33, 37–38, 45–46, 50–51, 60–61, 65, 84, 86, 89, 96, 138, 147, 149, 188, 190, 192, 194, 198
Arch Street Opera House (Philadelphia) 94
art 4, 6, 26, 40, 44, 68–69, 72, 76–77, 88, 95, 101, 103–105, 112, 117, 136, 194, 197, 199, 200; attitudes toward 42, 44, 110, 117, 126, 133, 163; gallery shows 32, 34, 37, 40, 44, 52–53, 72, 97, 192; Monte Carlo Casino 39; paintings 44, 72, 95, 102; sculpture 4, 24, 29, 37, 39, 40, 44, 62, 69, 70, 72, 95, 101, 105, 128, 153, 155, 174, 192; studio attire 39
art gallery shows 72, 95, 104
Arthur, Chester 22, 187–189, 191, 194, 198
Atlanta, GA 116, 119–123, 160; ticket sales 121

Bakhtin, M. M. 3, 187
Baltimore, MD 87–88, 164–165, 198; arrival 87
Beardsley, Aubrey 35
Beecher, Henry Ward 51, 53, 55, 194
Beerbohm, Max 196
Bennet, James Gordon 40

207

Bernard, Youle (Judith Van Hard) 1, 194
Bernhardt, Jeanne 13, 94, 124, 133, 139, 154, 169, 171, 189, 190
Bernhardt, Lysiane 9, 189
Bernhardt, Sarah: American characteristics 2–4, 20, 31, 64, 82, 107, 148, 169, 194; Americanization 17, 26, 44, 60, 144; arrival in America 25; author 5; business acumen 2, 11, 16, 95, 116, 168, 172; as a businesswoman 11, 95, 116, 168, 172; class issues 2, 4, 11–12, 16, 17, 22, 31–33, 37–38, 39, 40, 42, 45–46, 50, 53, 61, 69, 81, 89–91, 96, 100–101, 103, 106, 108, 113, 115, 117–118, 124, 134–135, 139, 148, 159, 164, 170, 172, 189, 192; commodification 4, 17, 22, 31, 47, 68, 80–83, 89, 91, 102–103, 105, 123, 128, 159; company members 11–12, 22, 24, 42, 46, 49–50, 69, 74, 77, 83, 94, 103–104, 107, 110–111, 114, 116–117, 120–121, 124, 131, 133, 141, 144, 146, 150, 152, 154, 155–156, 158, 160–161, 165, 167–168, 189, 190, 192, 197–198, 200; contract 2, 7, 12, 20, 33, 77, 89, 103, 119, 121, 139, 167, 168, 188, 191, 194; cultural conflicts 2, 3, 5, 7, 11, 13, 29, 31, 37–38, 39, 45–46, 49, 60, 65, 70, 80, 100–101, 103–104, 107, 115, 117, 129, 131, 138, 147–148, 156, 168, 187, 190, 195; cultural icon 3, 9, 59, 60; description 1, 4, 5, 11, 15, 20, 25–27, 29, 33, 46, 48, 55, 66–67, 73, 76–77, 79, 81, 87–88, 91, 99, 103, 105–106, 113–115, 117, 119, 124, 129, 130, 138, 142, 145–148, 151, 153–154, 156, 158–159, 162–163, 166, 168, 174, 188, 190–192, 197, 199; dining habits 24, 27–28, 64–65, 67, 72, 97, 104, 117, 120, 122–124, 133, 143–144, 153–154, 195; domestic habits 6, 16, 48, 101, 114, 199; economic prostitution 5, 31, 33–35; education 1, 6, 17, 20, 39, 74, 133, 190; father 116, 135, 139, 150, 162, 187, 190; fondness for animals 10, 195, *see also* menagerie; foreignness 2, 4, 10, 12, 17, 22, 25, 29, 45, 49, 51, 55, 58, 66, 81, 83, 89, 100, 101, 115, 129, 131, 134, 156, 164, 174; injuries and illness 66, 76, 99, 119, 167; life as theater 9, 12–14, 16, 26; lifestyle 4, 11, 15, 20, 37, 39, 44, 77, 95–96, 100, 102, 124, 174, 187; lovers and suitors 2, 13, 16, 20, 34, 39, 40, 48–49, 55, 77, 84, 111, 116, 120, 133, 145, 158, 189–190,192; luggage 24, 29, 103 139, 199; marital status 90, 101; mode of travel 14, 16, 26, 55, 65, 68, 83, 88, 97, 109, 110, 116, 121, 126, 131, 139, 143, 150, 157, 160; mother 1, 2, 17, 20, 37, 58, 86, 111, 115–116, 126, 142, 158, 172, 174, 189, 199; motto 7, 67, 91, 102, 195; myths 10; professionalism 3, 11, 13, 16, 17, 20, 24, 33, 39, 50, 51, 58, 69, 80, 96, 113, 170, 188, 189; religious upbringing 1; son 2, 6, 16, 20, 31, 32, 40, 55, 70, 94, 96, 120, 137, 168, 172, 189, 190; temperament 10, 15, 83
Booth's Theatre (New York) 22, 34, 42, 48, 147, 163, 169, 170, 188, 190–191, 198
Boston, MA 59–62, 64–70, 72–74, 76–77, 79–81, 83, 90, 95–98, 101, 106, 108, 109, 121, 146, 152, 158, 160–161, 170, 188, 191, 195, 197; arrival 49, 65, 67, 80, 90, 160, 194; departure 80
Bowry Theatre (New York), 49 194
Brabender, Madame de 20
Bradford, PA 153–154
Brooklyn Tabernacle 51
Buffalo, NY 153, 159; ticket sales 159
burlesques 26, 70, 79, 94, 101, 161, 163–164, 189

Calvé, Emma 188
Camille (Dumas; see *La Dame aux Camélias*) 48, 76–77, 81, 85, 88, 91, 99, 106–107, 115, 119–121, 128–129, 132, 137, 141, 143, 146–150, 152–154, 157, 159–160, 162, 163, 166, 192–193, 197
Carpenter, George B. 99
Central Music Hall (Chicago) 65, 99, 138
Chang 70, 196
Chestnut Street Theatre (Philadelphia) 89, 95, 165, 166
Chic 15, 17, 27, 29, 34–35, 37, 40, 42, 44, 46, 49, 51–53, 55, 61–62, 65, 69, 72, 76, 86, 95, 103, 144, 189
Chicago, IL 68, 89, 90, 95–103, 106,

108–110, 112, 115, 117–118, 120–121, 145–146, 165, 170, 196, 200; arrival 97; departure 102; receipts 98
Chicago Exposition Building (Chicago) 97
Cincinnati, OH 98, 109–117, 120, 129, 143, 165
Clairin, Georges 40, 192
Claxton, Kate 200
Cleveland, OH 121, 150–153; arrival 150
clothing 2, 12, 16–17, 19, 20, 22, 24–25, 28–29, 39, 44, 49, 53, 68, 72–73, 77, 83, 90, 97, 102, 105, 113, 118, 124, 127, 133, 142–143, 145, 151, 161, 166, 172, 194, 198, 200; gloves 19, 24, 83–84, 118, 123, 132, 147, 150; trousers 6, 39, 107
Colombier, Marie 13, 25, 79, 91, 102, 111, 116, 154, 158, 169, 189, 190; *Les Mémoires de Sarah Barnum* 26, 70, 79, 101, 189
Columbus, OH: arrival 130–134; ticket sales 85, 153
Comédie Française 1, 2, 11, 12, 20, 67, 74, 133, 156, 194, 195, 197, 200; Perrin, Emile 11, 12, 197
Comstock, Anthony 52, 132, 194
Conkling, Roscoe 53, 55, 194
Conservatoire de Musique et Déclamation 1, 17, 20, 74
consumerism 3, 17, 35, 85, 89, 122
Coppée, François see *Le Passant*
costumes 4–5, 10, 12, 17, 22, 29, 46, 49, 50, 84, 85, 97, 100, 107, 112, 123, 127, 140, 146, 151, 155, 161, 174, 191, 192
Croizette, Sophie 74, 99, 197
Crowinshield, Frederic 72, 197

Daily Graphic 25–26, 40, 42, 48, 169, 170, 171, 190, 191
Daly, Augustin 192, 198, 200
La Dame aux Camélias (Dumas; see *Camille*) 19, 37, 48, 86, 198
Davenport, Fanny 81, 114, 148–149, 192, 198
Dayton, OH 131–134, 139, 144; arrival 131
Detroit, MI 147–149; ticket sales 147
Doche, Eugénie 81
Doré, Gustav 1, 39, 192

Dumas, Alexandre (fils) 40, 99, 158, 161, 167, 169, 170, 198; see also *Camille*; *La Dame aux Camélias*; *L'Étrangère*

Eames, Emma 188
Edison, Thomas Alva 59, 66, 70, 72, 195
Englehardt, Fred 146
Erie, PA 153–155, 157; arrival 154
L'Étrangère (Dumas) 99, 170
Euclid Avenue Opera House (Cleveland, OH) 151

Fabre, Bishop of Montreal 86
Fall River, MA 161, 163
Fechter, Charles 81
Feuillet, Octave see *Le Sphinx*
Fifth Avenue Theatre (New York) 24, 168, 191, 192
finances in America 3–4, 11, 14, 16, 33–34, 38, 44, 50–51, 55, 82, 84, 103, 130, 132, 134, 152, 159, 163, 166–167, 169, 198; contract 34; import duties 22, 24, 46; receipts (see city names) 4, 34, 73, 80, 82, 87, 90, 95, 98, 102, 112, 122–123, 138, 140, 163, 165, 168, 170, 191; ticket prices 33, 73, 81, 90, 111, 119, 164
finances in France 11, 12, 116, 127, 156, 189, 193, 197–198
Fontaine, Jean de la 74, 197
Frechette, Louis 85–86, 198
French, T. Henry 168
French realism 100, 107, 129, 137, 148, 153, 162, 169–170
Freud, Sigmund 16, 17
Froufrou (Meilhac and Halévy) 16, 45, 47–48, 74, 85–88, 98, 106, 115, 118–119, 122, 128, 131, 133, 136–137, 140, 146, 148, 151, 157, 160, 163–164, 167, 170

Gaiety Theatre (London) 11–12, 50
Garfield, James 42, 51, 191, 194
Garnier, Charles 39
gender attitudes 2, 4–6, 11–16, 20, 25, 28–29, 31–33, 39, 40, 42, 46, 48–49, 51, 58, 60–62, 68–69, 73, 74, 76, 79, 84, 88–89, 97, 99, 105–106, 110, 112–113, 116, 118, 126–128, 134, 137, 141,

143, 145, 147, 157, 158, 162–169, 188–189, 191, 198–199; femininity 2, 7, 11, 15, 16, 29, 39, 70, 73, 94, 127, 160–161, 169, 190, 198
Gilded Age 3, 38–39
Grand Opera House (St. Louis) 107, 119, 147, 157, 188
Grisi, Julia 114, 199
Guérard, Madame 20, 111, 116, 199
Gymnase Theatre (Paris) 20

Halévy, Ludovic see *Froufrou*
Hartford, CT 68, 80–82, 83, 85–86, 90, 111; arrival 83
Haynie, J. H. 111, 144, 158
Hernani (Hugo) 26, 46, 69, 73–74, 79, 86, 88, 91, 100, 107, 161, 194
Heron, Matilda 82, 198
Holmes, Oliver Wendell 69, 195
Houssaye, Arsene 138, 200
Howells, William Dean 69
Hughes, Ball 67, 124, 196
Hugo, Victor 1–2, 46, 69, 73, 86, 89, 91, 99–100; see also *Hernani*
humor 11, 15, 26–28, 38, 45, 48, 50, 55, 65, 78, 81, 94, 106, 109, 113, 128, 142–143, 147, 149, 150, 155, 170, 189; caricature 4, 12, 17, 26, 29, 31, 33, 38, 45, 51, 60, 94, 98, 164, 191; rural 45, 147, 154; satire 4, 9, 11, 15, 25, 29, 33, 37–38, 40, 44–46, 51, 58, 69, 89, 103, 112, 121, 129, 134, 144, 161, 189, 199; urban 45, 65

immigrants 3, 11, 22, 24, 38, 45, 47, 50, 61, 194
Indianapolis, IN 111, 114, 134, 136–138, 153, 160; receipts 137; ticket sales 24, 82, 109, 124, 132, 137, 154, 159, 191
Ingersoll, Robert 51, 118, 126
Iphigénie (Racine) 195
Irving, Henry 95, 198

Janauschek, Fanny (Francesca) 74, 77, 197
Jarrett, Henry C. 1–2, 4, 7, 10–13, 15, 17, 27–28, 33, 42, 47, 59, 66–68, 72, 77, 79, 94, 103–105, 108, 110–114, 116, 131, 138, 141, 151, 155–156, 158, 165, 188, 191, 196
Jefferson, Joseph 95, 198

jewelry 5, 34, 40, 45, 61, 68, 70, 104–105, 110–111, 119–120, 131, 133, 142, 151, 165, 174
judge 15

Kansas City, KS 138–139, 142
Keene, Laura (Mary Moss) 82, 198
Kendal, Mrs. W. H. (Madge Robertson) 13, 189
Kirby, J. Hudson 49, 194
Kristeva, Julia 5, 188

Langtry, Lillie 13, 189
language 1–4, 7, 12, 17, 22, 24–26, 29, 34, 42, 45–46, 48–49, 51, 62, 64–65, 68–70, 77–79, 81–82, 85, 87–88, 90–91, 96–100, 102, 104, 106, 108–109, 111–118, 120–146, 148–151, 153, 155–156, 158, 160, 162–164, 166, 168, 170–172, 187–188, 190–195, 197–198, 200
Lathrop, George Parsons 200
Leavenworth, KS 134, 138–139, 140–143
Legouvé, Ernest see *Adrienne Lecouvreur*
Lehmann, Lilli 188
life 15, 28, 37, 60, 70, 83, 87–88, 189, 196
Ligne, Prince Charles Lamoral de 2, 20
Lincoln, Mary (Mrs. Abraham Lincoln) 13, 25–26, 144, 189, 198
Lisle, Leconte de 99
Logan, Olive (Mrs. Wirt Sikes) 110–111, 113–116, 118, 120, 122, 129, 137, 146, 199
Longfellow, Henry 65, 69–70, 196
Louisville, KY 109, 116, 121–122, 124, 126–130, 137; arrival 126; ticket sales 124
Lucca, Pauline 11, 188

Mapleson, Colonel 22, 139, 199–200
Marseillaise 24, 113
Mathieu-Roland, Meusnier 39
Mayer, Marcus 123, 138–139, 141, 158, 171, 200
Meade, Jim 191
Meilhac, Henri see *Froufrou*
Memphis, TN 104, 115–116, 119, 122–124, 126–128, 132; arrival 124; ticket sales 123, 128
menagerie 10, 12, 48, 105, 156
Merritt, General G. A. 22, 24

Metropolitan Opera House (New York) 188, 192
Milwaukee, WI 134, 138, 145–146; arrival 146; ticket sales 134, 138, 145–146
Mobile, AL 119
Modjeska, Helena 74, 82, 88, 137, 149, 160, 197–198
Molière 12, 74, 188
Montreal, Canada 58, 85, 86–88, 90, 94, 98, 110; arrival 86; departure 87
Morny, Duc de 2, 20
Morris, Clara 77, 82, 88, 106, 114, 146, 153, 169, 192
Moss, Theodore 168, 198
Moulton, Mrs. Lillie 69, 196

Nashville, TN 116, 120–124
Nethersole, Olga 13, 189
New Haven, CT 80–84, 86, 96, 111–112, 114; arrival 83
New Orleans, LA 116–118, 122, 133, 140, 143, 170; arrival 116; receipts 118
New York, NY 1, 3–4, 6, 9, 22, 24–26, 28–29, 35, 37, 42, 44–46, 50–53, 55, 58–61, 65–68, 70, 72, 74, 76–81, 83, 85, 87, 90–91, 94, 97–98, 101, 108–110, 114, 118, 121, 129, 144, 147, 153, 158, 161, 163–165, 168–172, 174, 188–192, 194–195, 197, 200; arrival 12, 169
Newark, NJ 163, 164–165; ticket sales 163
newspaper reporters 4–5, 7, 19, 24–28, 44, 50, 66, 73, 74, 76–79, 84–85, 89, 95, 97, 100, 103, 107, 109–111, 113–115, 118, 120–124, 126, 131–132, 138–148, 151–152, 154–55, 158–160, 164, 168–169, 171–172, 191, 193, 195, 200
Niagara Falls, NY 153, 157
Nilsson, Christine 11, 188

Opera House (Pittsburgh) 152
Opera House (Springfield) 143
Opera House (Syracuse) 160
Opera House (Titusville) 141, 153; Calmeel 164

Park Theatre (Newark) 163, 170
Passant, Le (Coppée) 99
Patmore, Coventry 16
Patti, Adelina 114, 199
Phèdre (Racine) 16, 49, 66, 76, 91, 94, 99, 118, 165, 193, 197

Philadelphia, PA 24, 28, 45, 47, 55, 66, 89, 90–91, 94–99, 103, 108–110, 163–167, 169, 170, 188, 194, 196–197; departure 97, 99; ticket sales 29, 89, 150, 152–153
Pinkerton Detective Agency 68, 97, 110, 142, 144, 151
Pittsburgh, PA 94, 152–153, 195
Princesse Georges, La (Dumas) 40, 158, 161, 167, 169, 170
Providence, RI 163
Puck 15, 29, 31, 33, 37, 42, 46, 48, 55, 59, 73, 77–78, 84, 95, 99, 116, 118, 170, 189, 192, 199

Quand même 7, 67, 91, 102, 195
Quincy, IL 134, 138, 140, 143–144; arrival 143

Racine, Jean Baptiste 76, 195; see also Iphigénie; Phèdre
Reed, Isaac G. 28, 154
religious controversy 1, 28, 58, 78, 86, 87, 90, 96, 107, 141, 157, 200; denunciations 58, 85–86, 96, 99, 199; see also pulpit oratory, reviews
reviews: acting company 49, 76, 141, 167; moral critiques 48, 51, 70, 129, 148, 164; pulpit oratory 3, 51, 55, 78, 84, 86, 90, 96, 101, 107, 127, 129, 136, 137, 165, 174, 194
Rice, William Henry 94, 163, 170, 198
Ristori, Adelaide 73, 197
Rochester, NY 159
Roze, Marie 139, 159

St. Joseph, MO 134, 138–139, 140, 142–143, 200
St. Louis, MO 102–104, 106–111, 115–118, 128–129, 138, 189, 196, 198–199; arrival 103; ticket sales 103
Salvini, Tommaso 84, 197–198
Sarah Burnheart 163
Sarah Heartburn 94, 161
Sarcey, Francisque 11
Sardou, Victorien see La Tosca
Sarony, Napoleon 138, 168, 200
Scalpers, ticket 33, 69, 73, 82, 89, 102, 110, 118, 120–121, 123–124, 128–130, 132, 136, 152, 153, 159, 163, 168, 170
Scams 103, 110, 117, 142

Schwab, Fred 198
Scribe, Eugène see *Adrienne Lecouvreur*
sexuality 5, 31, 32, 35, 39, 46, 53, 128, 148, 189
Siddons, Sarah 95, 198
Sikes, Mrs. Wirt 110–116, 118, 120, 122, 129, 137, 146, 199
Sims, Frank H. 60, 61
Smith, Henry 67, 188
Soudan, Jehan 40, 111
spectacle 11, 13, 17, 19, 39, 46, 50, 66, 68, 73, 77, 80, 82–84, 94–95, 97–98, 104–105, 108–110, 112–113, 117, 126, 129, 137, 148, 151, 155–156, 160, 188, 190; *see also* advertisement
Le Sphinx (Feuillet) 20, 47, 74, 91, 98, 106, 119, 193–194, 197
Springfield, IL 133–134, 138, 143, 145–146, 149
Springfield, MA 87–88; departure 88, 96
staging 17, 128, 148
Stebbins, James 40
stereotypes 5, 38, 45, 65, 96
Stetson 73, 168, 191
Syracuse, NY 160

Talmage, De Witt 28, 51, 55, 78, 84, 90, 107, 127, 157
Terry, Ellen 13, 189
Thatcher & Ryman's Minstrels 94, 161, 198
Theatre Comique (Providence, RI) 163, 188

thinness 4–5, 10, 15, 20, 26, 28–29, 31, 33–35, 44–45, 49, 53, 60, 62, 69, 76, 79, 81–83, 88, 99, 106, 108, 114, 122–123, 126, 130–131, 141, 143, 147, 151, 154, 160, 164, 170, 191
Titusville, PA 153
Toledo, OH 130, 147, 149, 150, 152, 154, 158
ticket prices 149
Toronto, CAN 157, 196
La Tosca (Sardou) 16, 192, 198
Troy, NY 159

Union League 37, 40, 44, 52–53, 72, 131, 136, 159, 192

Wales, Prince of 1, 12, 105, 112, 190
Ward, Genevieve 13, 189
Washington, D.C. 24, 88, 164–165, 197
whale 60, 67–68, 72, 79, 83, 97, 146, 152, 158, 160, 196
Whitman, Walt 31
Wieland 24
Wilde, Oscar 1
Worcester, MA 97, 111, 119, 121, 132, 150, 161–163, 166, 169; arrival 161; receipts 142, 163
Worcester Music Hall (Worcester, MA) 140, 161

Zandt, Marie Van 11, 188
Zangwill, Isreal 195
Zola, Emile 40

www.ingramcontent.com/pod-product-compliance
Lightning Source LLC
Chambersburg PA
CBHW032054300426
44116CB00007B/736